Trinity Tales

Trinity College Dublin in the Eighties

Trinity Tales

Trinity College Dublin in the Eighties

edited by KATY McGUINNESS

THE LILLIPUT PRESS
DUBLIN

First published 2013 by
THE LILLIPUT PRESS
62–63 Sitric Road, Arbour Hill
Dublin 7, Ireland
www.lilliputpress.ie

ISBN 978 1 84351 409 1

1 3 5 7 9 10 8 6 4 2

A CIP record for this title is available
from The British Library.

Set in Minion with Akzidenz Grotesk display titling by Marsha Swan
Printed and bound in Spain by Grafo

CONTENTS

EDITOR'S PREFACE

THE RECEIVED WISDOM is that Dublin in the eighties was grim, but I don't remember it as such – and there is very little by way of misery memoir in the contributions that go to make up this, the third volume of *Trinity Tales*. Then, as now, Trinity was a great place in which to sit out a recession.

The previous *Trinity Tales*, also published by The Lilliput Press, gathered together contributors who had been in college during the sixties and seventies. By the eighties, Trinity was no longer a controversial choice for Catholics, and many students were drawn from the Dublin middle classes. Heidi Haenschke, arriving in Trinity from the US for her year abroad, was surprised to find so many of her classmates living at home and commuting to college. For this cohort, summers abroad such as those described by Linda Hickey, Jane Mahony and David McWilliams, allowed an escape from under the parental roof. Migrant Trinity students found their freedom in the factories of Germany, and the bars and restaurants of London and New York.

I had already visited Trinity on numerous occasions before I enrolled in the Law School in the autumn of 1979. As co-editor (with my school friend, Paula Flynn) of the *Wimp Wonder Comic* fanzine, I had been blagging my way into gigs all over town since I was fifteen. I saw the Buzzcocks and The Worst in the JCR, and The Clash in the Exam Hall. And, unlike many who claim to have been there that night, I can prove it, thanks to a clipping from the next day's *Evening Press* in which I'm wearing a fetching plastic bag celebrating HM Queen Elizabeth II's Silver Jubilee. 'Spitting At The Band, In Trinity's Hallowed

Cloisters' read the caption; it caused a stir when it appeared on the noticeboard in Holy Child Killiney the following Monday morning.

My brother, Paul, had attended Trinity a decade before me. (He writes about this in *Trinity Tales: Trinity College Dublin in the Seventies*, edited by my sister-in-law, Kathy Gilfillan.) He left Trinity without a degree, not that this appears to have been any impediment to his subsequent career as the manager of U2. My other brother, Niall (who died in 1993), had also failed to graduate from the University of Loughborough. And so the weight of parental anxiety weighed heavily on my shoulders. My instructions were clear. I was to attend all my lectures, have nothing to do with Players, where Paul had apparently spent far too much time, and I was to stay away from Brendan Kennelly, who had refused him academic credit at the end of his third year, meaning that he could not sit his exams and lost his grant. Reading over the accounts of this golden age of Players in the accounts of Lynne Parker, Declan Hughes and others, I have some regrets now that I was such a biddable child. My path never crossed Kennelly's.

I met Sarah Bailey on a library tour. She was so grown up (matching shoes and handbag) that I assumed her to be a mature student. In fact, she was seventeen, like me. We went for coffee in Switzer's afterwards, and spent much of the next four years gossiping in either the Kilkenny Design, or the Bailey, or O'Neill's or Murph's, often in the company of classmates Eoin McCullough, Michael Cush, David Cox and Nicki Harvey. I am lucky that they are all still my friends. Sarah was to be avoided at exam time, however, as her bluffing skills in relation to arcane legal rules were legendary and could wrong-foot you. We lawyers avoided student politics, by and large, and had little time for SU president Joe 'Duffle' Duffy and his speechifying from the steps of the Dining Hall.

I went to my first Trinity Ball in a long, jade-green, Grecian-style dress and very high heels. Arriving at the pre-Ball drinks, I was greeted by veterans Simone Stephenson and Adrienne Foley in simple silk camisoles, trousers and flat pumps. I made that mistake only once.

My father died suddenly during the summer after my first year. Money was tight and my hopes of getting rooms were dashed. By way of compensation, a white Renault 5 was purchased, and I careered around Dublin without much consideration of the drink-driving laws, such as they were at the time. Paula (by then studying fashion and textiles in NCAD) and I set up Dublin's first singing telegram business, and drove the performers – law students Anne O'Neill, David Cox and John Coulter, and Players' 'talent' including Gary Jermyn, Una Clancy and Arthur Riordan, to their appearances. The money I earned, as well as from selling advertising for *Piranha* and waitressing in Barrels in Dalkey kept me going.

I spent a couple of summers in New York, and my head was turned. After four years in Trinity I knew Dublin and everyone in it far too well, and could not leave soon enough. I was on a flight to JFK the day after my final exam. For the next decade, I was one of those ex-pat yuppies breezing into the Shelbourne for Christmas drinks with the old gang from Trinners that Alan Gilsenan remembers resenting. And by the time I returned to live in Dublin, and walked through Trinity once again, it felt as if I had never been a part of it at all.

The two concluding essays are by Patrick Healy and Gerald Dawe, neither of whom is a Trinity graduate, yet both very much part of the college community. As before, the royalties from this book go to the Long Room fund of Trinity College.

At The Clash, TCD Exam Hall, 21 October 1977. Left to right: Paula Flynn, Katy McGuinness, Paul Byrne and Rachel Pigot.

Katy McGuinness (TCD 1979–83; Legal Science) studied for an LL.M. in trade regulation at New York University School of Law and was admitted to the New

York Bar. She practised law in New York before moving to London, where she was head of business and legal affairs at Palace Pictures. Back in Dublin, she produced several feature films. She holds an MA in English (creative writing) from Queen's University, Belfast. As a journalist, she has written for **The Irish Times, Irish Independent, Sunday Tribune** and **Sunday Times,** and is the restaurant critic of **The Gloss**. She is co-author of **The Irish Beef Book** (2013). Katy is married to architect Felim Dunne; they live in Dún Laoghaire with their four children.

FOREWORD

mary mcaleese

MY MOTHER and her siblings have sixty children between them. I am the oldest of nine. Where two or more of us siblings or cousins are gathered together, discussing our parents or grandparents, the variety of memories and opinions, the conflicting views and analyses, could make a body wonder if we are talking about the same people and places. Well, we are and we aren't. From the oldest to the youngest of the sixty of us, there is a difference of over thirty years. A lot changes in thirty years. Add personalities and interests and the vagaries of life to the mix and the shared genetic landscape of familiar noses or build or colouring cannot conceal the strong gravitational pull of differentiation – in sixty different directions. And so it is with gathering memories of Trinity College. This book is the third in a series of contemporary reminiscences about an institution that has had a place in Irish society for over four hundred years. Its boundary walls have long since created a unique island at the heart of Dublin city.

Tens of thousands of tourists, locals, students and staff meander through there every day, accreting memories as they go. Once it catered for a tiny elite and was no bigger than a small secondary school. Today its cramped campus is stuffed with elegant old edifices and brash new buildings cheek by jowl. The Campanile, the Exam Hall, Botany Bay and the Old Library are still more than a little righteously disdainful of the ugly Berkeley Library of the 1960s and the grim Arts Block of the 1970s, but these buildings mark the watershed between elite and mass education. They also mark the beginning of state investment in Trinity College, the growth of new disciplines and postgraduate education, the laying of the groundwork that would see the college transformed in thirty years into a serious high-level player on the global university stage. The eighties really were the start of something big in Trinity.

It seemed at times in the eighties as if the landlocked campus was destined to become a permanent building site and no doubt future volumes will speak of the new, smart, architectural gems that populate the Westland Row end of college, not least of which is the much-needed new Dublin Dental Hospital, which was endlessly discussed in the eighties but did not appear until the end of the nineties. Its existence is a testimony to the visionary persistence of Derry Shanley, the former dean of the Medical Faculty who masterminded the radical modernization of buildings and curriculum, while managing to look like a twelve-year-old altar boy.

However, all those swanky new builds of the nineties and noughties are for another decade of reminiscences; in the eighties most of them were just notions jump-started to life by the formidable raw energy, ambition and necessity unleashed by widened access to education. The old world of prim, presumptuous ease that was the alleged delight of former generations was put to flight with scary rapidity, leaving some bleating on wistfully for years about a putative golden generation that was truly educated as opposed to those who followed, blah, blah. This was for the most part self-regarding shorthand for the last tiny petted cohort of students that was rudely supplanted by the arrival on the scene of the more numerous first-generationers.

These were the education-hungry youngsters from humble and modest backgrounds, whose parents never had the chance of second- never mind third-level education and who were the real fruits of free second-level education. The doors of Trinity were thrown open to those 'intelligences brightened and unmannerly as crowbars' who 'would banish the conditional forever', to borrow from Seamus Heaney's description of the same phenomenon north of the border a generation earlier in his poem 'From the Canton of Expectation'.

I had arrived in Trinity in 1975 as the last of the sixties generation moved on and the cut and jib of things began to be refashioned in the image and likeness of the new owners of memories of Trinity. One major shift was in the pattern of Christian worship in college. Shortly before, Father Brendan Heffernan had been appointed the first-ever Catholic chaplain to Trinity. The beautiful Anglican College Chapel was generously offered on a shared basis to the Catholic community in college for daily Mass. Thus grew the strange spectacle of a not insignificant number of staff and students dashing from lectures across the lethal cobbles of Front Square to be in time for Mass at the eccentric time of five minutes past one each weekday.

The Catholic Church's ban on Catholics attending Trinity had been dispatched in 1970 to the same bin of historic vanities as the original college ban on Catholics and Dissenters. So the eighties, though characterized by some as an era when the college became homogenized and less cosmopolitan, was, in fact, a time of pelting new vitality for those who actually worked, studied or lived there. A buoyant, ground-breaking ecumenical spirit was the hallmark of Trinity's chaplains of various denominations. It was a lived communal reality of oneness, a terrific team ministry, which I was never to encounter to the same extent elsewhere in Ireland despite valiant efforts of the likes of Cecil Kerr's Christian Renewal Centre in Rostrevor, or Ray Davey's Corrymeela Community, or the Glencree Centre for Peace and Reconciliation.

Not until I encountered the Catholic Caravita community in Rome thirty years later, with its hearty ecumenical relationships, did I find such a relaxed and genuine Christian unity. In the eighties, however, uniquely on the island of Ireland it was Trinity College that led the way, more than playing its part in setting a new agenda for ecumenical parity of esteem. Through that difficult, violent decade it bore witness to the values of tolerance and mutual respect in contrast to the roiling sectarian conflict that continued to poison the atmosphere and paralyse the political maturing of relationships within the North, between North and South, and between Ireland and Britain.

Trinity's lively intellectual discourse showed evidence of real if not always well-informed interest in Northern affairs but the level of benign ignorance was no worse than elsewhere and there was always a challenging debate on in the Hist or the Law Soc, where passion and repartee took the place of forensic scrutiny rather like your average parliamentary debate only almost invariably wittier and more entertaining. One face, one voice, dominates my memory. The young baby-faced, multi-curled Brian Lenihan. He had won Schol at the end of the 1970s; his was a brain of legendary and amazing capacity. Funny, savvy, passionate and knowledgeable on a very eclectic span of subjects, he pretty much outshone the rest. That was no small feat for his peers were a bright and high-achieving bunch, many of whom have made a national and international imprint. But he had a very natural charm, decency and gracious-ness that alongside his brainpower was to earn him, in his student days, the widespread respect that characterized his later legal and political career.

The eighties saw the stirrings of computer literacy. There was reputed to be a Computer Something Department somewhere in college though we had no idea what went on there and no idea of how it would shortly revolutionize our lives. Our wonderfully maternal if occasionally scolding Law School secretary, Margot Aspel, was tormented by a brute of a typewriter, correcting fluid and those horrible black carbon-paper packs with 'flimsies' and other time-consuming tyrannies, which included all of us staff and students, for our favourite place was in her office drinking her home-made lemonade or eating her delicious little cakes. Unless, of course, she was in a mood, in which case most of us would have chewed our elbows to the bone rather than venture across her door. I still miss her.

Meanwhile, I mastered the first of Alan Sugar's cheap Amstrads and ventured not very boldly into the computer age. When at the end of the eighties I moved to the Queen's University of Belfast and enquired of the Northern Ireland Bar Library whether it offered online services and computer access to barristers, the tentative reply was that they had the electric plugs. How quickly it became unthinkable to teach without computers, the Internet, wi-fi, online libraries and all the rest. In the eighties in the Computer Something Departments in Trinity and elsewhere a new generation of thinkers and doers was, almost unnoticed, changing the trajectory of our lives. Golden genera-tions, one after the other and one more remarkable than the next.

Trinity Tales

Trinity College Dublin in the Eighties

A FLASHY PLAYER

tom doorley

I THINK I was only ten when I decided that I wanted to go to Trinity. On my weekly visit to a great-aunt in Pembroke Street I would wander through Front Gate, school satchel swinging, and amble along to Lincoln Gate. It was exotic; I liked that. I liked the squares and the buildings and their quietness and elegance. Many of the students – this was 1970 – looked as if they were refugees from the 'summer of love' and had just removed the flowers from their hair. My inability to achieve anything approaching a pass in a maths exam prompted my headmaster to point out that Trinity would not require me to have mathematics – provided I had a pass in Latin, something I could manage in my sleep. Egged on, I'm sure, by the entire maths department at my school, the headmaster suggested that I might give mathematics a miss at Leaving Cert. and concentrate on Virgil and Cicero. I didn't hesitate.

The TCD Matric was my salvation. It rather grandly ignored the Leaving Certificate syllabus in its entirety and I fell upon it, as Wodehouse would say, with glad cries, in 1976 when I was in the fifth form. When I was awarded the only distinction in English that year, I was convinced that TCD had, with laser-like acuity, recognized my peculiar genius. It must, I decided, be a distinctly superior kind of joint. But, of course, it never made the same mistake again.

I arrived to register in the School of History in the autumn of 1977, stepping off a yellow number 11 bus and into a campus of a mere 4500 students. There was no Arts Block; Fellows' Square was a big building site. We history students started our academic careers in the Museum Building, amidst the fossils and the skeletons. As far as academic matters were concerned it was, in my case at any rate, an example of youth being wasted on the young. Some of the finest brains in the land were on hand to teach us and yet I failed to be gripped by the story of the Guelphs and the Ghibellines and the emergence of medieval Europe.

But there were pleasant distractions. Most of us boys had been educated at all-male schools that smelled of sweat, ink and cabbage. Girls were galactic creatures who sprinkled the sidelines of cup matches at Donnybrook with fairy dust; they imparted a sensual frisson to even the dullest of inter-school debates. Now, they were classmates and we had to adjust to their regular proximity. People from my old school, Belvedere, made a point of eschewing each other for the first term or so, in an attempt to avoid falling into a clique. I recall the late Brian Lenihan saying in a very earnest stage whisper – to the puzzlement of everyone within earshot, i.e. most of Front Square – 'We mustn't keep meeting like this!'

Most history students laboured under the illusion that doing a BA (Mod) in history involved learning history. In the fullness of time, a majority realized that what we were learning was, in fact, a set of skills: the ability to research, refine an argument, marshal thoughts, think clearly. I was in my thirties before I realized that I had learned a great deal during my four undergraduate years. It just wasn't what I had been expecting.

At the time, however, I came to accept that I was going to end up knowing more and more about less and less. I developed a vast and wholly unexpected enthusiasm for the wool industry in medieval England – purely because my tutor, Dr Christine Meek, was a superb teacher. I ended up producing a mini-thesis on how the cloth industry helped to finance Edward III's military campaigns. I still have a mild sense of disbelief when I realize that I managed to pull this one off.

Some of us were lucky enough to be taught by R.B. McDowell, when he was still in full flight. When you stepped into his office you were – literally

– ankle-deep in papers and books; he had an aversion to using shelves. On one occasion, when I had gone to collect an essay, he told me brightly: 'You take that side of the room, I'll take this and I'm sure we'll turn it up eventually.' It took less than an hour. He taught a brilliantly random and exciting course under the broad title of 'Ireland in the Age of Imperialism and Revolution'. He had a marvellous talent for digression, a quality I have always regarded as undervalued. Some other courses failed to grip me. I drove Professor Louis Cullen, the great expert on Irish economic history, to distraction. On one occasion when reading a seminar paper on the price of potatoes in the nineteenth century, he asked me, rather sharply, to 'spare us the further details'. On another occasion, while struggling to choose a suitable essay topic from the wealth of material offered by twelfth-century Ireland, I made the mistake of telling one of the leading experts in the field, Professor J.F. Lydon, that I found the whole thing rather dull. The resulting explosion could have shattered windows as far away as the Pav.

The extramural part of our education involved nursing cups of coffee and talking. This kind of thing tended to be conducted in the café of the Kilkenny Shop on Nassau Street, with its fine view of College Park. Celia West, Michael Buttanshaw, David Hughes, John Wilson, Mandy Daly, Patricia Quinn, Catherine Stokes, Louise Broderick, Ann-Marie Harty, Mary Devally and many more formed what was quite a large *salon*.

Given that students are supposed to eat anything you care to put before them, it's a measure of the horrors of college food in those days that we had a Students' Union boycott of the Dining Hall and the Buttery shortly after I enrolled. As soon as we had got through Junior Fresh, we spent as little time as possible in the Buttery, 'the orange painted hell' as *Piranha* called it. It did, however, have two attractions. One was the Manhattans made by the lugubrious barman, Matt, who looked as if he had been painted by El Greco. The other was the chocolate biscuit cake, which was produced – and consumed – by the ton daily.

Towards the end of my time in Trinity, I became part of a kind of cooking co-operative, with Clive Lee, Dick Flood and a few other medical students. The idea was that we would take it in turns to feed each other in rooms, using two gas rings and such culinary skill as we could muster. My dish was a Hibernian sort of spaghetti bolognese; Dick's was T-bone steaks. Clive stuck doggedly with his own invention, curried Knorr minestrone soup, which was much better than it sounds. On one of the few occasions when a bottle of wine (Vin de Table de Plonk) was produced, and set in front of the gas fire to become – ahem – *chambré*, it curdled. I have never seen such a thing, before or since.

We historians were amongst the last undergraduates to sit, as a matter of course, September exams. This relic of a more gracious age was fraught with one major potential problem: if you went down, you had to repeat the whole year. I panicked the night before my British medieval exam and went to bed in the hope that I would wake refreshed and clear-headed. Not so but somehow I managed to pass.

The following year, some of us started to conduct tours for visitors, with the blessing of the Senior Dean, J.V. Luce, who drawled his approval in that detached and sleepy voice of his. He even went so far as to say that college would not take so much as a tithe from our takings; we could keep the loot.

Pausing in mid-tour one day in the Museum Building, I pointed out the memorial plaque to Edward Cecil Guinness, first Earl of Iveagh, a benefactor of the college whom, we hazily understood, might have something to do with the free Guinness on Commons.

A gum-chewing American tourist asked suddenly, 'Was he a Jew?'

'No,' I said, 'I think he was an Anglican.'

'So,' said the tourist, 'who was the Tullamore Jew, then?'

Tourists would often ask if the busts lining both sides of the Long Room were of graduates 'of this school?'

'No,' we would reply, 'Socrates was a bit early for Trinity …'

I wasted a great deal of time on the Hist and I'm not sure why. I was a poor-to-middling debater and the hard core – I rose to the dizzy heights of being censor and secretary – were obsessed with what one of them, during Private Business, described as 'this society, which is greater than all of us'. It was also a hotbed of skulduggery, intrigue and bitchiness. As an antidote to all the law students at the Hist, I spent more and more time with people from the 'science end', especially medics. The Hist folk tended to frequent The Stag's Head, while the scientists and nascent doctors favoured the Lincoln, with its *Dublin Opinion* cartoons, sticky carpet and outstandingly tolerant barman, Pat

Healy, who later went on to have The Blue Light in the foothills of the Dublin mountains.

During the approach to my finals I decided to defer my departure from Trinity by the simple expedient of trying for teaching and the H.Dip.Ed., a course that, with very few exceptions, was taught by eccentrics, incompetents and the bone idle. In some cases, all three.

I found myself teaching in the mornings at St Columba's in Rathfarnham, and sleeping quietly in the Edmund Burke Theatre in the afternoons. When we sat our exams at the end of the course we were astonished at how little of any value we had learned. And when, during our first paper, a member of the department arrived breathless in the Exam Hall to tell us that, 'in question 3b, the word "aprents" should be "parents" ', the Revd Matthew Byrne, chaplain of King's Hospital, exclaimed loudly, 'Oh, that's such a shame! I've just written three pages on aprents.'

The strangest part of the H.Dip.Ed. was that I got a first in statistics. I'm still convinced that this was some kind of computer error. I continued to teach at St Columba's but decided that I would pursue a part-time M.Litt. Of course, it was not a foregone conclusion that I would be accepted for postgraduate work and I am eternally grateful to the School of Modern History that they decided to give me the benefit of the doubt.

The M.Litt. fizzled out over the next year or so (I blame the paucity of original source material, which is always a safe bet) and my name disappeared from the books of Trinity College Dublin. But I don't think I ever really left.

Tom Doorley (TCD 1977–83; History) did the H.Dip.Ed. (1982) while teaching at St Columba's College, Rathfarnham, and stayed there until 1985. Since then he has worked for the **Irish Independent, The Sunday Tribune, The Sunday Business Post** and **The Irish Times**. He is now food and wine critic and general columnist with the **Irish Daily Mail**. He has worked in advertising and, as PR adviser to Durex in the 1990s, saw condoms become legal in Ireland. Thanks to his work in television and radio he has become what **The Cork Examiner** once described as 'a minor celebrity' and divides his time between rural Munster and Dublin. He is married to Johann McKeever and has three daughters.

A DIFFERENT PLACE

aine lawlor

IT WASN'T a place I'd ever been until I sat the Matric. For years, it was the mystery behind the walls I'd walk past or glimpse from the top of a passing bus. The home of the Book of Kells, and the otherwise unknown. Nor was Trinity a place that girls from my convent school tended to go. There was no longer a ban on Catholics, but still the decision to go there brought the whiff of difference in a world where my father didn't quite get why a daughter would go to college instead of getting a job.

So, naturally, Trinity was irresistible to me.

For the first few weeks and months I felt hopelessly out of my depth; navigating the new Arts Block, getting used to and then loving the pall of smoke that hung over the Buttery, Matt throwing his eyes up to heaven behind the bar, Janet clearing the tables and proclaiming her views on the news of the day or the carry-on of the students around her. After a time you got to know her crooked smile, and the pleasure she took in friendship.

And the surprise at finding out how little I knew about the real world, the world outside of books – the markers of class that I hadn't learned to read, but that made such a difference. We'd grown up in Fianna Fáil land – a world where our parents worshipped de Valera and the Pope; both their pictures up on the kitchen wall. It was a world I'd been dying to escape from, but I didn't realize what a klutz I'd feel amongst those reared to take privilege and choices for granted.

On the other hand, there was the joy of meeting gay people, straight people, Northerners from both sides of the divide, black people, brown people and country people. Suddenly 'diversity' was lots of people I knew and called friends and not just a word in the worthy novels I tended to read back then.

In school, May was the month of Mary. In Trinity, May was the month of exams, yes, but also of the Trinity Ball, of sitting on a windowsill in Botany Bay on a sunny evening, or watching a cricket match while having a drink down at the Pav, as the buses roared past outside. During my first few years, the world beyond the walls disappeared, obliterated by the distractions of this new world: Players, the debates in the Phil and the Hist, and all the goings-on besides – the Cumann Gaelach, O'Neill's on a Friday night, the Palace, the Bailey and warm chocolate doughnuts in Bewley's. Dublin was dowdier then, the recession biting. But there was also a sense of a new Ireland rising: U2 and The Boomtown Rats; the Sheridan brothers and John Stephenson in the Project; gay rights and feminism; Tony Gregory. Dowdy yet exciting.

I got a job in the Students' Union shop, one of the few places in the country you could buy condoms over the counter. I remember there were four brands on sale, the cheapest, Black Shadow, at 70p. Those were popular with shy young men and furtive middle-aged ones. The older men I usually didn't like, my convent sensibilities put off by their spending less than a pound on the nasty black ones instead of £2.50 for the dozen of Featherlight. The young guys were sweet, in and out a few times to drum up their courage, and always asking for a Mars bar first.

Big days came and went on the Dining Hall steps. We occupied buildings around college in various campaigns, heady with indignation at the prices and standards of catering, or library opening hours. Once there was a warrant out for my arrest over an illegal occupation. I came home that night, I think it was April or May of 1980, expecting that the next day would see my arrest as a lowly member of the Students' Union executive. That was to reckon without my mother's swift intervention. The next day I was on a plane to exile with my aunt in Germany, while my father was left with the job of purging my contempt of the court injunction. So much for any attempt to be radical on my part.

The harsher realities of politics and life outside Trinity in the early eighties soon began to have an impact. I remember Bernadette Devlin speaking to a huge crowd in Front Square during the hunger strikes, the black flags that appeared on the way into college, the way the city resembled those news clips from Belfast on the way home at night – gardaí in riot gear jumping out of vans, buses on fire, O'Connell Street in chaos. Waiting for the news each morning to find out whether Bobby Sands had died, and whether anyone else had paid the price of a life or a limb in those bitterly sectarian days that intruded even into a Trinity student's bubble.

It was hard to avoid politics. Even during exam time, trying madly to cram three terms' work into three weeks, there was the distraction of the loudhailers on the election vans passing down Nassau Street calling on us all to arise and follow Charlie. You were with him and his Ireland, or against him, and Trinity, for all its faults, was an important oasis where you could see lots of different kinds of Irish people with different kinds of beliefs. *The Irish Times* became more important for morning coffee than a chocolate doughnut as it chronicled the grotesque and the unbelievable, the economic crisis, the sectarian and culture wars. Slowly, I was learning to see my country with adult eyes. My childhood was a world of great security and sunshine, with a sense of community I'd only truly value later on in life. But back then I had stood against its unquestioning loyalties, and its questionable ethics.

Towards the end arose the question of what to do and where to go. Somehow I decided that being president of the Students' Union was the next best step. And, despite the forty-seven engineers who also decided to run for president that year, and in no small thanks to my election agent, law student Ger Scully, and the barrel of beer I promised the engineers for their second preferences, I managed to get elected.

The bonus of student office was a year in rooms, a summer of falling in love while they filmed *Educating Rita* outside my bedroom window, artificial snow falling under an August sky. With term time came the chance to learn how Trinity worked behind the scenes, a glimpse of its political mechanisms, but most of all the pleasure of getting to know the eclectic groups of academics and staff who kept it all going. What had seemed distant and formal and archaic before became personal and funny and humane. I discovered how often the staff were really on the students' side. Before, I'd only known the academics who taught me or those who'd hung around the Buttery or the debating and meeting rooms. But now I also had the chance to come to know those involved in running departments or sitting on committees. The Students' Union fought the cuts and went on marches but student protest mattered less to me now; what was going on in the country became a greater preoccupation. The internal machinations of student politics quickly seemed pointless but that year of living in college was one of my highlights.

And then it was all over, and time to head back outside Front Gate. I took with me what mattered most, a relationship with Ian Wilson, who married me and is with me still, the friends who are still friends, and a belief in curiosity and diversity that I try to hold on to.

There's less of a divide between Trinity and the Ireland outside its gates these days, which is as it should be. Both the country and the institution needed to change. But there was a time when, to me, Trinity's singularity represented something important, it was a place in which there were choices about being Irish. It was more than an academic institution. It was a place that welcomed all kinds of different people whose reality was denied in the Ireland of my childhood. And that's what mattered most.

Aine Lawlor (TCD 1978–82; English and Irish) was president of the Students' Union 1982–3. An Irish radio and television broadcaster, she co-hosts the **Morning Ireland** radio show on RTÉ Radio 1. She lives in Dublin with her husband Ian Wilson, a producer in RTÉ 2fm, and her four children. Her interests include gardening and growing and cooking her own food. She was presented with the Trinity College Alumni Award in 2008. Other awards include PPI News Broadcaster of the Year 2012 and **Tatler** Woman in Media of the Year 2012.

NORTHERNERS, POETS AND NOT BEING BEATEN BY THE RECESSION

hugo macneill

I SUPPOSE one should be careful not to over-romanticize the past. I don't think my memory is too selective but when I look back on my Trinity days, my sense is of a magical time.

And yet the economic backdrop was dire. It is interesting to compare the situation of the early 1980s with that of today. The unemployment rate was 20 per cent and most of us emigrated on graduation. There was very little entrepreneurship. Those who stayed went mainly into the 'safe' professions. Start your own business? What if it went bust? What would your parents say to the neighbours?

I suppose we thought it would get better, or that we would cope with it one way or another. A recent *Irish Times* series on young people showed an overwhelming desire not to get sucked into anger and frustration at the current crisis but just to get on with things. Maybe that's one of the best things about being a student; you put things in a wider context. And in spite of the terrible state of the early 1980s, we did see a subsequent economic transformation with a profound and lasting change in terms of entrepreneurship. People who set up companies that failed set up others that worked. Unemployment went down and just about everyone I knew who wanted to come home, did come home. Myself included. Will that be the experience of today's Trinity students?

My Trinity rugby days followed the success of John Robbie's Leinster champions of 1976 and came before Trinity challenged again in the mid 1980s; in fact, during my four seasons we did not win a single match in the Leinster Senior Cup. Did I really enjoy it? After all, I had just come from the fanatical atmosphere of a Blackrock College Schools' Cup-winning team. Adversity bred great strength and friendship. We were all just out of school, without worries about jobs or families. Just sport, studies, meeting people and having fun. New friends and teammates were drawn from places that had until recently been our deadliest rivals: Terenure, St Mary's, Clongowes and De La Salle. Years later, I was privileged to tour with the British and Irish Lions and I had the same experience on a wider scale, getting to know and play with Scots, Welsh and English players, former adversaries from Twickenham, Murrayfield and Cardiff.

The day after a match was always special, a sensation of pressure released even if the mission had not been accomplished. Sitting in the Pavilion bar with friends, teammates and supporters, the prevailing feeling was not one of ecstatic celebration but just real satisfaction. There are few feelings comparable to being with friends and teammates the day after a victory. Subsequently, in the Irish teams we always made a point of meeting the next day with friends, wives and girlfriends before parting for home in various different directions. I had the shortest trip of all – the walk down from the Shelbourne hotel and in through the Lincoln Gate. You can't be a student and an international these days. I would have hated to have had to make a choice.

Academic and sporting life went hand in hand. Thanks to teachers like Dermot McAleese, Sean Barrett and John O'Hagan in the Department of Economics, I was fortunate enough to be elected a Foundation Scholar. With it came rooms, fees and Commons in the evening. The real benefit was that it enabled me to spend a year studying Anglo-Irish literature, just for the pure enjoyment of learning. Being introduced to James Joyce by the enthusiastic David Norris was a wonderful experience. I recall the quiet precision and dry Ulster humour of Terence Browne. And then there was Brendan Kennelly.

Spending time in his poetry classes and getting to know Brendan as a friend was one of the real highlights of my time in Trinity. Our first meeting was memorable. Having decided on Anglo-Irish literature, Professor Trevor West advised that I had to meet Brendan to explain that this was not an excuse to stay on playing rugby. Trevor was the most complete university person I have ever met and a special friend. He touched so many aspects of university and wider Irish life – scholar, sportsman, gifted teacher, university senator and peacemaker in Northern Ireland.

We had a great night in O'Neill's of Suffolk Street and then went back to Brendan's rooms. West and Kennelly started arguing about who was the better sportsman. This could not be left to theoretical speculation but had to be verified empirically. So off across Front Square to College Park they marched at half past two in the morning. I was the starter for the 400-metre chase between the Professor of Mathematics, senator and chairman of DUCAC in one lane, and the Professor of Anglo-Irish Literature in the next. Off they sprinted with West taking an early lead around the bend by the law library. The benefit of Kennelly's Gaelic football youth kicked in and he took the lead down the back straight and towards the Pavilion. In a last desperate throw, West tried to take advantage of the gloom and the Cork mathematician bisected the bend towards the finish line. He didn't make out the cricket net and flew into it at top speed as Kennelly came down the home straight, raising his arms, laughing all the way.

During the international rugby season, Brendan and I would meet on the Monday night following each game. You are quite insulated when you are playing, physically and in every other way. You are unaware of the wider context that makes those weekends so special. Hearing about Brendan's adventures on a rugby weekend enhanced my own experience of playing for Ireland.

The team used to stay in the Shelbourne and Friday mornings were normally free. Even when I had left Trinity, I would often drop down to Brendan's poetry class on the Friday before training. In 1985, I got Brendan two tickets before the Triple Crown and championship decider. On the Monday night, he was in good form but seemed a little awkward. The country had been celebrating for the previous two days. His mood seemed quiet. He finally confessed that he had headed out for the big day and stopped at a pub in Beggars Bush. He met a lovely English couple, on their first trip to Dublin but a little down because they could find no tickets. Brendan gave them his and then went and watched it on TV. He was worried that I would have minded. How could I?

In recent years, I have become involved with the National Institute for Intellectual Disabilities in Trinity where students do a two-year course and receive a Certificate of Contemporary Living. It is truly inspirational and one of the greatest initiatives I have seen in Trinity. Brendan captured its spirit perfectly when speaking on the Institute's prize day. He thanked it for 'removing the mask of disability to reveal the extraordinary ability that lies beneath'.

Two other things made Trinity special for me. First was the stepping stone to Oxford and the second was the link with the North of Ireland. Trinity at the time was not very cosmopolitan. Students from the North, the Anglo-Irish tradition of the South and a few random overseas students was pretty much it. In 1981, Oxford made their first visit to Trinity for many years. As captain of Dublin University Football Club (DUFC), I waited in the Pavilion with other players and club officials for the coach to arrive via the Holyhead ferry, and the Oxford contingent eventually appeared in their dark-blue blazers. Over that weekend I got to know some of the most remarkable people I have ever met, many of whom became close friends and teammates.

At the time there was much debate in Ireland as to whether the Irish rugby team should tour the still-apartheid South Africa at the end of the season. It was my first season in international rugby. Despite his love of rugby, South Africa's Chris Hugo-Hamman advised against playing South Africa as long as the apartheid regime was in operation. I subsequently chose not to go.

The North has always been important in my life. Some of my earliest memories are of the annual family holiday to the seaside at Bettystown, which always included a day trip to Newry where we could buy 'English' sweets. At Blackrock we had played RBAI, Campbell and Methody. That was my first real experience of going north. It used often be said that the great thing about rugby in Ireland was that players could come together from North and South and 'the Troubles' were never discussed. I always thought that was fine as far as it went. But if people who knew and respected each other could not try to understand the other's tradition, how could we expect kids from polarized ghettos to do so? We did talk about 'the Troubles', and that bred mutual respect.

The IRA ceasefire broke down when it bombed Canary Wharf in London in 1996. Trevor Ringland and I organized a 'Peace Rugby International' where the Barbarians brought many of the world's leading players to play the Irish team. It was meant as a statement against the IRA and other terrorist violence. Large elements of 'middle Ireland' were speaking out against this violence for the first time. It was quickly organized with inspirational help from many people and was probably the most emotional of many days at Lansdowne Road. The guests of honour were children touched directly by violence; a young Protestant boy who lost both parents and a brother in the Shankill Road chip-shop bombing; a young Catholic whose brother died in a reprisal shooting in Greysteel; an English boy whose best friend was killed in the IRA bombing of Warrington.

Players who had created some of the greatest moments in rugby came to Dublin to lend their voices to those working for peace in Ireland. David Campese, Australian World Cup winner; Philippe Sella and Laurent Cabannes, Grand Slam champions for France; Rory Underwood and Dean Richards of England; and Francois Pienaar whose photo with Nelson Mandela after South Africa's World Cup win in 1995 went around the world. It was a very special day and summed up the best about rugby and Ireland, North and South.

I recently passed through Trinity during Freshers' Week and saw freshmen walking through Front Square and others coming out on College Park to begin their own special adventures. Clubs and societies were luring new members with all kinds of promises and enticements. The economic gloom seemed to have been left at Front Gate – for the time being, at least. There was noise and possibility and optimism in the air. I think that's what made Trinity special to me – that great sense of possibility. A possibility that extends to a much wider audience through the various access programmes now available. Traditions are renewed and built upon, redefined in the Ireland of today and tomorrow as well as by the splendours of days gone by.

Hugo MacNeill (TCD 1978–82; Economics; Diploma in Anglo-Irish Literature) studied economics at Oxford until 1985. He worked in London for Boston Consulting Group and then Goldman Sachs. He returned in 2000 to take responsibility for Goldman's investment banking business in Ireland. He is also chairman of the Ireland Funds, vice-chairman of the British Irish Association, member of the advisory board of the Institute of British Irish Studies at UCD and board member of GOAL UK.

FISH ON FRIDAY

dermot horan

I **ENTERED** Trinity College in October 1979, at the tail end of a decade of oil crises, rock bands who released albums, not singles, and some of the worst fashion the world had ever seen – flared trousers, platform boots and poly-cotton shirts with large, rounded collars.

I was part of the first generation of Dublin Catholics who applied for Trinity rather than UCD, and felt no guilt about entering an institution banned in previous decades to Catholics by John Charles McQuaid. For me and several school friends, it offered a venerable and historic alternative to the windswept concrete jungle that was Belfield in those days. It was also situated in the middle of a capital city, away from the leafy suburbs of Blackrock, Monkstown and Dún Laoghaire where I had spent my teenage years. Dublin was a smaller city then and you often bumped into people walking down Grafton Street, but if you felt it was too vast or noisy, or even dirty, you only had to walk through one of the many gates into the Trinity campus and you felt part of a unique and protected community.

I studied (or, to use that more traditional term, 'read') history and clas-sical civilization and there was plenty of reading in both subjects. The lecture schedule was light and most of my academic time was spent in the Berkeley Library preparing for and writing essays, which were handed in and assessed in tutorials. Tutorials turned out to be far more important than lectures. These were where you would have your essays critiqued, and where in small groups of six or seven you would engage in dialogue with the academic staff.

One lecturer, Ian Robinson, would continue our discussions over coffee in Brown Thomas, which occupied the building now home to Marks & Spencer. These were the days before Starbucks, Insomnia and Costa Coffee. There was Bewley's, and cafés in department stores, and that was it.

Brown Thomas, being the cosmopolitan place that it was, served Rombouts coffee. This was coffee from a single filter placed directly over the cup. The waitresses wore crisp uniforms. Waitresses also featured in Bewley's up the street, where I went for my second cup of coffee every afternoon after three o'clock lectures. Bewley's had an honesty system of leaving a cake stand full of delicious buns on each table and asking how many you had consumed when settling your bill. Many a Trinity student had selective memory loss when it came to these declarations.

The Berkeley was the home of law, history and classics. It was a non-lending library, full of specialized tomes that you had to read on site. You had no class or locker room so the library became your residence on campus but you were not meant to take ownership of a desk. In truth, most of us pretended we were still there, by leaving an A4 pad with some notes on it together with several large and heavy reference books left open. That ruse generally worked and you could head off for a lecture and a coffee afterwards pretty secure in the knowledge that 'your' desk would still be there, ready for reoccupation. My one foe was Conor Cruise O'Brien, who used to write a column for a national newspaper at the time and researched and wrote it in the Berkeley. He knew exactly what I was up to and took regular pleasure in moving my carefully prepared assortment of books and notes to the edge of the desk, forcing me to apologize quietly and move to a free desk if one existed.

Going for coffee and buns meant having money. My parents were generous in granting me an allowance, and from this I was meant to budget for every-thing from clothes to Clearasil to bus fares, coffee and drink. I also had various summer jobs and for the last year I sold advertising for the illegal pirate radio station Radio Nova. Any money I earned or that was given to me was lodged in the Bank of Ireland student branch, which was in the Bank of Ireland opposite

Front Gate. There were no cash machines. Students used to queue up, particularly on Fridays at lunchtime, to withdraw £20 from an old-fashioned cashbook, the withdrawals from which were handwritten into your little book by the teller.

In those days, once you opened an account with Bank of Ireland, AIB or Ulster Bank you would be with them for life; banks were extremely keen for you to open an account. The Bank of Ireland was a regular advertiser with *Piranha*. The magazine has gone through various guises over the years and is still in existence, but when I started working on its staff in second year it was only three years old. Antony Sellers had founded *Piranha* in 1978; I would work with him some years later at Granada Television.

Its name suggests it was a satirical magazine, and it was, in parts. There was a back page called 'Grapevine', where the great and good were lambasted, but always couched in terms that would avoid legal proceedings. There were law students on the staff and in my day these included the likes of Katy McGuinness and Eanna Molloy, now a noted Senior Counsel. They made sure we were on reasonably safe ground when we published anything scurrilous. There were frequent threats of legal action, of course, usually made by other law students flexing their intellectual muscles.

When I edited *Piranha* we operated out of an office in Front Square almost beside the Students' Union and with a view of College Green from the window. We brought out around two editions per term. The weekends we went to press were hectic and exhilarating. We had articles and artwork commissioned a few weeks in advance, and waited in anticipation for them to arrive.

The phrase 'cut and paste', which we use on a daily basis on our computers, was a reality then. We laid out the magazine on plain A3 pages, on which we would cut out and paste articles that had been typed up on enormous golf-ball typewriters. The paste was a Pritt Stick and the cutting was done with a scissors. These 'going to press' weekends were often all-nighters, with the eventual magazine laid out very late on Sunday. On Monday morning I would walk around to the printers, and on Thursday would collect the several hundred copies, reduced to A4 size and much the smarter for that.

Piranha always went on sale on a Friday. 'Fish on Friday' was its catch phrase and we would hang posters all over the campus during the week, advertising its imminent publication. On the Friday morning we would have staff members selling it from Front Gate to Nassau Street to Westland Row. It cost 10p, the coin that – by coincidence or accident – had a fish on one side. On a good day we would sell out by lunchtime.

My other major extracurricular activity was acting, directing and writing in Players. The early eighties boasted a rich vein of dramatic talent in Trinity. The likes of Lynne Parker, Declan Hughes and Arthur Riordan would go on to found the Rough Magic Theatre Company. Darragh Kelly, Michael Ford, Stanley Townsend and Pauline McLynn trod the boards. Renaissance man Gary Jermyn would act and then do his party piece – Lucky's speech from *Waiting for Godot* – at the wrap parties.

On Fridays and Saturdays there were late-night performances at 11 pm, our second performance of the night. Gangs of engineers and medics would block-book seats and have several pints on them before packing out the tiny theatre. The actors needed thick skins and also the ability to improvise as rice and bread were thrown on the stage and non-stop heckling was constantly audible, above a general hum of post-pub banter.

No party, meeting or even society meeting was complete without alcohol. In my Freshers' Week in 1979, every society was handing out the latest drink – Guinness Light. It was probably ahead of its time, but it sank without trace that autumn. As we became more sophisticated, wine began to feature. The trouble was that almost all of it was the worst kind of plonk. Most of us had never studied German, but we all knew the word 'Liebfraumilch' – a sickly-sweet white wine, developed by the Germans for the export market. The most famous brand was Blue Nun, which was pretty horrible, but there were cheaper, viler versions for sale in the supermarkets and off-licences.

In my final year I was lucky enough to live on campus. It was difficult to get rooms, especially if you already lived in Dublin. I took Room 16.23 in Botany Bay. The facilities were Spartan; an electric kettle would blow the fuses for the whole building. I had a flat with a decent-sized living room looking out over the square, a tiny kitchen with a table-top gas cooker, and two bedrooms. The bedrooms had no source of heat and faced due north. They were absolutely freezing in winter. For all its failings, living in rooms was great. You were in the centre of town, and yet cloistered deep within the campus. You did not have to eat in the Buttery, which in those days had a dreadful reputation. Botany Bay was then the preserve of young men only. The squares were segregated, with rooms in Front Square reserved largely for women. The facilities and wiring in some of the other squares, such as New Square, were better and this attracted staff, including the Junior Deans. Back in Botany Bay you could make noise, stay up all night and get up to most manners of mischief without any censure: the Junior Deans were simply not bothered to make their way to our frozen and inhospitable square.

Making mischief in those days generally consisted of having parties and playing loud music. The hit albums of the time were Michael Jackson's *Thriller*, *The Lexicon of Love* by ABC, *Let's Dance* by David Bowie and *Sweet Dreams (Are Made of This)* by Eurythmics. Big singles included 'Don't You Want Me' by The Human League, 'Just an Illusion' by Imagination and, of course, 'Come on Eileen' by Dexy's Midnight Runners. There were no legal commercial radio stations; most people took their music cues from BBC's *Top of the Pops* and then bought the albums. Those not 'into' pop music indulged themselves with LPs by bands such as Led Zeppelin and Pink Floyd. Botany Bay was a cacophony of different music tastes.

Four years after I'd arrived, I left with my degree and emerged into the real world. There are so many memories. Playing cricket in College Park on summer afternoons. Falling asleep regularly at three o'clock lectures and being told by my classmates that I had been snoring. Getting home at 9 am after the Trinity Ball and trying to sleep, knowing that when I awoke it was two days before my exams. Attending twenty-firsts – at which the parents and their friends often got more drunk than the students – on almost a weekly basis in third and fourth year. Dressing up in vintage dress suits bought in Jenny Vander, and learning how to tie a real bow tie so you could untie it and look even cooler. Now, thirty years after I graduated, my eldest son Jack has embarked on his own journey through Trinity and I sincerely hope his time is as varied and as much fun as my own.

Trinity Ball, 1980. Left to right: *David Cox, Dermot Horan, Francesca White and Denise Kinsella.*

Dermot Horan (TCD 1979–83; History and Classical Civilization) is director of Broadcast and Acquisitions in RTÉ, where he acquires all the feature films and international programming. He previously worked as a producer/director in RTÉ and was also head of children's programmes. He started his TV career with Granada in Manchester. He is a board member of the St Patrick's Festival and is married with three sons.

A TRINITY INTERLEKT

linda hickey

MY LOVE AFFAIR with Trinity began when I chose it as a topic for a school project when I was about seven or eight years old. My dad took me to the library and we pored over tedious textbooks that recounted the exalted history of the place. Dad took notes, and I did whatever seven-year-olds do in libraries. Later, I struggled to make sense of his notes about Oliver Goldsmith, whose statue, he observed, stands outside Trinity College facing the traffic island. This translated in my finished project to: 'Oliver Goldsmith worked as a lollipop man outside the University.' I think I got a B, but more importantly the die was cast – there was only ever going to be one entry on my CAO form – economics and social studies (ESS) at Trinity.

Trinity College experienced a 'feminist spring' of sorts in the early eighties, or at least that's how I remember it. After the bra-burning and the contraceptive battles of the seventies, our generation was going to get the equal treatment it deserved. We were sure of it. Society had moved into a new era and was not going to revert to old ways of thinking. Looking back, we seemed to inhabit a special time when girls wore the feminist badge with pride and the only surprise to me now is that the fervour of our passion isn't shared by young women today. The unreconstructed feminist views that flourished in me and my friends in our Trinity years, and indeed never left us (and yes I mean you,

Mary Corcoran), now seem nothing more than a source of bemusement to younger female colleagues and friends.

I took myself and my specialist subject very seriously. I was quickly and correctly identified as being absurdly easy to rise, and my new male friends would take bets on how quickly they could send me into orbit by saying something ludicrously trite like 'Women are intellectually inferior to men.' I could never see that I was being wound up until I was in full flight and by then the guys were howling with laughter.

There was a pre-determined reading list for all self-respecting feminists in the 1980s that ranged from Erica Jong's *Fear of Flying*, which combined feminism and filthy sex in a guilt-free read, to Simone de Beauvoir's *The Second Sex*, which was intellectual and dry (and which, I am afraid to admit, I had never finished), to Germaine Greer's *The Female Eunuch*, in which she made the alarming claim that a woman couldn't say she was liberated unless she had tasted her own menstrual blood (I didn't). Given my obsession with such weighty matters, I didn't have much success with boys in my early college years. My father tired of telling me that my chosen look of dungarees, his shirts and a cropped haircut was unlikely to appeal to callow eighteen-year-olds. Today I'm sure I would be given a different label; then it was 'humourless feminist'. I wasn't really humourless, more overwhelmed with the responsibility of making everybody see the light.

Particularly exhausting for me was the fact that I was also fighting a class war. My new friends refused to accept my claim to being working-class on the simplistic basis that anyone who, say, liked classical music and had read Anthony Burgess couldn't claim the mantle, but working-class I was. We all experience one or two epiphanies in our lives; my first came in Freshers' Week 1979. I stumbled from one society welcoming party to another, trying to make friends as I knew no one else starting in Trinity. At DUBES (Dublin University Business and Economic Society) I met a boy who told me he had been to Blackrock College. At an event in the Junior Common Room the following day I met two more. When I came across my fifth Blackrock graduate I expressed my surprise that five boys from one school were all in Trinity. He looked at me strangely and said, 'Linda, there are about fifty from Blackrock starting in Trinity this year and the same number in UCD.' My school, Whitehall House, had been delighted to have three students going on to third-level institutions; it was a good year. I realized that I was lucky to have grown up in a house where we were encouraged to think we could do anything we wanted, but the boys from Blackrock didn't have to feel lucky, they just had to go to Blackrock.

The call for class war was harder to win converts to than the feminist one. At the time, it was fairly cool for guys to sign up to the feminist charter, but acknowledging a society where your opportunity set depended on being one of the 'lucky sperm', as Warren Buffet would say, was tougher to accept. Joe Duffy, president of the Students' Union 1979–80, was equally outraged by Trinity's inherent elitism and identified a battleground to rally support for his attack on the administration – access to the Dining Hall. Not quite Paris '68, but we had a cause. There was a sit-in. I was excited beyond belief. I was a sympathizer to a political action.

Armed with new vocabulary learned in Junior Fresh sociology, I went to war on the lumpen bourgeoisie (I still don't know what that means). I thought I had understood the Theory of Ideology. If I had really understood it I wouldn't have persisted in trying to change my friends' minds. Now I know it's futile to try to change an eighteen-year-old's understanding of society and his or her place in it. We were all hard-wired by that stage and the battle lines were drawn. Happily, a Bachelor of Business Studies degree in the early eighties didn't require the student to take many business courses, a reflection, no doubt, of the faculty's disdainful view of business at that time. I was able to indulge my passion for the class war by slipping courses like 'Welfare Economics' and 'Public Sector Economics' into my business programme.

The problem with being brought up to think you can do anything is that you spend a lifetime being disappointed at all the things that you simply have no talent for. I joined Players in my first week and auditioned for the first play of the term; I have no memory of what it was. In any event I wasn't chosen for a part – I was either fortunate or unfortunate to have started at the same time as Pauline McLynn and Lynne Parker – I suspect I never had a shot. I thought I would slink away quietly after the auditions but I was told I would be on lights. This didn't involve sitting in a booth fiddling with switches, but rather shimmying up a ladder hoisting dangerously heavy lighting fixtures and attaching them to ceiling gantries. I decided very quickly that my future did not lie on either side of the floodlights.

In 1980, I went to Berlin to work for the summer. At night we would climb up the viewing posts and stare silently over the wall, which looked fairly innocuous on the west side. The vista that greeted us on the other side was one of armed East German soldiers, thirty feet of no-man's-land and high security fences. In true Irish fashion, there were about eight of us sharing a one-bedroomed flat, so we got to know each other very well. In the case of me and John Wilson, also from Trinity, we got to know each other very well indeed. Romance blossomed and I had a college boyfriend at last. When my father saw the photograph of us at the Trinity Ball, he asked if John had red hair. 'No,' I said, 'it's the colour of ripening corn.' I've never been let live that one down. The relationship lasted a year, but the slagging from my family has endured for thirty.

The richness of life outside the lecture hall was an unexpected bonus of college life and I embraced it with gusto. I served on the committee of DUBES, which in those days was a bit of a slackers' society. We met at Tuesday lunch-time and there was free soup and sandwiches. We always struggled to get speakers but the late Paul Tansey filled in when we were stuck. I was an enthu-siastic attendant and occasional speaker at the Hist and the Phil. All my inter-ests came together in one bright shining evening when the topic was to do with female equality, probably something like 'women are intellectually inferior to men', and speaking in favour of the motion was Oliver Reed. The great thes-pian was outrageously drunk and entertained the crowd by adopting the cobra position on the speaker's table. I, of course, spoke against the motion and tried to bring some seriousness to the evening. I still hadn't learned – this was no room to be won over by Simone de Beauvoir. Today I'd probably try my hand at some yoga positions instead. After the debate ended, and I don't recall, but I suspect the proposers triumphed, I asked Oliver for his autograph; he was famous after all, if an extraordinary chauvinist. He signed it with love, and addressed it to 'Dear interlekt'. I read later that he struggled learning scripts because of his dyslexia.

After exams wrapped up in fourth year, I went in search of a lecturer to give me a reference. I had always had a crush on John Bristow. He was English and challenged us to think for ourselves. He was happy to oblige and told me to come back a few days later. When I collected it the following week I was pleased to read his praise for my writing skills, my class participation and my performance as one of his tutors. Unfortunately, I never got to use it as it started with the line, 'Although not outstanding intellectually, Linda was well above average as a student'. I couldn't see any upside in highlighting my intellectual mediocrity to prospective employers. Luckily, I had requested a reference from a second lecturer so all was not lost, that is until I opened it. It started with 'Linda has a very bubbly personality' (yes, it actually said bubbly), and on it went in a similar effusive style, enough to prompt a sensible reader to think that our relationship had moved beyond the strictly academic. That one went in the bin, too.

References from Trinity have thankfully played a small part in any progression I have made in my career over the years, but I suspect that the lessons learned, mostly outside the lecture halls, have been an important factor.

Linda Hickey (TCD 1979–83; Business Studies) worked in New York for seven years in venture capital and stockbroking, spending her last four years there with Merrill Lynch. Returning to Dublin in 1990, she joined NCB in institutional sales, moving to Goodbody in 2004 as head of Corporate Broking. She remains a card-carrying feminist and is indulged in her occasional rants by her husband Kevin Keating, a proud graduate of UCG.

AMONG CULCHIES

carl nelkin

I CAN still picture the scene as if it were yesterday: a debating chamber in the Graduate Memorial Building at TCD where a quiz was in full swing. I had just completed a round of questions on my specialist subject of the Old Testament and was now fielding a second round of general knowledge questions.

'What do you call people from Cork?' asked the quizmaster.

'Culchies,' I replied, without a moment's hesitation. The erupting laughter almost brought the house down.

It was the autumn of 1979 and I had just entered Trinity's School of Law. I was lucky to be alive at all. The previous February, I was involved in a motor-cycle crash and suffered two broken thighbones. I had just started to walk again that autumn after several months in a wheelchair and life was good.

I was born and bred in Dublin and, as a member of the small Irish-Jewish community, I had attended Stratford College in Rathgar – the only Jewish school in Ireland. At that time, Stratford was an entirely Jewish school and, consequently, I had never spent much time with non-Jewish children (apart from playing with kids on my road). Nonetheless, there was nothing to worry about, as my religion and background were never an issue in Trinity.

As I lived nearby I did not need to stay on campus so probably missed out on a large part of college life. Nevertheless, it was a thrill to walk around Front

Square during Freshers' Week, when all the clubs and societies were touting for new members. I joined a few clubs but I no longer remember which ones.

I hadn't a clue about how one studied law, as was evident from my first assignment in criminal law. A set of facts was presented to us, with the task of identifying the legal principles involved and their application to the case. I had simply read the facts, felt sorry for the accused and declared him innocent. At each lecture, students were presented with a list of the cases that had been cited. At the end of class, there was a stampede to the law library to procure the case books as copies were limited.

Looking back now, I am critical of the lack of a proper introduction to the methodology. Instead of being taught how to glean a point of law from a case, one was simply left to one's own devices. One of the first cases we were given was an enormous Supreme Court judgment containing several complex opinions running to dozens of pages. The net point we were supposed to extract was contained in one or two short paragraphs but, since nobody pointed this out to me, I ended up reading the entire mind-numbing case and getting nothing out of it.

The library was a great place for meeting people and chatting – I am not sure how much studying was done. As a new student, it was one's own decision as to how much time to invest in reviewing law reports and the other materials meted out during lectures. There was one girl (who shall remain nameless) who buried herself under a pile of books from 9 am to 5 pm, Monday to Friday. I found this somewhat intimidating as it suggested that I was not studying enough. On the other hand, there was another student who probably never knew where the library or the lecture theatre was. This chap just showed up once a year for exams and passed with flying colours. Most of us spent several hours a day in the library but study was punctuated by chats and going for coffee around campus.

Jewish prayers are recited three times a day. The Afternoon Service must be recited before dark and, during the winter months, this coincided with my study time in the library. In the theology section on the top floor, I found a Hebrew prayer book. Each afternoon, I would go to the appropriate shelf and recite the prayers while pretending to browse. I was always afraid that someone would come by and ask what I was doing but they never did.

Apart from lectures, law students were obliged to attend tutorials. Sometimes the discussions became rather intense and, on one occasion, I nearly ended up in a fist fight over some obscure legal point. Video games had just made their entrance on the student scene. On the first floor of Regent House, which sits over Front Gate, was the Junior Common Room (JCR). At first glance it looked imposing, but, in fact, housed Space Invaders, Galaxian and other popular video-arcade games. Many's the time I would be trying to study in the library when my friend, Adam Taylor, would approach and make Galaxian noises in my ear. I shudder to think how much I spent on those games but I was, for a time, a champion Pac-Man player!

After second year, law students could choose some of their subjects. Because it was seen as an easy option, I chose land law. The lecturer was Eldon Young Exshaw, whom I remember as a quiet and rather gentle person. Mr Exshaw had taught the course for many years and had committed the year's lectures into note format from which he read his lectures. Unfortunately, a past student had obtained a copy of these notes and made further copies available in the Students' Union shop. I remember looking ahead a page or two during lectures and asking Mr Exshaw a question. He would say irritably, 'I was just going to tell you that.' Mr Exshaw's two or three standard jokes also appeared in the notes. I am not sure if he ever realized what was going on.

I was a member of the Hist and the Phil and regularly attended debates at both. On one occasion, a debate was interrupted by somebody sweeping into the room to announce that the government had just fallen as a result of their attempt to impose VAT on children's shoes. One of the standard topics was Israel and the Palestinians. Instead of debating the issues, each side would fling as much mud as possible at the other. I remember being approached by two Arab students following a particularly acrimonious debate. They were conciliatory and friendly but I was so angry and wound up that I rebuffed them. I have regretted this action ever since and I have long wished that I had shown them the same friendliness. If we, in faraway Ireland, cannot have a civil debate about Middle East politics, what chance is there for peace on the ground?

During my Trinity days, I joined the Rathmines and Rathgar Musical Society and sang Gilbert and Sullivan operettas and musicals at the Gaiety Theatre. Because I was (and still am) an orthodox Jew, I was not able to attend performances on Friday nights. The society would have been completely within its rights to decline my application for membership on the grounds that I would be absent on one of the busiest nights of the week, musically speaking. Instead, it made special arrangements for me to be absent as required. I have never forgotten this kindness.

My years at Trinity drew to a close when the Irish economy was on its knees. I intended becoming a solicitor and, given that many (if not most) of my fellow students were planning to emigrate, I was terrified at the prospect of being locked into a profession with few job prospects. In those days, an Irish solicitor's qualification offered little scope abroad.

After four years, it was wonderful to graduate and prepare for the big world outside. Commencements were held in the Exam Hall and were conducted in Latin. I was very proud to have my grandparents present while I was conferred with a BA (Mod) in legal science.

Trinity taught me to embrace different cultures and faiths. I also formed friendships that have lasted to this day. While Trinity has been described as an academic playpen with no real bearing on reality, those years marked my passage from childhood to adulthood and prepared me for the real world. I will always retain fond memories.

Carl Nelkin (TCD 1979–83; Legal Science) qualified as a solicitor with the Dublin law firm of McCann FitzGerald. In 1988, he joined GPA Group plc as internal counsel and has specialized in aircraft leasing and financing ever since. In 1994, Carl set up his own aviation law practice in Dublin and represents clients all over the world. In his spare time, Carl is a singer of Irish and Jewish music (www.irishjewishmusic.com). He has released two CDs and gives regular concerts both in Ireland and abroad. He is an active member of the Irish Jewish community and has done his bit to keep the community from shrinking by importing his wife from the United States. They have two daughters.

TRINITY DAYS

shane o'neill

MY FIRST CHOICE on finishing school was law at Trinity, but I didn't get it. I was offered a place at UCD instead and reluctantly accepted. Five days in, I came home and my mother said that a letter had arrived for me; it turned out to be an offer from Trinity to read law. Having started at Belfield, I wasn't that keen on switching, but I decided to take a walk into Trinity to have a look. I was bowled over: it was so far removed from UCD's concrete jungle. While I was there I ran into Hugo MacNeill, who had been two years ahead of me at Blackrock and was a big rugby hero to boys of my generation. He, it turned out, had done something similar, switching to Trinity after a year at UCD. He said, 'You've got to come to Trinity – just look at this place.'

That afternoon I went over to the admissions office and accepted the offer.

On the Monday I showed up for my first day of lectures, I was completely overawed. There were only sixty people in my class, but it was much more diverse than my class at UCD. For one thing, there were far more Northerners. For another, there was a bunch of very strong women who exuded the sophistication and self-confidence that I lacked.

But I knew no one. That first month, I would buy my lunch and go wandering around the campus looking for someone to have it with. A lot of my Blackrock mates had decided to repeat the Leaving to get better results.

Only one of them – John Coulter – had come to Trinity, and he was doing engineering, so for that first month I was a little lonely. However, there was just so much to distract you, it didn't take long to build up a circle of friends.

I had a particular approach to study for the last eight weeks before exams. During the day I did all there was to do, but at midnight I would go to my room with a cup of coffee and study through the night. Once I got into it, I would really focus and work hard. I almost enjoyed it. Then I'd sleep from 6 am until midday and head into college for a day of socializing. And it worked; I got all of my first-year exams.

They called it the Senior Freshman Blues: in first year everything's new. You make friends, it's different; it's exciting. You come back for your second year, expecting the party to continue, and it doesn't. Depression is too strong a word: I remember it as being on autopilot, just going through the motions; getting up, going to lectures, going to lunch, getting on a bus, going home. I felt a vague sense of being lost, of being disconnected from everything. Over time, it passed.

In second year I hung around with a group that became known as the Northern Girls. Truth is, before I went to Trinity I'd never met anyone from Northern Ireland. Though only a hundred miles up the road, they were like an alien tribe. I made a number of firm friendships with people from Northern Ireland while at Trinity. Both my roommates were Northerners. I enjoyed their irreverence and humour; also the sense that there was something much larger going on in their lives but which we couldn't talk about. In large measure they were at Trinity to escape the Troubles.

We had only eight hours of lectures a week. We had some tutorials, but not many. We were expected to spend time in the library researching cases and, to pass the exams, you really did have to do this. I was a crammer; I did almost nothing for the first six months of the academic year, and then worked intensively for the last two.

I started playing rugby in my second year. We hardly ever won, but we had fun. The routine was the same each weekend; win, lose or draw it was back to the Pav at 5 pm to meet the other Trinity teams. We'd while away the next two to three hours, drinking pints and reflecting on the game, before heading into town for food. As sportsmen, we were very focused on our diet. We'd only ever eat McDonald's, or Burdocks, the premier fish and chips in Dublin.

Afterwards we returned to the Pav, by which time the evening crowd would be in and things would really be cooking. Invariably, the rugby crowd would start singing, and by the end of the evening it was messy, with beer spilt or thrown and everyone locked. And that was our Saturday night, all that year and the next.

At the end of term they had elections for the following year's rugby officers, and I was elected as junior secretary. The great thing about this role was that you got to live in rugby rooms, the only way a third-year could get to live on campus; most had to wait until fourth year. I was assigned rooms in Rubrics. Rugby rooms were on the top floor. There was a rudimentary galley kitchen and two bedrooms, but no bathroom. Midnight loo visits were a real hassle: you had to descend four flights of stairs. I don't know which one of us started it, but after a while we abandoned the stairs and pissed out the window instead. Believe it or not, this was not the worst thing to come flying out our window that year.

My roommate was Gery Juleff, or 'Juff', senior secretary of the Rugby Club. He was from the North and, although his Unionist tendencies had been softened by exposure to the 'Free State', he had served in the part-time Ulster Defence Regiment (UDR) before coming to Trinity. He was a very popular character in the Rugby Club. With Juff, what you saw was what you got. On the first night, he laid out some security ground rules. If we ever got a late-night knock on the door, I was to ask whoever it was to identify themselves, other-wise not to open the door. Given the explosive state of Northern Ireland at the time, his fears were not by any means unfounded. The H-Block hunger strikes were ongoing; sectarian killings were rife. It was one of the most tense times of the Troubles. What spooked Juff was the possibility that having been in the UDR he might be a target for the Sinn Féiners in Trinity. Once those ground rules were established, we never discussed politics again.

The lack of stress, the cosy, enveloping bubble of Trinity, the easy access to friends, the gentle rhythm of the day, suited my personality. Until I had a family, this was undoubtedly the happiest I had ever been. We had an idyllic life and we knew it. We did, however, nearly kill someone.

The third E's rugby team became the first Trinity team to win a Leinster Cup in several years. When the Pav closed at 11 pm it was decided, probably not by Juff and me, that the party would repair to our rooms. A mere hour later, the place was destroyed. I'd never seen such feral partying: people were peeing out of windows, getting sick and generally running wild. It culminated in someone throwing our fridge out the window. Juff and I could barely believe what was happening but were not in a fit state to do anything. Eventually, the Junior Dean, John Gaskin, arrived, which had the impact of clearing people out quickly. He said he would see us in the morning.

The following day we woke to a scene of utter devastation, and slowly the reality of what had happened the night before began to seep into our hungover brains. In the cold, sober light of day we were forced to admit that we had actually risked killing somebody. John Gaskin thankfully took a lenient approach. He said that he understood how winning a cup was a big occasion, but that we had to take responsibility for the fact that the party had spiralled out of control. He fined us a hundred pounds – a huge amount. During the day, several of the people who'd been at the party called on us to apologize and to offer to pay their share.

At the end of third year, I was on the lookout for someone to share rooms with in fourth year. I bumped into Paul O'Neill, who was a classmate, and asked him if he had sorted out someone to share with. He hadn't, so we agreed to room together. It was as simple as that.

Back at Trinity after spending the summer of 1982 in Cape Cod, I moved into rooms with Paul. He was a musician. At the time I met him he had already put out a single called 'Rock 'n' Roll Queen', which had got into the lower reaches of the charts. The other guys in the band used to come and go and leave their instruments in our rooms. Sometimes after I'd had a few drinks, I would take a guitar out of its case and warble along to it. Paul would tease me relentlessly about this, but he did show me a few chords. That was my introduction to the guitar, which became a source of enormous pleasure and enjoyment over the next twenty-five-odd years.

I resigned from the Rugby Club in fourth year; it was taking up too much time. This was no great loss to DUFC, but it did mean a pretty major alteration in my social life. In order to fill that gap, I auditioned for a musical called *Salad Days*. Because it was the only thing I could remember the words to, I decided to sing 'Silent Night'. I gave it my best Sinatra tones and was cast as the singing policeman.

About this time, Paul, who was always a little secretive, had started to go out with a girl called Sheelagh Pyle. I knew this not because Paul had told me but because someone else in the circle asked me if I'd met Sheelagh. I hadn't, but I soon would. At the next rehearsal, I was hanging around in my policeman's uniform when someone handed me a programme for the show. As I sat idly scanning it, I noticed Sheelagh Pyle's name; she had the role of the dancing nun. I looked to my left and there was a girl dressed as a nun, so I turned and introduced myself.

I got to know Sheelagh well over the next few weeks. We started going for drinks together at O'Neill's after rehearsals, and very quickly became mates. I remember one Sunday morning Paul told me that he was going to break up with her. I remember saying, 'You must be mad. She's gorgeous ...'

The summer of 1983 was the most important of my life. I went back to New York. Sheelagh was working in a bar called Limericks, and I used to drop in at around 11 pm. She'd usually have an hour of her shift left and, while I waited, she'd feed me gin and tonics. I'd walk her back to her Manhattan apartment, then I'd catch the subway home. I was staying with Paul far out in Brooklyn, near Coney Island. On a couple of occasions I awoke on the subway all the way out in the Bronx.

I had no job in New York, so eventually had to go to Cape Cod to earn some money. I had promised myself two weeks in New York before I returned to Ireland, but once I got back, I couldn't find Sheelagh. She'd changed both job and apartment, and nobody had a number for her. A couple of days before I was due to fly home, I ran into her friend, Anne Sheridan, on Fifth Avenue, and learned that Sheelagh was working in Durtie Nellie's, a nearby pub. I headed straight there and we made a plan to meet in Greenwich Village that evening.

I clearly remember the moment she walked into the pub. I felt a pang of delight. I realized at that moment just how attracted to her I had become and how much I had missed her. The pub filled up with other friends, but we stayed deep in conversation all evening. At one point we walked down West Fourth Street, arm in arm, to find a less crowded pub. It was the most magical of evenings and marked a major turning point in my life.

My finals went okay. I got a 2:2, a result that closed some postgrad doors for me, but the reality was that I didn't want to pursue law as a career. I wanted to be a businessman like my father. I needed to get a business qualification so I applied to Arthur Andersen and Stokes Kennedy Crowley, the top two accounting firms in Dublin at the time. I thought I interviewed well at Andersen's but they only accepted people with 2:1 degrees so SKC took me in.

Work was a shock to the system. I went from a crazy romantic summer in New York and from being top of the heap in college to being the lowest of the low, trudging through warehouses on industrial estates, counting carpets and packets of crisps. After long days in the freezing grey winter of 1983 I would have to catch two buses home. I remember saying to my father in October of that year, 'Dad, I've made a serious mistake.' He encouraged me to stick it out and not make any rash decisions, but those desolate winter mornings, when my breath fogged the glass as I looked out through the window of the bus at other disconsolate commuters, were pure misery, and on top of that I had a week of evening lectures to contend with.

The only light in my life was Sheelagh. I would meet her a couple of evenings a week and most weekends. There is a photo of us at Karen Finnegan's twenty-first birthday party from around then, and whenever I see it, it brings me back to the love and contentment of that time, despite the mundane daily grind.

My memories are of four wonderful years spent in the beauty and splendour of the oasis that is Trinity. Of the friendships begun there, many have lasted throughout my life.

Shane O'Neill (TCD 1979–83; Legal Science) qualified as an accountant with Stokes Kennedy Crowley before leaving soon after for a working holiday in Australia that lasted nine years. He worked for Macquarie Bank and later for Goldman Sachs with whom he transferred to London in 1996. He left Goldman to work for a client company, now Liberty Global, as chief strategy officer. He was chairman of UPC Ireland, and founder of Lessons for Life, a charity that provides funding for education for children affected by HIV/AIDS in Africa. He died in London in 2012, aged fifty.

Sheelagh Pyle and Shane O'Neill at Karen Finnegan's twenty-first birthday, 1983.

THE BALLOT BOX WITHOUT THE ARMALITE

eoin mccullough

MY MEMORIES of 1979 to 1983 are fragmentary and confused. I am not sure about events, or the order of events. This was before mobile phones, and still longer before mobile phones had cameras, and there is little to jolt the memory. There are some photographs and basic written material that help put the picture together, but they give little assistance in recreating what I thought or felt at the time. There is sadness in being able to establish so little emotional connection with experiences that were once clear and vivid.

Not a great deal was demanded by the Law Faculty of its students, and so we had plenty of time to do whatever else we wanted. I spent a lot of that time in the Graduate Memorial Building (GMB). There was a romance to the activities of the College Historical Society, although it was not strictly socially glamorous, and certainly attracted some odd characters. But public speaking is challenging, and can be thrilling when the audience is large or a speech goes well. And there is undoubtedly an attraction in the process if not the substance: the Hist has been in existence since 1770, with an arcane system of business and its own language and culture. A ballot box, the committee room with centuries-old records, an auditor in direct succession from Wolfe

Tone, the antiquated form of address, an order of business pursued late into the night. It felt important, and although I must have known that it was not, there is nevertheless a kind of magic to tradition and ritual that makes even the most cynical suspend his critical faculties.

The annual reports for those years record debates, lists of officers, and details of elections. Some of the topics of discussion speak of the interests of an age long forgotten, but others continue to engage. There was a deep level of interest in the role of the Catholic Church, which would seem misplaced now. That topic, together with three others – Northern Ireland, South Africa and abortion – was discussed every year.

The first meeting I attended is a reminder that we have come full circle: the motion for the Freshers' Debate in October 1979 was 'That real improvement in the educational system must wait on economic recovery'. In February 1980, there was a debate on abortion, featuring John Bonnar and Anne Connolly, when the house favoured decriminalization. Context is important. In 1983, a prohibition on laws permitting abortion was added to the constitution; in 1992, the X Case was decided; in the same year a recognition of the right to travel and obtain information relating to abortion was added to the constitution, but the same statute whereby abortion is criminalized applied until earlier this year.

Other meetings were on topics now long irrelevant. Questions of whether this house would participate in the Moscow Olympics, or whether the reaction of the West to Russian expansionism had been dangerously inadequate, speak of the Cold War. The society was particularly worried about religion, debating in that one year whether Articles 2 and 3 of the constitution required repeal, whether the Church had crucified modern Ireland, and whether Ireland needed an ayatollah.

I must have gone to many of these, but remember none. I recall the impression rather than the details of the inaugural meeting, on the topic of 'Abuse of Power'. It was, to me at least, an occasion of considerable glamour: the Examination Hall, a large crowd, dinner jackets, ceremony. Alex Owens was the auditor, now a good friend but then a distant and powerful person. Sean Moran, another good friend, now GAA correspondent for *The Irish Times*, was auditor for the 211th session. I was elected as fourth member of the general committee. The election itself is another blank, but I must have been pleased to be in a position of power: access to the committee room as of right, attendance at meetings, dry sherry, sitting on the bench during debates. This year featured two meetings about Northern Ireland, one being the motion that the house supports the aims of the Provisional IRA, and the other being that the house would yield to the hunger strikers. The mood was not republican and both were defeated, but the society had sufficient radicalism in January 1981 to support the proposition that divorce should be legalized. It seems hard to believe from today's perspective that it took the people another five years even to reject that idea, and that it was not until 1995 that the constitution was amended to repeal the prohibition on divorce.

Brian Lenihan was treasurer. He had a talent for intrigue and a detailed knowledge of rebel songs. He was clever and quick-witted, and had been awarded a scholarship the previous year. I knew him again later as a fine barrister, and his political career does not need to be set out here. It is very sad that such a talented man should have died so early.

The dry annual reports cannot convey the intrigue, the bloodletting or the bitterness that inform student politics. Bill Maguire and Brian O'Moore were leaders and fine speakers, and one part of the society saw that the natural order was for the former to follow the latter as auditor. Bill, however, stood against Brian: this was not about policy but about power. The sadness and drama of the H-Block hunger strikes had begun in March 1981. Bobby Sands died on 5 May, and there were riots in Dublin that night. On the same night, Bill was elected auditor for the 212th session and I became treasurer on the same ticket.

More of much of the same followed. Northern Ireland was debated twice: the society refused to reject republicanism (with Jim Kemmy and Padraig Flynn as guests) in November 1981 but in April rejected the idea that the solution for Northern Ireland lay in a United Ireland. John Bonnar and Anne Connolly were indefatigably back to discuss abortion: it is hard to interpret what the attendance meant by rejecting the idea that abortion was a necessary evil. An abiding interest in South Africa was demonstrated in the discussion on the topic of violence being the only answer to apartheid, featuring Kadar Asmal, then a lecturer in law and later a minister in the South African government. Bill Maguire's inaugural address was entitled 'Authority and Freedom'. Speakers included Ivan Yates, Albert Reynolds, Jack Jones and Owen Carron, who had been Bobby Sands' agent and elected in his stead as MP for Fermanagh-South Tyrone in August 1981.

I was elected without opposition as auditor of the society for the next session. When Jack Lynch addressed a meeting in late October 1982 on the motion that this house reveres the memory of Eamon de Valera, he was met with a standing ovation before he'd said a word. The affection that those present felt for him was a reflection of his decency, but also of what had happened in his party since he resigned as taoiseach in 1979. Charles Haughey was governing under the terms of the Gregory Deal; the GUBU press conference had occurred in August; in early October, Charlie McCreevy's motion of no confidence in Haughey as leader of Fianna Fáil had been defeated and was followed by thug-gish scenes outside Leinster House. That government was to fall in November 1982. Sean Haughey was one of the other speakers that night, and must have had a tough time.

Abortion featured yet again, with a debate on the proposition that the (then contemplated) abortion referendum was a cosmetic exercise. We discussed the introduction of extradition for political offences, and the rather extreme notion that the media's first duty was to the state. Later in the year, Seamus Mallon and Robert McCartney were guests on the perennial Northern Ireland issue, which was said to require constitutional and not institutional change.

There was a new government under Garret FitzGerald by January 1983, and we debated the motion that the house had no confidence in that govern-ment. Bertie Ahern, Richard Bruton and Cllr Eamon Gilmore spoke, and the motion was carried: it is astonishing to think that the same people could debate the same motion almost twenty-five years later. There was a literary debate on the rather mysterious topic that 'The Muses no Longer Dance on the Bog of Allen', addressed by Homan Potterton and Colm O'Briain. Although I was undoubtedly present at all of these, they sadly provoke almost no memory.

The inaugural meeting took place late in the session, in February 1983. The security staff was on strike, and neither the tánaiste, Dick Spring, nor Donal Nevin, who had agreed to speak, would cross the picket line. For what appears to have been the first time since the society was expelled from college for debating subjects of political interest in 1815, the inaugural meeting had to be held elsewhere. We ended up in the Mansion House. Declan Costello, an SDLP politician named Paddy O'Hanlon, and Conor Cruise O'Brien also spoke. Although I do not doubt that I was very pleased with myself, I cannot really recall either the details or the feel of the occasion, save for one strong memory of being interrupted consistently by a drunk from the rear of the hall. The acoustics in the Mansion House, however, are so hopeless that no one else may have noticed.

It is hard to say that it was four well-spent years. A lot of time was spent plotting, organizing and talking about things of ephemeral interest, and nothing was changed one way or the other. No doubt they are talking about roughly the same things still. But I enjoyed it enormously, which is enough to be able to say about anything.

Eoin McCullough (TCD 1979–83; Legal Science) was auditor of the College Historical Society for the 213th session. He qualified as a barrister and has been a Senior Counsel since 2001. He is married with three daughters and lives in Dublin.

A LOVE STORY BEGINS

jackie kilroy

I SHOULD NOT be writing this. It should have been my husband, Alan Ruddock. He was the clever one, the writer, the journalist. I only got into Trinity on minimum entry requirements and chose subjects I thought might be easy. I was always a lazy student. Being a girl, I was told in school that I could be a nurse or a teacher, but given that I had no science subject, nursing was out of the question. I focused on French – I already spoke the language, having lived in Belgium as a child – and also chose Russian because it was easy to get into as no one else wanted to do it. Russian was a big mistake, much more demanding than I had realized. I failed it and switched to sociology.

Out of the Russian Department, however, came a couple of friendships that have lasted to this day and it was one such friend, Anne Laidlaw, who orchestrated my first meeting with Alan. She invited me to her sister's twenty-first birthday in Castleknock on New Year's Eve 1979. We had been in college for three months at this stage but I don't think we had socialized much so the invitation came as a surprise. I was reluctant to go by myself but had nothing better to do. It was my first black-tie party, which was a bit daunting, not to mention the fact that I didn't really know anyone. When I arrived at the house I nearly turned around and drove away again – it was huge and these people were obviously posh.

I decided to brave it and found Anne who introduced me to some of her old school friends. I had never come across these kinds of people before. Straight out of a Julian Fellowes novel, they had an air of money and privilege. I realized when I got to know them that while the privileged backgrounds were real, they weren't all rolling in cash. I spotted a guy sitting on the stairs who was quite drunk but vaguely charming and handsome. We talked for a while and then danced, or I tried to dance and he stumbled around. As it turned out, it was probably one of the few times we danced in our thirty years together. Alan always claimed that I made all the effort after that party to try and meet again. He was probably right but if I'd left it up to him nothing would have happened. He always believed that things – and people – should come to him.

The Arts Block was fairly new at the time and a great place to hang around in the hopes of spotting a friend. There was always someone available for coffee and a fag; you could smoke anywhere on the concourse and keep an eye out for people coming out of lectures. The problem was that it was far too tempting not to go to lectures at all in case you missed someone and, in Alan's case, what I failed to realize was that he didn't actually go to any lectures. He possibly attended the odd tutorial but his timetable for history was light, which made it very difficult for him to remember when lectures were on.

Our relationship did progress, however, mostly thanks to Anne and the Lincoln's Inn. It turned out that all of these Old Columbans spent most of their time in the Lincoln and so he was easy enough to track down. The Lincoln was our pub while we were at Trinity. It was tatty and the ladies' loos would not pass Health and Safety these days but there was always someone in there you knew. In the Lincoln I met all of Alan's friends and we have remained friends since. Some of them – Keith Archer and Nicky Roche, Anne Laidlaw and Anthony MacFarland, Patrick Cooper and Juliet Wheeler – married each other.

For the next four years we were together in Trinity. Officially I still lived at home, but in reality I was either in Al's flat in Rutland Street or in Botany Bay, when he moved there with Jonathan Cooper. Anyone who lived off-campus ended up there for lunch but there was never anything but bread or cheese. Of course, going back to lectures was out of the question because a game of poker or backgammon might start up. The games would end when it was time for training. Alan was very serious about his hockey despite his rare appearances at training for the Trinity First XI. I was very involved in his hockey as well but only because I had a car and there was never enough transport for the team. It was quite unusual to have a car unless you were from the North and were on a grant; all the Northerners had fancy, fast cars. My falling-apart Renault 4 could take seven at a push as long as two people sat in the front but we'd try to keep it to five.

Some of the away games were strange. There was a certain bias against the 'posh students' from Trinity and strenuous efforts went into taking them down. The most notable away game was a cup match against the RUC in the North. It was the height of the Troubles and the hunger strikes. Trinity had to travel to the RUC's home ground; some of the Trinity players had very personal reasons to dislike the RUC and everyone was on edge. Security was tight and there were dogs and machine guns around the side lines. Against the odds, Trinity won – we couldn't get out of there fast enough in the Renault 4. The Troubles hadn't really affected us much apart from the occasional hunger-strike march that Alan went on, but those guns made it very real.

Our group of friends was probably seen by some as a bunch of pretentious tossers. I can only assume that we were thoroughly disliked by Joe Duffy and the other Students' Union leaders – a serious bunch of lads who wore duffle coats and ran for office against our chosen 'Toga' party leader, Conor McElroy, who was carried around by young men on a litter. We didn't take much notice of student politics although national and world politics were always important. Student life for us was about having fun, not about fees or library opening hours.

Parties were black-tie. A party could start in or near Dublin but end up in Kerry, because drinking was no impediment to getting into a car. It was a hedonistic life, which didn't require much money but a lot of stamina. Al and I were well known for fading early and disappearing but there were plenty of late nights or all-nighters. I worked weekends and some evenings in the Berkeley Court hotel for most of my student life, but Al didn't appear to have time for a job so I kept us both going, just as he would do when I stayed home with the children after we were married.

Alan graduated a year before me in 1983. Using a vague connection, he headed to Johannesburg and I stayed to finish my final year. We kept in touch by letter and the occasional phone call. By some miracle, I managed to get my degree and followed Al to South Africa where he had established himself as a journalist.

After a career in journalism in South Africa, London and Dublin, including editorship of *The Scotsman* and the Irish edition of *The Sunday Times*, and the occasional battle with cancer, IVF and Albert Reynolds, we settled with our three sons in County Carlow from where Al wrote his columns for the *Sunday Independent*. I became a guidance counsellor in protest at the totally inadequate guidance that we had received in school. On 30 May 2010, Alan died suddenly at forty-nine. He was playing his favourite game of cricket and was batting when he collapsed. His funeral was full of old friends from Trinity, many still married to each other. Trinity was a place of superior learning but it was also a place where many of us fell in love and were very happy together.

Jackie Ruddock (née Kilroy; TCD 1979–84; French and Sociology) lived in South Africa 1986–8, working for Agence France Presse, and London 1988–9, working for the English Cricket Board and Lowndes Lambert Insurance Company. After a decade of having and looking after children she did a Higher Diploma in guidance and counselling in NUI Maynooth in 2000. She has since worked as a guidance counsellor for Carlow VEC and now for Rathdown School. She has three sons and lives in Tullow, Co. Carlow.

THE MIDDLIN' SCHOLAR

pauline mclynn

I FETCHED UP to Trinity College Dublin a greenhorn in the autumn of 1979. I was seventeen years old (just), had grown up in Galway, and I knew no one else at college and nothing about a lot of things. Four years later, I departed the august institution knowing *some* stuff (though not necessarily all degree-related and, of course, convinced I knew it all), with a group of friends, collaborators and acquaintances that abide to this day. So, a splendid education got 'got'.

I was at Trinity to read English and history of art, ostensibly. Before the academia kicked off, and during Freshers' Week, two things occurred: first, all introductory lectures I attended seemed designed to point out that a job was the last thing one should expect out of a degree; second, I joined DU Players, the drama society, and my path for the next four years was truly mapped.

How did that pan out? Well, I graduated and was delivered into the last great recession in Ireland – there were no jobs, degree or no; and some thirty years after graduation I am still an actor.

In those long-gone days, Players had a theatre in Front Square and I remember how my breath was taken away to see front of house that very first time: all the mugs hanging from hooks above the serving counter, then climbing the steps up to the theatre door and, on the other side, down into the tiny theatre itself. Later, I would spend hours under the stage preparing for a production, or doing paperwork in the office, or using the payphone, or hunting out props and costumes – all subterranean.

I threw myself into the nuts and bolts of the society and eventually became treasurer and chair. I was extremely bossy. I was partial to a high-necked garment and word would often arrive ahead to committee meetings that I was 'wearing a Pauline Blouse', which, apparently, was a warning as to my mood.

I became part of a group that is still very active in the professional theatre world today, in Ireland and beyond. We were passionate. We were *surely* the first ever to feel as we did about theatre ... *ever*. We were driven. We were invincible. I suspect we were, also, a *nightmare*.

I was so involved with Players that the two academic departments I should have been haunting began to send my assignment notifications directly to the theatre. Actually, I always regretted not attending more lectures and tutorials when I began to swot up for exams because, the fact was, I really did go to university to learn more about those subjects and I particularly loved history of art. I eventually got the hang of juggling the dual strands of my college life, though I remained 'a middlin' scholar only'.

One of the great joys of my time at Trinity was that Anne Crookshank was still professor in the History of Art Department. I had the enormous pleasure of taking a trip to London with her for my final-year specialist topic, eighteenth-century British art. And there was the occasion when Anthony Blunt was outed as a Soviet spy and she, as one of his favourite pupils, made the front of the evening papers with the headline 'Is *THIS* the Fifth Man?' – thrilling and hilarious times.

These days, I open the odd exhibition and have written fictionally about art in some of my novels; I hope that answers the 'Do you never use your degree, at all?' question. Anecdotally, I hear my photograph is, or at least was, on the main noticeboard of the History of Art Department as one of the graduates who has gone forth – though not into the 'history of art' world.

I lived in various rooms throughout campus and that is surely one of the highlights for any Trinity student. From 1979 to 1983, I discovered that pasta is not just tinned spaghetti hoops in tomato sauce. I learned to love charcoaled food – the two-ring 'cooker' in Front Square rooms had a flame-thrower by way of a grill. I often survived on cheese and bread and whatever soup was left over after the lunchtime shows at Players. I saw a lot of matinee movies. I once fell asleep in the sunshine on the grass opposite the Lecky Library, halfway through reading *Waiting For Godot*. I got mentioned a few times on the back page of *Piranha* – the height of notoriety. I never visited the Book of Kells.

As I was leaving, the authorities began proceedings to move Players out of Front Square and into a new custom-built theatre. There were many impassioned meetings about the pros and cons of the proposal. At one such gathering (which I don't remember, although he does) a young man, who had just arrived into TCD, spoke against the move and I told him, quite succinctly, that he didn't know his arse from his elbow. I suspect I was wearing a 'Pauline Blouse' at the time. Reader, fourteen years later, I married him. Ah yes, Trinity, the college that keeps on giving!

Pauline McLynn (TCD 1979–83; English and History of Art) is an award-winning actor, and a writer with nine novels to her name. She is still married to Richard Cook, the guy she met at Trinity, the one with the arse/elbow issues.

LOWERING THE TONE

lynne parker

TO SOMEONE who had made the journey from Belfast to Dublin in 1979, leaving behind the dull tension and cultural curfew imposed by the Troubles, and a struggling welfare state about to be destroyed by Margaret Thatcher, walking through Front Gate was like entering paradise.

On the way down I had gawped at the litter still decorating the road from the airport into the city, fresh from the papal visit. You wouldn't get that in my leafy suburb of east Belfast, thought I. What you also wouldn't get was the easy *savoir faire* of the truly bohemian city that was Dublin in the eighties, its last gasp as a shambolic but charming outpost of intellectual Europeanism.

So, a mixture of paradise and Paris? Steady on. Dismal bedsits and shared semi-ds lay ahead, but for my first week in Dublin I was billeted in the YWCA on Baggot Street, and got a small taste of something akin to convent life. Fortunately, I was soon absorbed into the relative luxury of Trinity Hall, which made first year a lot more palatable. There I met Deirdre Madden and Pauline McLynn, and we formed an unlikely trio in the English Department over the next few years. Did I mention that I came to study English literature? If I did, I'm a liar and a damned liar. I came to join Players.

The myth so devoutly trusted by my parents – that a university education inevitably leads to prosperity, security and happiness – is just that, innit? I got a good degree from my stint in TCD, but so far that isn't what has opened doors to career advancement. What I also got from my four-year sojourn in paradise was a *modus operandi*, a splendid bunch of friends and colleagues, and a trade. In short, a life.

I'd visited Trinity at the age of fourteen when I came to Dublin to see the first production of my uncle Stewart Parker's play, *Spokesong*, at the Dublin Theatre Festival in 1975. So from the start, Trinity was linked with the idea of theatre, and when I left school Trinity offered a route to what seemed to me the only job I was fit for, or interested in doing. When I met my tutor Nicholas Grene in my first term, he asked if I had any idea what I wanted to do and I replied unhesitantly that I wanted to work in theatre. To his eternal credit he supported me throughout my undergraduate years and beyond, overlooking my deep deficiencies as a student and allowing me to incorporate work in Players into my course wherever possible. I did manage to glean some prized academic insights from him and the wonderful, aged Professor Walton, whose classes on Milton were as much a pleasure for his delicious nineteenth-century-ness as the subject itself.

One idea that has never left me was a simple and profound insight from Paula Simmonds, who taught me Anglo-Saxon literature. All art, she once said, is based on pattern. This idea really chimed with me, and may have fed the fascination with pre-Romantic music and literature that formed so much of my creative bent. It reaches into much of the work I still do in music theatre, structured dramatic prose and poetic dialogue, and touches on the funda-mental connection between science and art and speech and mathematics that I'm currently exploring. I've no notion where Paula Simmonds is today, but I've used that idea as a compass for years, and I thank her for it. In what can frequently seem like freefall during the construction of a work of art – particu-larly in the vulgar and mischievous form that is theatre – it is reassuring to remind yourself that underlying the expression of emotion and imaginative thought is a formal pattern, a logical structure.

This seems a bit highfalutin when you look at what we were getting up to in No. 3 Front Square. Drama wasn't the half of it. Nowadays, of course, Players has been amalgamated into the Samuel Beckett Centre and sits alongside the Drama Studies Department. That course didn't exist when I came to Trinity and if it had, and I'd been accepted onto it, I wonder if my life might have taken a different direction. Perhaps if I'd studied theatre as a formal subject I might have ended up in journalism or something else, in reaction. Hell's bells, I might have become a theatre critic.

In fact, I'm a huge admirer of Trinity's work in drama studies, and took the drama option as part of my joint honours English course. That option was a precursor of the drama degree pioneered by John McCormick, then an inspirational lecturer in the French Department. McCormick's production of the Brecht/Weill opera *Rise and Fall of the City of Mahagonny* was the first thing I saw in Players during Freshers' Week, and it astonished me – the greatest revelation I'd experienced since seeing *Spokesong*. This was a level of theatre unknown in Belfast, and it was performed by students, so I grasped that it was possible to make great theatre with visionary direction, young actors and minimal resources. Without that example, some of the achievements of the next four years in Players and the foundation in 1984 of Rough Magic Theatre Company might never have happened. The musical director was an eighteen-year-old pianist called Helene Montague, who worked on a huge number of shows with Players and became a founder member of Rough Magic.

But for me the glory of Players was its extracurricular nature. I was a sorry student of English literature, but as luck would have it my passion for theatre focused on work that was frequently in sync with my supposed studies. And that grotty, rat-infested little box that was Players Theatre gave me an open forum to learn first hand, by heroic misadventure, creative hubris and bitter experience, what this bizarre practice of theatre-making actually meant. What it lacked in elegance it made up for in atmosphere, the thing that so frequently eludes contemporary theatre architects. No one was there to advise us, we made it up as we went along. This is not necessarily a recipe for success; what made a difference for us was our extraordinary peer group.

Pauline McLynn and I joined Players in 1979. We came in at the tail end of a very glamorous generation that included John Comiskey, Jonathan and Nicola White, Robert O'Byrne, Gabrielle Reidy and other bright lights. They appeared unutterably stylish and confident, apparently all from upper-middle-class intelligentsia, articulate, informed and superior. Posh 'Old Dublin' in essence, although some were actually blow-ins from the North and elsewhere, just like me. Lofty as they were, they seemed genuinely glad to see us. In retrospect, my impression was certainly coloured by my own sense of inadequacy, but there was an undeniable sea change in the composition and nature of Players during that era, and that might even have been true of Trinity in general. Around that time, Joe Duffy and Aine Lawlor were being threatened with jail for staging protests, not what you'd expect of an institution characterized as the Anglo-Irish ascendancy. We weren't the first commoners to cross the cobblestones but the demographic of third-level education in Ireland was changing, just as it had in the North a generation before. Trinty was still perceived as snooty, but it was about to welcome a pluralistic and diverse intake that would strengthen its character and celebrate its traditions and architectural beauty.

Pauline and I – how shall I put it – began a 'lowering of the tone' in DU Players that was compounded by the influx the following year of a wave that included Declan Hughes, Anne Enright, Darragh Kelly, Ian Fitzgibbon, Arthur Riordan, Michael James Ford, Gary Jermyn, John O'Brien, Rosemary Fine and many others. Our Freshers' Co-op production (my first attempt at directing) marked the debuts of Stanley Townsend, Martin Murphy, Jonny Speers and Alan Gilsenan, all of whom, including the aforementioned, continued careers in theatre and/or film. Playing the role of ringleader was the very posh 'Old Dublin' figure of Julian Plunkett Dillon, who, after grad-uating, left a promising career in Dublin to produce movies in LA for the likes of Mick Jagger. Julian staged a production of Anouilh's *The Lark* in the early eighties that *absolutely everybody* was in, and set the tone for an acting ensemble and approach to staging that Declan Hughes and I borrowed freely when we set up Rough Magic.

We began to work, unintentionally and informally, as a small theatre company. It wasn't just the work itself, although programmes built on every-thing from Wycherley to Stoppard, from Shakespeare to Sartre, are a pretty good platform for a life in theatre. And we toured! Michael Ford's adaptation of 'Guests of the Nation', directed by Julian, and Robert O'Byrne's one-man show, *Poor Dear Brian*, ended up going to the Edinburgh Fringe in tandem with John McCormick's outstanding production of Racine's *Phèdre* for the French Department. What seemed like about fifty of us slept on the floor of the Labour Party HQ, and shared one toilet.

Two years later I found myself in a basement disco somewhere off the Royal Mile at ten o'clock in the morning with my production of the medieval morality play *Everyman*, starring Anne Enright in the title role. There were three people in the audience and I began to realize that life outside Players might be chillier than we imagined. (It is.) And there were the Irish Student Drama Awards and golden memories of a glorious trip to Cork, which probably wasn't such a great experience for anyone sharing a train with us.

The activity wasn't confined to term time. A common practice was for a bunch of students to set up companies that used the theatre over the summer break on a semi-professional basis. Stage One, Trapdoor Theatre Company and the cabaret duo Isosceles were among these and provided models that we used in setting up Rough Magic. The beauty of Players was its location; situated beside Front Gate, with easy access to the unwitting tourist, we were able to wheedle them into the lunchtime theatre experience, using Players' mucky front of house as a soup kitchen in the blissful days before Health and Safety regulations. That prime passing trade (if you could nab them before the sharks in the History Department, which, at that time, had a monopoly on guided tours and made a fortune) would buy their tickets for Yeats or Behan or whatever you cynically served up with the unspeakable soup; that would pay for the more experimental and costly evening shows on which these fledgling companies were cutting their teeth. It would be no exaggeration to say that a great deal of the independent theatre made in Dublin in the explosion of activity during the mid eighties owes its existence to that system.

I wish I could say that I took up all the opportunities on offer at Trinity. I should have joined Choral, I should have joined the Hist or the Phil, I should have attended more lectures … I did, strangely enough, sign up to Cumann Gaelach for a week. This was because when I walked through Front Gate in October 1979 there was a guy in green tweed selling membership at the Cumann desk and it became clear that he was a Northern Prod without a word of Irish straight out of a Belfast grammar school, just like me. His name was Jonny Speers, and he'd walked through that gate for the first time about ten minutes before I did. I'd probably guessed what I now know. That it's okay to immerse yourself in theatre at the expense of other pursuits, because theatre covers all bases. Whatever I know about financial markets, sixteenth-century

Spain, mental illness and nuclear physics, however cosmetic, I've learned by doing plays. And that educational journey, which began in No. 3 Front Square, TCD, is ongoing.

Cast of Freshers' Co-op, 1980. Back row left to right: *Stan Townsend, Martin Murphy, Michael Ford, Jonny Speers.* Front row: *Lynne Parker second from left.*

Lynne Parker (TCD 1979–83; Medieval and Renaissance and Modern English Literature) is artistic director of Rough Magic Theatre Company, which she founded with Declan Hughes in 1984. She has also produced plays for the Abbey, Gate, Galway Arts Festival, Opera Ireland, Theatre Lovett and Lyric, and for theatres in the UK including the Bush Theatre, the Almeida, The Old Vic, the West Yorkshire Playhouse, the RSC, Traverse Theatre and the Birmingham Rep. She was an associate artist of Charabanc. She won the **Irish Times** Irish Special Tribute Award in 2008, and in 2010 recieved an honorary doctorate from TCD.

WHEN THE RUGBY CLUB MIXED WITH THE STUDENTS' UNION

john reid

I **SUPPOSE**, in retrospect, that 1979 was framed for me by the beginning of the Thatcher years in Britain; the end of the Shah of Iran; Ireland suffering its worst year of industrial disputes in history; the break with sterling and entrance to the EMS; Lord Mountbatten's death; and a burgeoning U2 playing the Dandelion Market while the RDS hosted artists from Queen to ABBA.

I left the home comforts of Belfast for the relative liberalism of life in Dublin two days before the Pope's visit. I thought at the time that the country went relatively bonkers over it, and it was a quick lesson to me, a hitherto relatively conservative Belfast Prod, in the strength of the Church south of the border. A fellow graduate of Methodist College Belfast, Gery Juleff ('Juff') and I had each other and the security blanket of the Rugby Club to enter what could easily have been a new continent, not a city only a hundred miles down the road from home.

Dublin University Football Club in those days was almost a parallel universe to that of academia. Even as the amateur sport that it was then, you could eat, live and sleep the game, which was run by local heroes such as Donal Spring and Hugo MacNeill. My first week in Trinity was spent on the pitch in

College Park, and in the Pavilion bar, with the occasional break for Freshers' Week activities. It's a measure of the bonding period it was that two of my closest friends (along with Juff) to this day – English import Mike Lynn and Kerryman David Fitzgerald – were among the first people I met.

Living in Trinity Hall that year made leaving home relatively painless. Later I moved into a flat in Blackrock with a couple of others. My last two years in Trinity were spent in rooms, first Botany Bay and then New Square. We had no idea how lucky we were.

I imagine the same student pranks exist worldwide, but one unique memory for me is of the morning that two engineering students discovered a trapdoor in their Front Square rooms, which led down to the college wine cellar. We got the knock on our door at eleven on a Sunday morning, summoning us to a wine and cheese party immediately. I don't believe there was much cheese. I'm sure the provost's dinner parties have never had quite the same choice of vintage claret since, and security in the tunnels under Front Square is somewhat more stringent now.

The business studies class of 1983 was housed in the Arts Block and attracted a great cross-section of Irish students as the popular growth subject in the early eighties. Michael O'Leary was one of those great character foils to the south-Dublin Blackrock College mafia that was so dominant, and it was also the class where I met my only real college girlfriend, Margo Quinn. It's an indicator of how I ordered my priorities in that period of my life that this is about all I can remember of academia-related matters.

Even the relatively lightweight work schedule of two eight-week terms, followed by a five-week summer term, looked relatively onerous when compared to the history degree: third-year history students had no exams. Memorably, a number of students showed up and signed the register that October and then disappeared with a bag of books on some sort of gap year. History also seemed to attract that other badly kept secret (unique to Trinity among the southern Irish universities) of British army-sponsored officers doing their degrees before entering service. Incognito went out the window after a gallon of Guinness in O'Neill's or Lincoln's Inn and various second lieutenants blew their own covers. This increased the personal paranoia of those officers in 1981, with the local backdrop of the hunger strikes, and marches in Dublin to support the H-Block protests. I remember one particular British officer, Denny Kemp, studying for his degree between bouts of political activism and marching for various causes. He graduated, but had only a short army career before becoming a socialist politician in England.

Some school friends in Belfast had formed a band, Silent Running, and from time to time I used to return home to help them carry gear, set up sound and light systems and so on. I don't know what inspired this interest, but it was the beginning of a lifelong career in the music business. It led me to help out on Ents events in second and third year. Being a rugby player, I had no other interaction with the Students' Union, and when Eamonn Daly (Ents officer 1981–2) suggested that I run for the post the following year, I thought he was wide of the mark.

It was still the era of left-wing-orientated students' unions, with annual Mexican stand-offs with the authorities over the Buttery, and the use of the Exam Hall and Arts Block for gigs. I was a bit outside my comfort zone of the Pav, where the deepest political discussion focused on team selection. However, there was a new mood in the air and a fresh approach to student politics from one of the candidates for the Students' Union presidency, Aine Lawlor. I liked her and agreed to run for Ents. The Rugby Club was pressed into service, printing and distributing posters and leaflets and wheeled out to vote for the first time in most of their lives.

The next year was at times a somewhat ludicrous juxtaposition of Friday and Saturday nights spent running gigs in town, at whatever venue we could get access to, and playing First XV rugby for Trinity, with the occasional social game on a Sunday. During the week I trained in College Park and got paid to run the Students' Union shop, book bands and DJs, and do my political service for the Students' Union.

I had great mentors, Brian Murray and Ian Wilson, who helped me through the various punch-ups with the college authorities and dealings with the entertainment industry. As an introduction to and training for my future career, being Ents officer could not have been better. I learnt from local masters of the live business such as Denis Desmond, with whom we promoted shows in the dark days of no access to college facilities, and talent agents such as Terry O'Neill. I realized where a college gig like mine stood in the big picture when, having secured a new act called Culture Club for the princely sum of £200, I watched them perform their Number One record on *Top of the Pops* after a call from their agent that morning to cancel the JCR gig because of 'a flu bug'. I got a quick lesson in the value and enforcement of copyright in the pre-digital era when I chose to exhibit a pirated pre-release copy of *E.T.* – the movie event of that year – to sell-out audiences for a week in the Buttery, and was swiftly shut down by the studio after a front-page story in the *Sunday World*.

That great year came to an end and I spent the summer running shows for Denis Desmond in Ireland and earning a lot more than I ever had in my life. I hadn't thought about leaving college until the July day I sat in my Portakabin at Phoenix Park Racecourse, where I was production manager for U2's first Irish outdoor show. There was a rap on the door and in came Pat McCabe, my tutor. I hadn't crossed paths with him for a year or two and was delighted to see him, but I couldn't for the life of me work out why he was there. We had a cup of tea, and I realized that he had gone to the trouble of tracking me down and travelling across town to talk to me about my future: he'd come to see if I was going back to finish my degree.

I asked if he thought I should, and he looked out on the semi-organized but impressive backstage area, and asked me if I intended being an accountant. If not, it looked to him as if I should just stick to what I was already doing. It's still the best bit of career advice I have ever been given – thanks, Pat!

John Reid (TCD 1979–82; Economics and Social Studies) ran major record companies in Canada, the USA and the UK, and the global business for Warner Music. Preferring muddy fields and pop festivals, he left the recorded music business to become president of Live Nation, where he has proved to be much more valuable to his teenage daughter when it comes to concert tickets.

MEMORIES OF TRINITY

katie donovan

I **SPENT** much of my miserable teens dreaming of how my life would change when I got into Trinity. I drove myself demented studying for the Leaving Cert. to make sure I would get in. And lo, in 1980, as soon as I started cycling to the lovely campus from the 'burbs of Dún Laoghaire each windswept morning, my life began to make sense at last. No matter that unemployment was 20 per cent and my joint honours arts degree was not going to get me a job. (All the career guidance counsellor could tell me was that London would be a good place to start.) No matter that Dublin was in the midst of a heroin epidemic, that I had my bike and bag stolen, that there was nothing to do in the city after 11 pm when the pubs closed except go and drink sour expensive wine in tiny nightclubs on Leeson Street. I had Arrived.

I loved the mix of buildings, from the cobbles and Campanile to the sleek slab of the Arts Block. I went to meetings of the Literary Society in Front Square where we had a room for writing workshops and boozy parties. Fellow members included poet Peter Sirr, film-maker Alan Gilsenan, journalist Victoria White and film editor Liz Walsh. Norbert Col, Rosemary Dawson, Mark Hutcheson, Peter Sellers and his enigmatic girlfriend Jo Higgins, whose idea it had been to start the society in the first place, were other regulars. We invited writers such as Seamus Heaney, Derek Mahon, Harry Clifton and

Jennifer Johnston to give public readings. I remember when Heaney came: the excitement of hosting him to a meal at Commons, and his retreat after to our Lit. Soc. room so he could prepare for his performance. He was actually a little concerned that no one would show up! Needless to say, we got a full house in the largest lecture hall in the Arts Block, the Edmund Burke, and he gave a marvellous reading.

Being neurotically analytical meant that I was tortured by self-doubt and prone to reading all sorts of hidden meanings into the most banal of encounters. Trying to look and act suave in the Arts Block, while simultaneously knowing that such posing was ridiculous, was a bit of a challenge. Course work could be intimidating, too. I remember one lecture by the inimitable Brendan Kennelly where he asked us to recall first lines from novels. Not one of us could think of a line until a handsome older exchange student from Harvard stood up and quoted *Pride and Prejudice*, leaving us feeling relieved and ashamed: 'It is a truth universally acknowledged, that a single man in possession of a good fortune, must be in want of a wife.'

Unlike literature students today, I pursued my reading without the heavy weight of theory, learning to articulate my own interpretations. With the razor-sharp Peggy O'Brien who taught American literature, I fell in love with William Faulkner's *The Sound and the Fury*. Anne Clune gave me the opportunity to read the Brontë sisters and Virginia Woolf, with a course on women writers (not commonly available then). Ian Ross put up with my tears over a Wordsworth essay. Terence Brown gave me my first window onto Beckett.

My second subject was initially a hurdle. My fascination with analysis had led me to pair English literature with psychology. In those days, the department was in thrall to behaviourism, crudely translated as the sort of study that centred on a rat salivating if shown a piece of cheese. I was not charmed to learn that by third year I might be lucky enough to have my own rat. Also, every week we had to do a test in statistics. I hadn't come to Trinity to study maths and feed rats. So in spite of having met two of my dearest friends in psychology, Sydna Farrar (later head of social care at Ballyfermot College of Further Education) and Sarah Finlay (long-time arts administrator and now cranio-sacral therapist), in second year I replaced psychology with history.

Although history was not a subject I had really been interested in pursuing at third level, I didn't have much choice. I had got an A in the Leaving because of my excellent history teacher at New Park Comprehensive, the late Dr John de Courcy Ireland. That grade enabled me to skip straight into second-year history. Third-level history was daunting. I never had the time or attention span to master the reading involved.

The course that really made an impression was David Dickson's Georgian Dublin. The indefatigable Dr Dickson took us students all over the city, from the faded glory of Henrietta Street to Dublin's oldest pub, The Brazen Head, where we imagined the heroes of 1798 having secret meetings to plot the rebellion. When he wasn't showing us ornate plasterwork on site, he encouraged us to undertake original research, meaning that we got to grips with the workings of the National Library and felt very independent altogether. Being in the city centre every day meant that I could see at first hand the huge variety of people who have, since Georgian times and earlier, made up the populace of Dublin. There was a refreshing sense that I, as a pampered and privileged student, could shelter from the less palatable aspects of this by walking through the gates of Trinity.

However, the reality of poverty, drug addiction and depression could not be ignored and I became a volunteer off-campus with the Samaritans, attempting to emulate my elderly great-aunt Phoebe Donovan, who had been with them for years. With very little life experience to draw on, I used my listening skills and fervently hoped that I could make a difference. On campus I joined the St Vincent de Paul. Members included my friend and green campaigner Clare Watson, then studying social work as was Christine Magee, and Austin O'Carroll, now a GP in inner-city Dublin.

Extracurricular activities took up a great deal of my energies. I wonder now how I found the time to study and churn out essays, but somehow deadlines were met, even when I had to take on part-time jobs in Quinnsworth (now Tesco) and later, for a horrible six months, McDonald's. It was easier in fourth year when I had no part-time job to distract me and no long cycle to contend with: I got rooms in the GMB overlooking Botany Bay. I had my own little kitchen to concoct tuna stews and other low-budget student delights. I had no fridge and the seagulls had great sport attacking the milk that I left out on the windowsill to keep cold.

One of the satisfactions of fourth year was pursuing theatre studies. At the time, Trinity Players was dominated by the talents of Lynne Parker, Darragh Kelly, Anne Enright, Stanley Townsend and many more, who went on to form Rough Magic. Plebs like me didn't stand a chance of getting parts, although I did appear in Alan Gilsenan's production of *Murder in the Cathedral*. By choosing theatre studies I had a direct route to writing and directing my own play, *Perspectives*, heavily influenced by a Hugh Leonard split-stage technique I had seen, and also by my parents' failed marriage.

In the meantime, there were TCD society parties, impromptu parties, twenty-first birthday parties (where we always seemed to be dressing up – on one memorable occasion, we came as babies) and, of course, the Trinity Ball. My first experience of this was a disaster: I had been set up with a friend's older brother, who soon lost interest and abandoned me halfway through the night.

By fourth year, I had an actual boyfriend to bring – my time at Trinity involved a lot of angst about acquiring such an item. I began to feel stressed about the future; I wanted to keep studying English literature but I wanted to travel, too. So I started applying to MA programmes in American universities and ended up getting an exchange scholarship that Trinity ran with the University of California at Berkeley. There my education, academically and in the broader sense, continued. Berkeley's English Department forced me to see literature in a whole new light. To balance my brain, my poetry writing intensified and I went to poetry readings by Robert Bly and Allen Ginsberg.

My years as a Trinity student coincided with widespread and often vicious arguments about abortion. The SPUC-ers with their grotesque posters of foetuses were a common sight. This all culminated in the anti-abortion referendum of 1983. My one and only speech at the Hist was as the result of a dare with a friend – that we would present the two sides of the abortion debate. I was vehemently in favour of a woman's right to choose; he was vehemently against.

People from my time in Trinity have remained part of my life as the years have passed. As my peers have been turning fifty, there have been reunions and reminiscences. We have all seen a lot of life since then. Success, disappointment, parenthood, bereavement. A certain unwillingness to acknowledge we really *are* that old dissolves into mutual reassurances that we are still dynamic and taking the world by storm. Only right and proper for graduates of good old Trinity.

Katie Donovan with her father Richard Donovan at her graduation, 1984.

Katie Donovan (TCD 1980–4; Modern English and History) was a founder member of the DU Literary Society. After an MA in English literature at the University of California at Berkeley, she taught English in Hungary for a year before working as a journalist with the **Irish Times** features department. As assistant features editor, she took voluntary redundancy in 2002 when her daughter Phoebe was born, and trained as an Amatsu therapist. After her son Felix was born in 2004, she combined her Amatsu work with teaching creative writing. She was writer-in-residence for Dún Laoghaire–Rathdown 2006–8, and now teaches creative writing at Dun Laoghaire Institute of Art, Design & Technology. She has published four collections of poetry with Bloodaxe Books and reads her poetry at venues and festivals in Ireland and abroad. She has co-edited two poetry anthologies, with Brendan Kennelly and A. Norman Jeffares.

IN 4.32.A, THEN O'NEILL'S

declan hughes

We are the vanguard, but of what?
—Isaac Babel

THE TRICK was to drive yourself into a state of advanced nervous exhaustion, with maximum intensity and plenty of shouting. That was the only way the play would work. So I had stayed up half the night on the Saturday helping with the construction of the set. Stanley Townsend, whose father ran a timber merchant's in Baggot Lane, was the chief set builder, ably flanked by Jonny Speers. The only snag was, by the time the previous show got out Stan was usually asleep, and it generally took a while to wake him up. Nothing to do with drink. Stan liked to sleep is all it was. Since I could barely hammer a nail, I was deputed to wake him. That was how I helped.

You got in on Saturday night and plotted lights on Sunday morning and teched in the afternoon and dressed on Sunday night. And there I was, nervous and exhausted, convulsed over a notebook in the front row of the tiny theatre in House No. 3, with a cast that included Stan, Darragh Kelly, Martin Murphy and Ian Fitzgibbon, watching the dress rehearsal of *Gimme Shelter* by Barrie Keeffe, the first play I had directed on my own. I had been in Players for two years now, since the Hilary Term of my first year.

I had acted in a dozen or so productions, co-directed a couple, even had a show at the Edinburgh Fringe Festival. I was the secretary of Players and Pauline McLynn, the chairperson, was my girlfriend. But it wasn't enough. I knew I couldn't really act, not the way Stan or Darragh, Ian or Martin, Pauline or Rosemary Fine or Anne Enright could. What I most wanted to do was write, but I wasn't really sure how to start, and, even if I had known, I lacked the confidence; it may have been the eighties but I still belonged to the 'It's Only Me' generation. So I thought I'd try directing. I felt I knew what certain playwrights were saying, and I had a feel for rhythm, and for how a line should be delivered, even if I couldn't deliver it that way myself. And I thought I understood what passion was, and how to communicate it, and I believed that passion was what it was all about. When you're twenty, it usually is.

The dress rehearsal came to an end, and I addressed the cast with overwrought intensity, as if I could somehow embody them with the dedication and conviction I thought necessary to carry off the play. I was cross, I was critical, I shouted. None of it was good enough, and we only had twenty-four hours to go. Seated behind me were Lynne Parker, Pauline McLynn and Jonny Speers, experienced Players hands all. One of them, while not actually coming out and saying, 'Jesus, Declan, give them a break,' made some noises to the effect that it was actually looking really rather good. I turned around and saw an expression on their faces that I had never seen there before; not quite respect, not quite admiration, although there were elements of each of those. No, the expression I saw – and I realized when I saw it that I had been seeking it my entire life – was recognition. We liked you anyway, and enjoyed having you around, they seemed to be saying – and I later discovered this is indeed what they were saying, and so were several members of the cast – but now we understand the point of you. You can do what we do. You are one of us. We are your people, and you are ours.

People used to say, 'God, you Players people take yourselves very seriously, don't you?' And it was true. The clue lies in the phrase, 'seeking it my entire life'. I had come to Trinity to get involved in Players. An English degree seemed like the easiest way of not interfering with that plan. At first, it seemed that not being very good at acting was going to get in the way. But I had found something else, something that gave me a sense of satisfaction and excitement

I had never felt before. This was what I had been seeking. Some people go through life without ever finding it. Why wouldn't you take that seriously?

THE FIRST SHOW I did in Players was a lunchtime production of *If You're Glad I'll Be Frank* by Tom Stoppard, directed by Rory McMillan. Lynne Parker and Martin Murphy were in the show but they seemed impossibly important and unapproachable. I made friends with David Cox and Amanda Pratt. And Maev Kennedy in *The Irish Times* said that I was melancholy and very nice, or, at least, that my performance was. It was a good beginning, but I still felt I was on the outside.

The big director in Players then was Julian Plunkett Dillon, and at the start of the following year I was cast in his new show, Jean Anouilh's *The Lark*. Julian was a slightly camp, gangly Gonzaga boy with a flair for gathering people together and firing them with enthusiasm. He knew more about staging a play than the rest of us put together, and had a confidence and authority at which I could only marvel. *The Lark* was a big hit; notable among the cast were Gary Jermyn, Jonny Speers, Ian FitzGibbon and Jonnie Goyer. David Cox and I did a double act as a brace of bishops. Julian later admitted that he had cast me because Pauline McLynn had liked the look of me. The casting couch, from the outset! Pauline, who would play Lady Fidget in *The Country Wife* later that term, was the most outrageous, funniest and loudest woman I had ever met. She taught a self-absorbed young man repeated lessons in how to take himself a little less seriously.

David Cox had brought a friend, a tall, extremely good-looking chap on a year's break from St John's College, Oxford. Hugh Schofield should never have been allowed join Players at all, but as soon as he set foot in No. 3, the women, once they had recovered their composure, barred the doors and refused to let him leave until he agreed to be in every show that term. The next one up was *The Country Wife*. Hugh played Harry Horner and I was the doctor who vouchsafed his (lack of) credentials. Lynne Parker directed it in two weeks. It took some members of the cast two weeks to read the damn thing, and several were never entirely sure what they were saying, so this was good going. Lynne was a tiny, big-eyed explosion of curls and creativity with an intuitive understanding of stylish comedy and a Belfast tongue that could put you in your place if you needed it. Not alone could she direct, she designed sets, costumes and posters, all to the highest standard. She also had the capacity of sensing talent in others and urging them to develop it.

The Country Wife was a bit shambolic but great fun and another success. It marked the Players debut of a certain Anne Enright, who was clearly the cleverest person any of us had ever met, as well as being a terrific actor. Anne got together with Martin Murphy in fairly short order, and they became 'MartinandAnne' from then on. Martin, who was in my philosophy class, had become an early friend and ally: as chairman and secretary of Players in our final year, we ended up sharing rooms in House No. 2, the natural stopping-off point for anyone coming or going to rehearsals and the default location for a cast party.

My first potential 'big break' came when the nicest man in Trinity, Gary Jermyn, dropped out of *Angel City*, and Martin Murphy and Fiona Donnelly, who were co-directing, asked me to replace him. We took *Angel City* to ISDA, the student drama festival, which was in Cork that year. The year climaxed with Julian Plunkett Dillon's epic production of *Coriolanus* in the Exam Hall, with its high scaffolding towers from which Gary Jermyn, in the title role, would fall to his death. I had spent hours in Players' subterranean office making sure secondary schools knew about the show, and we played to packed houses. Among the cast were Alan Glynn, Paul Murray and a charismatic young actor who had made an explosively funny debut weeks before in *The Real Inspector Hound*, Darragh Kelly. I played a comedy citizen with dyed pink hair.

We wore second-hand suits and frocks from Jenny Vander, or army surplus and Doc Martens, with silk scarves and paste jewelry. We survived on one meal a day: fish and chips from Burdocks, or the £1-salad bowl in the Granary, or seafood chowder in the Powerscourt Centre, where you could get a glass of wine and drink through Holy Hour if you had started early. We drank in O'Neill's, downstairs in The International, The Stag's Head and, in the summer, Kennedys and the Pav. We drank a lot, no doubt too much, although not as much as we would have if we'd had more money, or any money at all. And you had to be sober to rehearse, let alone perform, so that helped, or got in the way, depending on how you felt.

All the talk now was of the summer company JPD was going to lead in Players. He would direct a pastiche musical, *Dames at Sea*, Lynne would do

Travesties and I would adapt some selections from Joyce's *Portrait of the Artist* for the lunchtime show, the magnificently titled *Joycerpts*, which would be performed twice daily for six weeks and then taken to the Edinburgh Fringe for a further two. The hit of the season was *Travesties*, with a stand-out performance from Martin as Henry Carr. Anne Enright and I played the Lenins, bride and groom, and Una Clancy and Fiona Donnelly were a sparkling Gwendolyn and Cecily. *Travesties* had been booked to play the Everyman in Cork for a week, accommodation and meals included, and beer money, too; it seemed improbably fancy for a bunch of twenty-year-olds and we no doubt began to think we were the very fellows. We did a sell-out run in Players during Freshers' Week, then celebrated by blowing whatever money we'd made on a full-dress cocktail party, which ended in a lurid orgy of fighting, weeping and technicolour yawning, a nice and fitting judgment on our premature delusions of grandeur.

And somewhere along the way, I had bought a copy of *Gimme Shelter*.

LYNNE AND I were in the Granary one afternoon during Trinity Term 1983 when we decided to start Rough Magic. We didn't know what it would be called then, and the idea had been floating around in the ether for a while, but this was the first time we agreed to go for it. There was the strong sense that the work we had been doing, and the talent of the actors involved in that work, was too good not to be continued. There was the knowledge that no one in Irish theatre would employ us. And there was our belief that the Irish stage was a mausoleum of celibate bachelors and weeping mammies and farms and bogs and Sacred Hearts and pint bottles and half-doors and it said nothing to us about our lives. Lynne was fresh from her triumphant production of *A Midsummer Night's Dream*, her graduation show, so to speak, and about to attend to the minor matter of her finals. Then she would head to London and work backstage at the King's Head Theatre for a year, while I caught up.

My final year boiled down to two shows. The first was an over-budget and somewhat out-of-control *Serjeant Musgrave's Dance* with a large cast of old reliables and some new faces, including David Taylor, Donald Clarke, Quentin Letts, John O'Brien, Barney Spender and David Nolan. I overdid the nervous exhaustion on this one, not to mention the shouting, and tried the patience of my closest allies.

Ian Fitzgibbon was an intense and focused actor whose roles seemed to haunt his day-to-day life; Darragh Kelly was a slow burner with a lyric gift who would build steadily and then explode on stage. The idea of doing a Jacobean tragedy without them was unthinkable. I managed to persuade them both to appear in *The Duchess of Malfi*, my last show for Players. Rosemary Fine was a fine Duchess, Barney Spender just right as the noble Antonio, and Ian and Darragh were utterly possessed as Ferdinand and Bosola. Jacobean tragedy is full of torture and cruelty, sex and death, malice and madness and revenge: at twenty-one it felt more like life than life itself. I loved every minute spent rehearsing it, and I recall it now as a particularly magical time.

That should have been it, but David Taylor of TCD's Engineering Department suggested to Martin and me that he direct us in Athol Fugard's two-hander, *The Island*. Martin had just completed his inspired production of *King John*, which he had interpreted as a hitherto unrecognized comedy.

Whatever doubts I harboured about my acting ability, I put them to one side; *The Island* was the most relaxed and enjoyable time I ever had on stage. It was a temporary swansong. Three months later, with Lynne back from London, I would be directing Rough Magic's first evening show under the same roof, doubling down for the road ahead.

While I was at Trinity, I also took a degree in English and philosophy.

Declan Hughes (left) *and Martin Murphy in* The Island
by Athol Fugard, Players Theatre, 1984.

Declan Hughes (TCD 1980–4; English and Philosophy) is the co-founder and former artistic director of Rough Magic Theatre Company. He is an award-winning playwright and screenwriter. He has been writer-in-association at the Abbey Theatre. Author of five novels, his books have been nominated for the Edgar, Shamus, Macavity, Theakston's Old Peculier and CWA Dagger awards. **The Wrong Kind of Blood** won the Shamus for Best First PI Novel, and, in France, the **Le Point** magazine prize for Best European Crime Novel.

BOATS AGAINST THE CURRENT

alan gilsenan

Gatsby believed in the green light, the orgiastic future that year by year recedes before us. It eluded us then, but that's no matter – tomorrow we will run faster, stretch out our arms farther ... And one fine morning –

So we beat on, boats against the current, borne back ceaselessly into the past.

—F. Scott Fitzgerald, *The Great Gatsby*

THE EIGHTIES was a dark time. Or so the story goes.

But that's not how I remember it.

When I first entered Front Square, late one afternoon during the Indian summer of 1980, it seemed the place was bathed in a kind of golden light, a timeless radiance that history alone cannot contain. There were echoes of the past, no doubt, but mainly the air seemed pregnant with the promise of future lives.

Beyond the walls, Dublin lay in ruins. Georgian houses stood boarded up and factories lay empty whilst itinerant children roamed across desolate wastelands, playing amidst the rubbish and the rubble and the burnt-out cars. The sunlight fell here, too, illuminating the landscape with a poetic glow.

We knew the country was in tatters, of course, it was just that we didn't quite know why. As the eighties dawned, few of us who walked through the gates of Trinity College really had felt the true and damaging impact of unemployment or emigration. We had a sense, though, that something must change. At some inarticulate level, we sensed the social unrest and there was a growing feeling that things needed to be done. By us. By our generation. Yet, for the moment, this thought would remain unformed amongst us privileged freshers. For Trinity still remained largely the preserve of the lucky ones; the chosen few.

Some fledgling students knew more than the rest of us. Those who had to pay their own fees or, at least, knew the price of them; or those desperate young women who searched out the numbers of abortion clinics in Britain scrawled on the doors of public toilets; or the gay ones driven underground, unable to purchase condoms openly while rumours of a gay plague spread from the great beyond; those from 'broken homes' who weren't allowed to be officially broken; hardened Nordies embroiled in a war that none of us Southerners either knew or cared about; and all the other outsiders and outcasts that no one really noticed as they slinked anonymously into Freshers' Week.

But we all shared a strange, unspoken understanding – most of us, anyway – that this was our time. Pope John Paul II had come to Ireland in September 1979 and told us how much he loved us. In Ballybrit and the Phoenix Park, we cheered and hollered and downed our flagons and smoked our joints. But we weren't cheering out of some orgiastic reverence for Catholicism. No, we were cheering because we were young and we were there. Maybe we cheered because we even loved him, as well, messed up and all though we knew he was.

Years later, we'd discover just how messed up he and his whole institutional charade really were. That, even as we cheered, some priest was probably buggering some child somewhere out there across this great nation of ours. Had we known, we might have mounted a protest or something, even have stormed the altar, anything. Or so I'd like to think.

Most likely we'd just have cheered.

We had cheered, too, when the Boomtown Rats appeared on *The Late Late Show* two years earlier. They tore the RTÉ studio apart and, in doing so, set our small, dark, seventies world alight. Then Geldof did that interview. Famously claimed he wanted to 'get rich, get famous and get laid', all of which he happily achieved and more, much more. For Geldof stood then against all the smiley-faced hypocrites, the closed minds, the back-stabbers, those who said that one couldn't or shouldn't. He blazed a path right through the dark recesses of the eighties and showed us all a way towards our possible, if improbable, futures.

So we entered the eighties – and Trinity College Dublin – with a sort of unfocused, misdirected idealism. We were not, as history would have it, a bunch of losers intent on getting a degree and then getting the hell out. The Industrial Development Authority seemed to agree with us. They told us we were 'The Young Europeans', the brightest, the most well-educated, dammit, the best-looking kids in Europe. But we laughed at the eejits in the IDA posters all the same. We laughed at the ridiculousness of it all but, somehow, we believed. Believed in ourselves; in our capacity for change. Later, with the Celtic Tiger (how ludicrous it sounds now) and all that it brought, they rewrote our history. Painted us as the lost generation. And some of us were. But we'll get to that.

Back then, it seemed like we were entering a fantastical universe. Romantic imaginings of Oxford and Cambridge, of Harvard and Yale, abounded, filled our daydreams with some fairytale of higher education. Our English friends, many with extravagant affectations – bless them – reinforced this perception. Having not quite made the grade in England, they would much rather come to the hallowed halls of Trinity than be lost to some anonymous and grim cement campus in Middle Britain. Still something of an island within an Irish Republic, Trinity retained a sense of its own history, of its own enviable allure.

The calendar was littered with quaint, antiquated titles and occasions: Freshman and Sophister Years, Scholars and Fellows, Commons and the Buttery, Players and the Hist, the Colours Match and, of course, the Trinity Ball. Even the names of the academic terms had an other-worldliness to them: Michaelmas, Hilary, Trinity. We embraced it fully, for these gentle traditions had a reassuring air to them and we sensed that we, too, were slowly being absorbed – as if by some magical osmosis – into this glorious past.

We were happy to play our part, donning silly clothes and taking on our roles with gusto. We took glasses of sherry with tutors and raced around the perilously wet cobblestones of Front Square in the 'Chariots of Fire' foot race. We laughed at the pompous fools – like ourselves – who pontificated in debates and snuck into parties in the Rubrics and drank pints in the Pav.

Yet, despite the pantomime, we were free to be ourselves. Mostly, our lives were not overly governed by image or convention or glamour (that was for future, more competitive, generations). We dressed badly and cheaply and with a ridiculous sense of style. Or lack of it. We fell in and out of love. We put on plays, made films, wrote poems, edited magazines. We dreamed ourselves into being.

Education, lest I forget, played no small part in this. We devoured books and ideas and ideologies. Webster, Camus, Whitman, Beckett, Tarkovsky, Dickinson, Borges, Synge, Marx, Blake, Lorca, Neruda, Jung, Mishima, Ibsen, Shakespeare, Foucault, Dante, Eliot, Lawrence, Yeats, Laing, Boccaccio, Faulkner, Keats, Bellow, Kubrick, Strindberg, Conrad, Goffman, Cervantes, Plath, Pynchon, Genet, Morrison, Picasso, Scott Fitzgerald, Behan, Garcia Marquez. We were lost in the rush of it but, above all, changed.

Sometimes, especially in the early morning light, Trinity would seem like a remote island; a tranquil place set apart. Rarely would the outside world intrude. There were times, of course, when even we could not ignore the clamorous din beyond the walls. I have little recollection of the beginnings of the republican hunger strikes in the Maze prison in October 1980, but when Bobby Sands died on 5 May 1981, everything seemed to change. Across Northern Ireland, people rioted for days. On the streets of Belfast and Derry, they banged bin lids when his death was announced and on hearing the news in Dublin I could almost imagine the funereal clash and clatter echoing from Ulster pavements as I walked through College Park. The light seemed more diffuse, the air heavier, and while we were not aware of the subtleties of what was going on, perhaps not even aware of why he (and the oft-forgotten others) had sacrificed his life, we knew it was momentous. That a young man could lay down his life for a cause, for a people, seemed noble and grand, even in the rarefied air of Trinity College.

It left its mark, the death of Bobby Sands. There was a sort of pride, too, in what it symbolized: an almost poetic, if tragic, gesture of renunciation and rebellion. There were widespread protests across Europe. We took surprising pride in the fact that the name of Winston Churchill Boulevard in Tehran was changed to Bobby Sands Street. During one of those long, inter-railing summers, I ended up in a hospital ward in Turkey. The local doctor, unable to speak English, issued two phrases when I said where we came from: 'Bobby Sands?' and 'Johnny Logan?' 'Yes,' I said, 'Yes. Ireland. Bobby Sands and Johnny Logan.'

We knew that Margaret Thatcher was now the enemy of freedom. The Iron Lady, with her bitter, pursed lips. The Miners' Strike, the Falklands War, Northern Ireland. But the lady was not for turning. With stark simplicity, Billy Bragg sang 'Between The Wars' and Elvis Costello sang the elegiac 'Shipbuilding' while The Beat pleaded 'Stand Down, Margaret'.

Even inside the gilded palace of Trinity College, there were small revolutions. In the summer of 1981, the Irish Rugby Football Union made the shameful decision to tour South Africa during the height of apartheid. I remember, as clearly as memory will allow, a heated, packed debate about that ill-judged tour and apartheid in the Graduate Memorial Building. Late in proceedings, the handsome, clean-cut figure of Hugo MacNeill edged his way to the back of the overcrowded room. He was something of a sporting god within college and also the current Irish international fullback. He announced simply that he would not be going with the Irish team to South Africa, and left. We cheered. It seemed then, as it seems now, a noble gesture that proved that one could make some small difference in the outside world.

And inevitably, that outside world was beckoning. Many left for foreign shores – over 100,000 emigrated in the mid eighties – but for those, like me, who decided to remain behind there was still a tangible air of excitement. The Ireland before us seemed like a scorched, broken landscape, a world where the past had been erased but the future remained unwritten. It was a challenging, dizzy prospect but it was, nonetheless, our time. Time to go to work.

The 'yuppies' (remember them?) found fame and fortune in London and New York, Paris and Tokyo, Los Angeles and Sydney. Others grabbed their degrees and their sports bags and headed for those very first Ryanair flights to God knows where. Less lucky or probably less well connected, they ended up working, sometimes illegally, behind bars in Cincinnati or on building sites in Birmingham or waiting tables in Melbourne. Later, they would end up bitter, in exile somewhere, lamenting the country that sold them down the Swanee to pay for Charvet shirts.

The 'yuppies' would, however, come home for Christmas. They could afford to. Shopping on Grafton Street on Christmas Eve, meeting the 'old gang' from Trinners for drinks in the Shelbourne. To be honest, I resented them, breezing in for the briefest 'taste' of the old sod while the rest of us got on with the business of trying to rebuild the country. But to be Irish abroad then was a kind of fashion accessory and they were happy to flaunt their Irishness else-where while contributing little to the country that made them.

When the 'Boom' came, many of them flooded back, buying up land and property to beat the band. The empty wastelands, which once seemed so forlorn, were refashioned into eerie-looking apartment blocks and multi-storey car parks and strange hotels and the ghost estates of the future. Soon the country was unrecognizable; its geography erased. We were exiles in our own land.

Our history was rewritten, too. The eighties was revised and re-presented as a time of despair and desolation. Our hope, our blossoming of possibility and change, was reinvented as the shadow side of this new vision. It justified the new regime somehow; the new orthodoxy. The bright and shining path of the Celtic Tiger. Sometimes, now, I bump into people from those Trinity days, in unexpected corners of the world. There is often an almost embarrassed moment of recognition, the memory of some fleeting intimacy of shared youth.

We meet in hospital corridors as well. One day – not long before he died – I met the artist Gerald Davis in the oncology unit of the Mater Hospital on Eccles Street. Gerald was a mature student studying English at Trinity in the eighties. His burning passion for literature and art and jazz put us kids to shame. He also ran a small art gallery on Capel Street and, every Bloomsday, he became Leopold Bloom, James Joyce's archetypal Dubliner who lived, some-what neatly, on Eccles Street, not far from the Mater Private. We talked of this and that, picking up easily where we left off twenty years before, laughing at our predicament, joking in the face of our own mortality and its cruel reminders.

When I think back on those years in Trinity – something I rarely do – I remember an afternoon close to the end. It was early June 1984 and Ronald Reagan was visiting Ireland and his ancestral birthplace in Ballyporeen. There had been protests in Dublin but we were planning our own welcome: a 'Reagan Rave', a childish, tongue-in-cheek celebration of all things American, a satirical send-up of the visit. We dressed up as garish Americans and gathered in a garden a stone's throw from the American embassy in Ballsbridge, and not far from my family home on Raglan Road in the charming, much-maligned and soon-to-change Dublin 4. At some point late in that golden afternoon, we decided the time had come to deliver our own handmade card of welcome for President Reagan to the embassy. We moved out on to the lane and then down on to Elgin Road. The streets seemed deserted except for a few edgy marines on duty outside the embassy.

We started to move towards it. Slowly at first, a reckless, motley bunch of fancy-dressed students, we gradually gathered momentum and soon began to run down the centre of the tree-lined road. Infused with the warmth of the afternoon and the alcohol and an unspoken sense that this was our last hurrah, we picked up speed. Finally, we seemed to be running frantically, faster and faster, intoxicated by the moment. We were running now with careless abandon into a future that we could only imagine but could not know. We would never be that free or alive again.

Or so it seemed to me, on that summer's afternoon, in the midst of the 1980s.

Alan Gilsenan (TCD 1980–4; Modern English and Sociology) was awarded the inaugural A.J. Leventhal Scholarship. He is a film-maker, theatre director and writer. He is a former chairman of the Irish Film Institute, served two terms as a member of the Irish Film Board, and is currently a member of the board of RTÉ. He lives in Co. Wicklow with his wife, Catherine Nunes, and their two daughters.

THE ISLAND

austin o'carroll

AS A YOUTH just out of a Christian Brothers education, Trinity whispered promises of undiscovered freedom, beauty and learning. In my seven years there (two studying law and five studying medicine) it fulfilled its promise in many ways, furnishing me with memories of manicured, sun-drenched lawns; boaters and garden parties; bow ties and lavish balls; Sunday mornings on the quiet, cobbled Front Square; hot evenings sitting outside the Pavilion; and winter afternoons in the Arts Block watching the poise, the fashion and the sweet beauty passing by.

However, it was not within that beautiful haven that the future direction of my life's path was set. It was in the borderlands outside those walls, those spaces between Trinity and Pearse Street, Trinity and Sean McDermott Street, Trinity and Ballyfermot.

It started when I wandered through Freshers' Week stalls, savouring the vast menu of possible pursuits (often sweetened with bribes involving kegs of beer and crates of cheap wine). I joined the St Vincent de Paul on my sister's recommendation that it was a great society for meeting people. We had a strong family history of volunteerism and, having a significant disability, sports clubs were not a real option for me to fraternize.

At our first meeting in a windowless, soulless room in the Arts Block I sat among the other freshers, faintly awed by the more experienced members, who ranged from clean-cut 'good' boys to shaggy-haired relics from the hippy era, as they related their experiences of visiting the wild east on Pearse Street. Throughout that year I did weekly visits, distributing handouts for electricity, gas and food bills; delivering Christmas hampers; converging with fellow VdePers on Corporation flats with paint, much enthusiasm and little skill; dancing slow sets at 'old folks' parties'; and bringing wild children to Sunshine House. Mostly, however, I worked in the youth club staffed by Trinity Vincent de Paul. Each week we would pick up the children in Markievicz and Pearse houses and walk them to the club, which was based in an old Georgian house on Herbert Street. This was the Dublin red-light district at the time, with 'brassers' parading down the street and manning the corners round the Peppercanister Church.

By the New Year there were only two students left, me and Nick Sparrow. We played table tennis, board games and street games – anything to divert the unbounded energy of the children into some structured activity.

In my parallel Trinity existence I was experiencing the headiness of being a freshman, with all its newfound freedoms. I attended the Hist, Phil and Law societies to hear raging debates and wondrous orations from well-respected (or, more excitingly, non-respected) public figures; garden parties in the spring; Players Theatre for soup and drama; Hothouse Flowers playing outside the Pav; the opulent Trinity Ball. And my sister's advice was sound. Friends flowed from the SVP coffers. I drank with Nick Sparrow, partied with Clare Watson, Katie Donovan and Christine Magee, and danced with Johnny Daly and Barbara Cullinane.

I got a job through SVP in my first summer in Trinity as the co-ordinator of the eight-week Pearse Street Summer Project, where I organized activities for children from the Pearse Street, City Quay and Townsend Street areas. On my first day, my south-side Trinity-boy sensibilities were tickled when I admired a pretty, blonde, four-year-old girl's new blue dress. After several compliments on the dress she looked at me with her big blue eyes and told me to 'go suck my cock'. Despite this comment, she retained her innocence while I lost mine.

That summer was like a carnival run in a poorly supervised crèche. We had sporting competitions of all sorts; twice-weekly hikes; a film club in the local hall; fancy-dress swims in the canal; ghost hunts for children; and water fights in the Corporation flats off Pearse Street with hundreds of children and mothers pouring water over their balconies. It was my introduction to the chaos of inner-city life. Even though that same chaos is responsible for family breakdown, drug addiction, violence and early death, I loved it from the start and have remained in love with it. To me it was full of fun, excitement, surprise and at all times has felt more real than the more ordered calm existence of the suburbs.

I used Trinity as a means of escape from the chaos of the Summer Project. There, on the sunlit lawns and dappled paths, I could find peace and harmony surrounded by academics, students and tourists, with not a hint of a Dublin-accented youth in my vicinity. When term started, I joined the steering committee of the SVP. That committee had a peculiar energetic dynamism fuelled by a diverse group of people, ranging from those of a deeply Catholic conservative persuasion to those who were agnostic and left of centre.

The following three years were an exhilarating, frenetic and inspiring time. In our first year, the ranks of the SVP swelled. We doubled in size and expanded our range of services. I decided to move away from developing youth clubs and concentrated instead on organizing hikes with local children. This allowed students to volunteer for a few Sundays, and allowed us to run weekly hikes from September to May. These were the days prior to garda vetting, insurance and the threat of being sued if a child sustained an injury.

My second summer was spent in Dublin Corporation playgrounds in Ballyfermot. Regular tea breaks and team meetings punctuated the chaos. It was only when adult joyriders came to show off their skills that the chaos threatened to spill over.

In our third year we met the challenge of Community Action. This group set up by the Students' Union adopted a more developmental/political approach to addressing the problems of 'the poor'. The engagement with Community Action changed our perspective in SVP as it caused us to debate the charitable nature of the work we did. As a result, we adapted. Rather than simply visit 'the disabled', we organized a 'Disability Access Day' on which we brought a number of people with disabilities into Trinity for activities in order to highlight its inaccessibility. We developed the idea of giving grinds to help local young people improve their educational chances.

We expanded the number of areas from where we recruited children to bring on hikes. We ran three hikes – one from Pearse Street, one from Ballyfermot and one from St Joseph's Mansions on Sean MacDermott Street. The children in St Joseph's Mansions had a particularly special and what ultimately proved to be poignant influence on my future life. This is a small flat complex built on three floors around a central square that accommodated a compact playground run by Dublin Corporation. When we first visited, it was a vibrant community comprised of people who originated in the old Dublin tenements. We would visit the older people and listen to their stories of how Dublin used to be and on Sundays we would take a dozen or more kids from the flats on hikes.

The lads would huddle together adopting poses at the front of the top of the bus, while the girls – dressed up in glittery gear and caked in make-up – successfully teased and shocked the not-much-older TCD students. They performed dance routines to Madonna and Michael Jackson on the top of a mountain, and ran in fear from cows, which some of them thought were horses. We organized weekends away in Glendalough, did treasure hunts in the forest and told ghost stories at midnight in the graveyard under the Round Tower.

When I started working in the inner city as a GP I called to see St Joseph's Mansions, which was locked up and abandoned, like a bombed-out building that had somehow remained intact. The Mansions had been at the forefront of the drugs explosion in the 1980s; a monument to those who died from heroin use stood on the corner, overlooked by the unlit windows of the abandoned flats. One lunchtime, I was asked to do a house call off Sean MacDermott Street to a man who was dying from cirrhosis of the liver caused by Hepatitis C infection, which he picked up from having shared a dirty heroin needle. I arrived at the door to be greeted with a hug and a kiss. It was Anita, one of the kids from the hikes, now in her thirties with her own kids. Her sister Margaret was in the kitchen. It was their older brother who was dying.

I asked after the group: it had been decimated. Almost all of them had left school early, to face a future filled with nothing. They replaced hope with drugs, and most of them had got caught up in the drug epidemic of the 1990s.

A number of those surviving had drug addictions and drug-related blood-borne infections as well. The girls had done best. Some had stayed clear of drugs and got jobs and worked their way out of poverty. Some had moved to the suburbs and one had gone to the US and 'got herself a good job'. None had gone to university. None had even thought of visiting that island in the middle of the city. Traffic between Trinity and the inner city was one-way.

So in many ways the island of Trinity is central to the experiences that led me to work as a GP with an inner-city community fractured by poverty and drugs, and with homeless and drug services. I became involved in the Disability Rights movement, and have shifted from a charitable approach to a rights-based ethos. However, I retain my respect for the motivation and efforts of those involved in charitable work. I have learnt that humanity does not run parallel to political persuasion and, while I espouse a socialist philosophy, I seek out humane people.

When one distils the essence of non-impoverished youth – its hope, its optimism, its sense of adventure and fun – and funnels that distillation into a peaceful glade filled with noble buildings within the bustling city, one gets Trinity College. Now, having experienced the hopelessness of impoverished youth, that island seems a separate state with four passport controls that subtly but effectively ensure the right type of citizen enters and leaves. It has little relevance to the people I work with. While I love the memories it gave me, I now wish that waves of protest could hammer its coastline and break down the barriers between it and the community in which it has been plonked. Sadly, such waves don't even lap its shore.

Austin O'Carroll (TCD 1980–8; Medicine) started in law, having been told he was unable for medicine due to his disability. In 1982, with the help of his tutor Mary McAleese, he transferred to medicine. He is an inner-city GP with extensive experience in working with inner-city deprivation, new communities, and the homeless and drug-using populations. He was the winner of the Time and Tide Award from the African Refugee Network and is founder and chairperson of Safetynet, which co-ordinates primary healthcare services for homeless people and members of the Roma community. He is also founder of the North Dublin GP

Training Programme. Austin is involved in education and research initiatives in the area of addressing health inequalities, and has been a disabled-rights activist and spokesperson for the Irish Thalidomide Association.

Austin O'Carroll (in foreground) 'mountaineering up Grafton Street' as a fundraiser for the Society of St Vincent de Paul, 1984.

YESTERDAY, TODAY AND TOMORROW

nick sparrow

AS A STUDENT, alumnus and member of staff in Trinity I have a kaleido-scopic perspective. Trinity is different now to how it was in the eighties (louder, bigger and more confident, with a wonderful diversity in the student popula-tion) and yet so much remains the same: Front Gate meetings, Freshers' Week, the Trinity Ball, bicycles everywhere.

Re-entering college as a member of staff was odd, to say the least. But it was nothing compared to the transformation that came with my first day as a student. I can't remember why I chose Trinity, but as Denis Burkitt (my Trinity hero) said: 'Irish by birth, Trinity by the grace of God.'

Having been educated at five different primary schools, I went through secondary school feeling somewhat 'apart' from everyone else. In reality, I was probably no different from any other teenager. Little did I know that Trinity would be a haven for the likes of me – people who felt that everyone else knew where they were going. We watched them disappear into the horizon leaving us to navigate our solitary ways. Mine took me to Front Gate.

If I'm to be honest, I was not born for physics. If I'm to be really honest, I'm not sure half my class was, either. I have a memory of being with a classmate after jointly working out a particular experiment. We were quite happy with how we had mastered our understanding of this little corner of nature but then he said, 'Yeah – but do you understand "physics"? I mean, the whole thing, how it kind of explains everything?' We looked at each other like two elderly monks who realized that after a lifetime of devotion, their faith was gone.

All the concepts and formulae – what was I thinking? I left school understanding Pythagoras' Theorem and thought I could play with the big boys. I'm not sure which decision was worse, mine or my good friend Anto Long's, a gifted musician and fellow physics traveller, who chose the course to complement his musical interests with the intention of concentrating on acoustics. No one told him that this was not going to be taught – ever. How was he to know? Our naivety at the time takes me aback. Today's students actually have the temerity to ask for a syllabus before choosing their course.

I recall being in the library and seeing students ask for copies of past exam papers. My disapproval was visceral – if they were real students on a real journey of enquiry they would not need such trickery and cheating. (My perspective 'matured' somewhat before I sat my September resits.)

While physics was challenging, the Physics Department was supportive and did its best to stretch my mind as much as it was stretchable. I still wake up in cold sweats trying to attempt one question on my final-year paper that remains firmly etched in my brain: 'If everyone in Ireland drove on the right-hand side of the road rather than the left, would the day get longer, shorter or stay the same?'

I mean, lads, come on! How about a question on right-angled triangles?

For most Trinity graduates, the academic side of our student lives is not really what we recall best and many of us had one or two societies or clubs that forged us. For me it started with the Judo Club, a brief flirtation that was not to last. We'll draw a veil over a few humiliating episodes on the judo mattress. We'll also draw a veil over other humiliating flirtations in first year – which never got near any mattress.

It was the TCD St Vincent de Paul Society that gave me my formative college experiences. This was true for many of us – and remains true for today's students. There I met the most astonishing people and many became close friends. I'm even married to one, Margaret O'Donoghue, who read German and history. Vincent de Paul met on Thursday evenings. With a shocking lack of knowledge about the real hardship in the inner city, we set about doing our bit to change the world. I remain to be convinced about the real impact of our interventions on those we visited. But I have no doubt that the engagement with our neighbours, living so close to the campus walls but with radically different experiences, expectations and life opportunities, changed us students for the better.

At meetings we organized practical help – much of it beneficial, but we were a bit clueless at times. We must have driven those we visited mad; they were probably either pulling their hair out with frustration or laughing at us behind our backs. On becoming treasurer, I realized we had a fair amount of surplus funds and so, with a magnanimity that even Bertie Ahern would have thought irresponsible, we agreed to increase our grants. Some months later, such short-term perspectives began to fade. Someone in the group had been reading Marx or some liberation theologian and (not understanding any of it) pointed out that all we were doing was 'propping up the system' and that we shouldn't give any grants. Imagine the response we got when we called to one of our visits in St Joseph's Mansions – a single mother with five kids – and told her that the fiver we gave her was undermining the political progress we needed to make Ireland a fairer place. You will not be surprised that our stance did not last long.

The innocence of our approach is what I celebrate. And just when it began to disappear, we welcomed new freshers to take our places on the committee with their own ideas, equally daft at times, but equally well meaning.

Integral to that innocence was a pure motive to help make Ireland a better place. And Trinity, consciously and unconsciously, always nurtured this. As my fellow SVP member and friend, Austin O'Carroll, said at the time, the real value in the SVP wasn't really in the works we did, it was in the formation of the minds of the people doing those works.

Of my SVP colleagues, many continue to work amongst the vulnerable in society. I name three, knowing that I should mention many more. Iseult O'Malley went on to bring the activities of FLAC (Free Legal Advice Centres) to a whole new level of effectiveness; Roch Maher dedicated his life to housing people in London; and Michael Dillon who, when he left Trinity SVP, visited his three 'old dears' for years (even taking them away for holidays). Today, TCD SVP regularly wins 'Society of the Year' in college and has grown to over a thousand members.

When my time at Trinity ended, I was both liberated and lost. I couldn't wait to leave but couldn't contemplate it not being in my life. Meeting today's students makes me reflect that, while so much has changed, the differences are immaterial – there is a bond reinforced by the shared familiarity that connects all alumni. In my role in the Trinity Foundation, I have the privilege of working with many alumni who have their own Trinity memories and experiences – many different but yet surprisingly resonant with mine. They want to keep their connection with this wonderful college and see it thrive. They know that Trinity did great things for them, and for the wider world. They know that Trinity continues to do great things for today's students, and society in general. And they know that this will continue – today and tomorrow.

Nick Sparrow (Trinity 1980–5; Physics) FCA is director of the Trinity Foundation. He left Newbridge College in 1980 to study experimental physics in Trinity. After joining KPMG and spending a year in Libya, he returned to Ireland and became administrator of Belvedere College, Dublin, where he cut his teeth fundraising, before joining the Trinity Foundation.

CURRIES, SPATS AND DENIMS

patrick wyse jackson

THE CHOICE was limited, according to my career guidance teacher. I attended St Columba's, a well-known school in Rathfarnham, which nestles beneath the rounded granite mountains that hem Dublin in along its southern edge. A classmate dared to ask about the matriculation requirements for UCD, a seemingly innocent question, and was greeted with a snort and the words 'We never send anyone to UCD!' This suited me just fine – my two brothers had entered Trinity a few years earlier, as had my father in the 1930s, and so the continuation of the family progression through Front Gate seemed logical.

In any case, my linguistic abilities were severely limited and I didn't have French and Irish, which were required for the 'other' institution. Confident in my academic prowess, I took too few subjects at Leaving Cert. and didn't get a place. Undaunted, I spent a year decorating a house in Ringsend while also engaging in pre-university studies at Lincoln's Inn. Second time around, I received an offer of a place in natural sciences and entered Trinity in October 1980, at the same time as my younger brother.

Almost the first person I met was Larry Stapleton, fresh up from Kilkenny. A group of nervous students was waiting in the Chemistry Building at the start of the pre-chemistry course that was supposed to get us up to honours level in two weeks. Larry was sporting a tweed jacket, on the lapel of which he had written 'U2' in Tippex, and carried the most enormous rucksack. I suspect that we spent most of the course talking, and soon afterwards decided to share a flat in Ranelagh, above a carpet shop.

Science students in the 1980s often looked rather jealously at their counterparts in the Arts Block. We had far more lectures and practicals, and seemed to have less money to spend on clothes. However, all Southern students were green with envy as our Northern colleagues were on large grants, most of which seemed to be spent in the Pav or other local watering holes.

In our first year, Charles Holland, Professor of Geology, taught us in the Museum Building. He had a master switch installed near the lectern, which, when thrown for latecomers, would plunge the room into darkness. In geography, James Killen taught us how to draw maps and charts of lavatory density in Ireland, and regaled us with stories of riding the rails across North America. Gordon Herries Davies was a larger-than-life character who lectured on the history of science and threw in gems of wisdom on nautical matters in particular. My present-day work is much influenced by him.

In chemistry, lectures were held in a huge lecture theatre at the far end of campus. Frank Jeal lectured in zoology and had the great ability of making the subject both fascinating and revolting at the same time.

To a freshman student, Trinity seemed a hotbed of intellectual and political activity, although I suspect that a lot of it was hot air. It was a time when Joe Duffy was to the fore of student politics, barricading himself with others into administrative offices in Front Square and making noises about the inequality of funds spent on staff services as against student services. Student politicians were usually counterbalanced by 'fun' candidates: 'Apollo' was probably the most celebrated.

I was never terribly interested in student politics – most students weren't – so it now seems totally out of character that in my Senior Freshman year I sought a mandate from the student body for SU president. This was the year that forty-seven engineers managed to get themselves listed on the ballot paper, and were joined by me (dressed in a hired gorilla suit), Aine Lawlor and one other, the latter two being the 'serious candidates'. I came a creditable fourth, with just over two hundred votes.

It took me two years to dispense with JF chemistry, and in my Junior

Sophister year I signed up to take geology, which had always been my intended moderatorship. The class was relatively small at fifteen, and was made up of some former schoolmates, and others such as Aidan Forde from Killarney who was a fearless climber, Pippa Jeffcock who acted as a matchmaker later that year, and Peter Casey whom we thought would be the first to strike oil and make his fortune. We rapidly bonded as a group, and much of this had to do with various field excursions to the wilds of western Ireland and Scotland.

The geologists organized their own student society, named after the noted polymath John Joly, and weekly lectures were followed with sessions in the Pav, or occasional parties in the Main Lab where the benches were loaded up with bottles. The department was intimate and we had some lecturers who clearly loved their subject, but seemed to us students to have a greater depth to their interests. Doug Palmer lectured on palaeontology, but also talked about art. George Sevastopulo was a fount of knowledge, although he was rarely able to tell you precisely which journal to consult. He would remove any of the more interesting fossils that were found by students, telling them that they were 'needed for the Geological Museum'.

As an escape from my geological colleagues, Seán Dempster, whom I had known from school, persuaded me to join the Hockey Club. Unlike him I had no real ability but quickly slotted into the right-back position for the TCD Fourth XI. We were a motley bunch and in my first year the team cheerfully propped up the lowest division in Leinster, but did succeed in reaching the semi-final of the Minor Cup. The following year things improved when Barney Purce was recruited. Barney was a rare breed: he owned a car, and so the team had transport.

Another form of escapism was the cinema. Three o'clock on a Thursday afternoon would see half the geology class head to the Screen on Hawkins Street for the afternoon matinee. It didn't really matter what was showing, so long as we could miss the practical class in metamorphic petrology. The TCD Film Club, which in my time was organized by Donald Clarke (now film editor of *The Irish Times*), Philip Owens (now a film editor in the US) and others, was another popular activity. At the beginning of the year the committee produced a programme of films and was guaranteed a packed house for any that promised nudity. Invariably there was little, but nonetheless the punters always seemed satisfied, or else were drunk.

I shared rooms with Dermot Dix in 13.1.1 Botany Bay for my final two undergraduate years. We thought we were sophisticated, playing backgammon and trying to cook unusual meals. I recall some great dinner parties, particularly those with David Webb, the former Professor of Botany, who was an instantly recognizable figure, identified by his mass of white hair and full denim garb. He was a mentor to my botanical brothers, Peter and Michael, and accepted an invitation to dine in Botany Bay. As a starter I served Brussels sprout soup, a watery-green invention of my own, which he later admitted to hating.

About six months before finals, Charles Holland asked what my plans were on graduating. I had decided to do an H.Dip.Ed. – he looked somewhat disappointed. After a year's teaching, I called in to see him and asked if I could start a Ph.D. even though my final grade was not brilliant. He generously accepted me as his student. A few years later he offered me my first, and to date only, job, and I have remained in Trinity ever since.

Patrick Wyse Jackson (TCD 1980–92; Geology) embarked on a career as a secondary-school teacher, but soon afterwards returned to TCD to study carboniferous bryozoans (small marine fossils) for which he gained a Ph.D. He was appointed curator of the College Geological Museum in 1988, then later a lecturer, and associate professor in geology, and elected FTCD in 2006. He lives in Rathmines with his wife Vanessa (née Risk), two daughters Susanna and Katie, and three cats.

A FEW FALSE STARTS

luke dodd

I **HAD** a few false starts after leaving school – there was a year at the Sligo Regional Technical College, one at NCAD and another working in Selfridges in London. I decided to give it one more try and had come to the conclusion that a BA would be fun, that you could study only what you might enjoy and if you got to the other end the rest would take care of itself. The 1980s in Ireland was not a very hopeful time – emigration was endemic, the political situation unstable and the situation north of the border seemed intractable. Why not have fun while getting a degree if the prospect of a job in Ireland was remote? My year at NCAD had sparked an interest in art history – it seemed a plausible and pleasurable way to pass a few years.

UCD, the only university other than Trinity that offered art history, seemed too big and impersonal. Plus all that concrete *and* it wasn't even close to the city centre. Trinity, on the other hand, was compact and unthreatening. The blend of uncompromisingly modern buildings with the historic ones was enlightened, as was the integration of modernist sculpture around the campus. Most important of all, when campus life became too much it was easy to escape into the streets of Dublin and leave it all behind.

Trinity only offered art history as part of a joint degree so I opted for that other wonderfully marketable discipline – philosophy. In the early 1980s, there was a marked intimacy about Trinity, or at least that part of it that I inhabited, the Arts Block. And the general atmosphere was one of quiet, very civilized, conservatism – the Philosophy Department was steeped in the empirical tradition of Locke, Berkeley and Hume, and connoisseurship ruled the roost in Professor Anne Crookshank's Art History Department. The pace was leisurely – I think we had about eight lectures a week and the occasional seminar – and the terms short. It was still possible to go to college without incurring any debt – I think my final-year fees were £900 – summer work paid for the rest of the year. It all seems so innocent in retrospect. Lecturers and professors generally went by their first names. The arts and humanities staff were predominately English, especially at senior levels, and there seemed to be definite preference for recruiting from the 'mainland'. By the time I left in the mid 1980s, no Irish person had ever been appointed provost or librarian. There was a tacit, if erroneous, understanding that Trinity was more or less the same as Oxford and Cambridge.

The first term was difficult, a lonely time – maybe this is the case for many undergraduates? I marvelled at those around me who seemed assured and confident. They acted as if they always knew they would end up at Trinity. They joined student societies and from day one seemed to rush about, leading full and exciting lives. I joined the Film Society, an inexpensive way of seeing relatively recent releases, albeit 16mm prints, but none of the others attracted me. It didn't take long to figure out that the Phil and the Hist as well as the Students' Union were for those who aspired to public office. And there were certainly many who seemed to have come to Trinity purely for Players.

The art history classes were much smaller than the philosophy ones and consequently less intimidating. Also, the academics in art history were eminently more approachable, friendly and available than their counterparts in philosophy. Trinity was, at one level, a kind of gentleman's club. Men far outweighed women on the academic staff and female professors were scarce. Some of the male academic staff had rooms – their permanent residence.

The library provided some refuge and, because the stock of books that could be borrowed was very small, a good deal of time was spent there. It was a deeply frustrating place: it was often easier to purchase a book than access the library copy. Although the books were catalogued using the Dewey system, there were five different indexes, only one of which was computerized. Huge reserves of books were held in off-site storage in Santry, adding delay and further frustration. But the library was full of light and the desks adjacent to the art history stacks were in the best position looking out at the Calder sculpture in its circle of cobbles, framed by the gaunt edifice of Burgh's Library. It was from these very desks that Pauline McLynn and I were ejected – we were studying for our finals – for laughing too much and too loudly.

Not really knowing anybody in the first term, there wasn't much to do other than concentrate on the academic work. My first philosophy essay was a refutation of the ontological argument for the existence of God. I have only the vaguest recollection of the intricacies of the argument but I have a very clear memory of the mental strain and anguish that writing and researching the essay caused me. And I could no more rehearse the argument now than recite the Bible. I worked very hard that first term and it wasn't all that much fun. But a few things happened early in the second term to bring about a change.

A cousin of mine had acquired an early-nineteenth-century folio of estate maps of the Sandford Estate at Castlerea, County Roscommon. While most of the maps were intact, the top right-hand corner of the volume had completely rotted away and the original binding was in tatters. Eddie McParland in the Art History Department arranged for me to visit the conservation laboratory, housed under the eaves of Burgh's Library. Somehow, it was established that I could work on the restoration of the maps under the supervision of the staff (these were the same people who looked after the Book of Kells!) and just pay for the materials involved. The director of the lab, Tony Cains, was an acerbic, somewhat awkward Englishman who was, initially at least, deeply sceptical that I would see the project through. He liked to test people with an intimidating manner but it was easy to see that his colleagues all respected him.

It took me almost two years of painstakingly repetitive work. There were sixty-odd pages so each stage had to be repeated sixty times. But the most memorable part was not the finished, restored volume: it was getting to and from the conservation lab. I worked on the repairs early in the morning before lectures started and the only way to get to the lab at that time of day was via the Long Room. Each morning I walked the length of that magnificent room at mezzanine level, absolutely alone and unsupervised. That was a very special privilege.

And, of course, I made friends. We always had a five o'clock lecture in the Thomas Davis and that's where I first spied Angela Mehegan in her trademark red beret and mac. She was usually the last to go in as she finished a cigarette close to the lift near the entrance. She had also knocked around a bit before ending up at Trinity and had a wonderfully wry humour that provided a useful antidote to some of our more earnest fellow students.

Of the countless lectures I had in those four years, most are forgotten or barely remembered except for Anne Crookshank's. She was a natural orator and performer. She was also very funny. One day she projected a slide of an early-Renaissance Annunciation in which a small, crucifix-carrying angel was travelling along a beam of light from God to the general area of the Virgin's privates. 'I have no idea where he thinks he's going with that cross,' she barked.

The Douglas Hyde Gallery was also an important part of my time at Trinity. In my first term, it mounted a wonderful exhibition about the Abbey of St Gaul, Switzerland. Shortly afterwards, the Virgin Prunes did a one-night installation entitled 'A New Form of Beauty' as well as a performance at the Edmund Burke – exposure to that kind of avant-garde, post-punk experience was rare in 1980s Dublin, much less at Trinity. I became one of the team of volunteer students that hung all the shows – we also sat on the committee that decided the programme of exhibitions. A Welsh woman called Jenni Rogers ran the gallery during most of that time, a relatively thankless job given the budget. But there were some memorable shows: I remember hanging work by Francis Bacon and Lucian Freud. And I spent an entire night in the gallery with James Coleman, trying to finish the installation of his mid-term retrospective. Having a practical, physical outlet to counterbalance the academic work was, I now understand, extremely important for me.

I am rarely in Dublin these days but I never pass up the opportunity to walk through campus. The physical space isn't much changed; the newly constructed Ussher Library is a bit ungainly but doesn't intrude too much. And the Long Room Hub is a welcome addition to Fellows' Square – the 1937 Reading Room was always too timid to hold that side of the quadrangle on its own. I don't much like the new entrance to Burgh's Library via the arcades facing the Lecky Library nor the opening up of a large public stairwell right in the middle of the Long Room – that room should only be approached from the east or west end where the full impact is at its most dramatic. Nobody can argue with using the Book of Kells to generate money to support the libraries. But I remember a time when students had free access to that room, and when a pair of nondescript display cases on the right-hand side close to the western end held two of the Gospels of the Book of Kells almost as if they had ended up there by accident.

Luke Dodd (TCD 1981–5; History of Art and Philosophy) went from Trinity to the Whitney Museum Independent Study Program in New York. From 1986, he worked for ten years at Strokestown Park, Co. Roscommon, restoring the house and gardens and establishing the Famine Museum in the stable yards of the house. This was followed by a stint running the Irish Film Archive in Temple Bar. Since 1999, he has worked at the **Guardian** newspaper on a variety of projects, the most recent of which is a documentary on the life and work of the photographer Jane Bown.

A LAD TURNS LEFT, SLOWLY

dermot dix

I ARRIVED at TCD in October 1981. As one might expect, given that I arrived at the usual age of eighteen, it was where I became an adult – or gave it my best shot. I read history, my favourite subject from an early age. I had great friendships at school, but had failed miserably at love. Friendships at TCD were a wonderful mixture of the intense and the matter-of-fact; I relished making friends across disciplines and interests and across cultural and religious backgrounds. I had my first serious romance with Maureen Tatlow, who had been brought up in what seemed to me a wonderfully vibrant, multi-cultural, exotic home and country (Hong Kong). One Christmas her father, a university lecturer and Brecht scholar, gave me a copy of Edward Said's *Orientalism*; I was not ready for its approach at the time, but a few years later, when teaching in New York, Said's writings became heavily influential.

My friends included Kim Bielenberg and Niels Aalen in history; Caroline Canning in ESS; Angus Buttanshaw, Conor Devally and Joe Lavelle in law; Willie McKinney and Klaus Harvey in German; and a large group of self-styled 'medi-bores' including John O'Dowd, Keith Perdue and David Orr. John was my closest friend at Trinity, and through him I began to realize the excitement of a new kind of friendship, one not based on a tribal sense of belonging: he was the opposite in every way of a straight, Protestant, hockey-playing, arts/

humanities, laddish fellow like me (though it was years later that he came out). He, David and I adored Van Morrison's *Astral Weeks* and *Moondance*, the start of a lifelong passion for Van's music.

For two happy years I shared rooms in Botany Bay with Patrick Wyse Jackson, geology student and son of a distinguished Church of Ireland bishop. We learned to cook, I from my *World Cuisines* cookbook and he from his own eclectic imagination – I still remember his spicy Brussels sprout soup. We played darts, hosted lunches almost every day and brought pints of Guinness back to our rooms from the Buttery to wash down our dinners. We made forays in the holidays to his family's Nissen hut on the Dingle Peninsula where we would play beach cricket with driftwood bats and tennis balls, swim in the icy water, take long walks up mountains or along the beach, and drink copious pints of Guinness in Ashe's pub.

In the summer before final year, John was diagnosed with Hodgkin's disease, but he, Maureen and I went ahead with a planned tour of Europe. Her father's connections got us a week at the Normandy house of the distinguished Brecht scholar John Willett. The Liverpool poet Adrian Henry was one of the other house guests, a warm, funny man. In Provence we rented a small house in L'Isle-sur-la-Sorgue for a week. We came home via Maureen's relatives in Munich. In those few weeks I had started to think of myself as European and not merely Irish.

There were several mature students in my circle. Two, Jim Smyth and Shea Courtney, spring to mind – each the seeming archetype of his city (Belfast and Dublin, respectively), two heavy-drinking republican lefties. Jim became a history lecturer at a major Midwestern US university in Indiana; Shea was a union-organizer and also a fine singer of songs of conscience. I met Jim again when we were both graduate students in Cambridge, and that is when our friendship truly started. I asked him and his wife, Mary Burgess, to help me look after groups of American visitors to Ireland – I was on a self-appointed mission to change the way visitors experienced the country, and Americans were the easiest to lure since I lived in New York. Jim, pipe in tobacco-black-ened hand, zip often halfway down ('you never know the moment'), would dazzle them with his wry brilliance – once they had learned to navigate his Falls Road accent. Shea would often enliven the groups with flying visits; out would come the guitar, and songs would flow about Joe Hill, the old IRA, the Spanish Civil War, Che Guevara. He used to tell me that even in our TCD years he felt I wasn't too much of a gobshite – mainly because my summer job was loading trucks, even if it was in my father's transport company.

Once given the choice, I gravitated towards modern rather than medieval history. John Horne's lectures in the modern European history survey course were studies in intensity; he was the first lecturer I encountered whose approach appeared to be at least partly informed by Marxism, and he was exciting for that. Helga Robinson-Hammerstein was the maternal figure of the department, a scholar of German history ranging from Luther to the Weimar Republic. David Dickson, in those days teaching economic history, was always incisive – and so cool in his leather jacket. I took a course on the French Revolution with Patrick Kelly, a vastly learned man. Aidan Clarke taught a highly engaging course on the Puritan Revolution; he had a lovely warm chuckle and his voice was so magnificent that, mesmerized, one just wanted to listen.

K.G. Davies showed us that history could be funny as well as vital. He told me the way I wrote rather reminded him of Anthony Powell, which I took as a compliment since I knew Powell was a favourite of his. Indeed, he lent me his copy of *A Question of Upbringing*, the first in Powell's masterful twelve-volume series, *A Dance to the Music of Time*. However, one thing Davies clearly thought Powell and I had in common was an 'involuted' style – and as if to illustrate mine, he wrote in one marginal comment alongside an especially unwieldy sentence from a draft of my thesis on seventeenth-century Virginia: 'Eleven words where two would do'.

I took my history quite seriously. But I also took my gallivanting quite seriously. As a graduate student at Cambridge I abhorred the twittish undergrads standing around in dinner jackets, pouring pints of beer over each other and guffawing; but at TCD, for at least part of my time, I moved in similar circles. One year the Hockey Club held a party to which participants were supposed to bring a bottle of Pimm's. Each. Those of us who shared a bottle between two thought we were acting in moderation. The party, held in the rooms of Walter Hemmens and Peter Pim, rapidly degenerated.

A few of us, imagining ourselves superior to such ructions, locked ourselves into Tim Nicholson's smaller room next door to play backgammon – well, to drink and play backgammon. Towards the close of proceedings next door, a drunk was flinging empty Pimm's bottles through the Georgian windows, smashing all the panes one by one. Called in front of the Junior Dean the next day, Walter and Peter put on suits and prepared their fruitiest Protestant accents. The interview went as well as can be expected. A rite of passage? I suppose so, but I find myself in those years embarrassing to look back on. This was the Ireland of the hunger strikers, and here was I swigging Pimm's in a dinner jacket, *playing backgammon* as a side protest. Deeply unimpressive.

I graduated less than thirty years ago, yet too many of those I remember are no longer alive. Not just some of the academics, who in the nature of things were older, but contemporaries – Alan Ruddock, Peter Pim, Jonathan Cooper, Rodney Overend, Shea Courtney – all of whom died before their time.

Dermot Dix (left) *with his brother Peter at their brother Ian's wedding, 1984.*
Peter died on Pan Am 103 in the Lockerbie bombing in 1988.

Dermot Dix (TCD 1981–5; History) later studied at Pembroke College, Cambridge. He is headmaster of Headfort School in Kells, Co. Meath. Dermot has published research on British imperial ideology in the eighteenth and nineteenth centuries, with particular reference to India, Ireland and America. Before joining Headfort in 2003, he taught for sixteen years in New York City, latterly at the Dalton School in Manhattan. Between 1994 and 2002, he ran his own summer school, An Irish Sojourn, which introduced mainly American visitors to Ireland's history, literature, landscape, music and culture. He is married to Chandana Mathur; the couple have one son, Conall Kabir.

SPARKS

anne enright

WHEN I WAS fifteen years of age I cycled in to town and, it seemed, straight to the gates of Trinity College, where I stood, myself and pal, and looked over the cobbles. It was summer. Memory has it not only deserted but also misty, as though we had arrived just before dawn. This is very unlikely, but I remember how silent it was and that we did not presume to walk further in to Front Square, but just looked for a while and left. A year later I had a scholar boyfriend with rooms in the GMB and that silence – the popping of his gas fire and the bell of the Campanile outside – seemed not so much romantic as destined. The bell was also a signal to head for the last 15A in D'Olier Street, a loud corridor of beige Bombardier buses, rich with the smell of leaded petrol. The wall was lined with couples snogging before the last farewell. In those days, you didn't have a last fag at the bus stop; you lit up inside, after you had looked down from the top window and waved.

In fact, it was the 15A and not the Campanile bell that rang my destiny when it came to a choice of college. Because the 15A went door to door, and my mother, who made so many sacrifices – so many unbought carpets and cheap cuts of meat – to put us through college, was fed up and outraged by the 17 bus route to UCD that never got her elder children to lectures on time or home, either. After the four painful years of my degree she realized that this was not the fault of the buses but of the children because, of them all, I was the worst, for sleeping late or sleeping somewhere else altogether, and although I produced the right exam results at the right times, whatever dream she had of youthful innocence and achievement was slightly soured by the fact that I would not do it on her terms, so it seemed my success was only to thwart her. Which maybe it was.

But first, there was what might be called now my 'gap years'. Back in 1979, still a schoolgirl, I went one Saturday afternoon from my boyfriend's room in the GMB to an interview in the Arts Block for a scholarship to an international school in Canada called Pearson College. I wore a sky-blue pencil skirt and a pale-pink fine cotton blouse and I sat and discussed the connection between Impressionist painting and early-twentieth-century mathematics, a subject I had learned all about, apparently, and a little to my own surprise, in that room in the GMB. I got the scholarship (I thought it was the skirt that did it) and left Dublin for two years, after which international spree I traipsed back, a little unwillingly, to catch the 15A to college.

I was by now a citizen not just of Dublin, you understand, but of the world. In my first week at Trinity, I wore a poncho. More accurately, I wore a blanket from Kilkenny Design, with a slit cut into the middle of it, and it was a very nice blanket and quite warm. It was, in 1981, the only poncho on the 15A and perhaps in all of Ireland. I was wearing it when I walked up to Players' table, which was in a line with the other societies' tables in Front Square. I took, with a swirl of the poncho, a leaflet from Julian Plunkett Dillon. Julian was a pale young man who hid his alarm behind a faint and very precise display of good manners. I thought it was my poncho, but in fact it was the way Julian was all the time, in those days.

Six months later, he cast me as the communist 'First Citizen' in his production of *Coriolanus*, staged with great verve and showmanship on a scaffolding stage in the Dining Hall. I was surprised to discover he thought I was sort of working-class. Sort of. I had never really thought of myself as having a 'class', but I was pretty sure it wasn't this one. In retrospect, it seems to me that posh children were more anxious about class than the rest of us in the impoverished seventies and eighties, when Catholic money was on the ropes, or seemed to be, and ascendancy money couldn't pay for the heating. So, though I learned a little about class in those years, I never quite learned to care. I should have done, I think – fluency in these things is one reason people send their children to college.

The fabulously talented Julian Plunkett Dillon would leave, like nearly all of my generation, for America, in his case for LA and a life of sunshine and excitement that was far from his Irish upbringing. But in 1981 he handed me a pen, and with a further swirl of my poncho I signed up for the Freshers' Co-op, a production designed to introduce new members to the theatrical society that was DU Players.

I was ready to fall in love that first week – and every week, indeed, until Christmas. I had as high a turnover of sentiment and lust and larking about as anyone, and was always happy to call it 'love'. I thought Stanley Townsend, one of the directors of the Co-op, had a gorgeous deep voice, and I thought Martin Murphy, the other director, was far too English and a bit of a bloke. I did not think that I would fall in love with him. But Lynne Parker and Pauline McLynn were the queen bees of Players and they liked Martin for reasons I could not yet discern. There was a bit of matchmaking, let's face it. There were also fifty-hour working weeks in the theatre of No. 3 Front Square, with its grey plastic seats on a stepped wooden rake, the lights cracking as they warmed up, the smell of turpentine and of costumes going stale.

Sparks flew. Sometimes literally. Sparks ran blue along the bars of the rigging. The lights box hummed and gave the occasional bang, as you 're-patched' – switching plugs at speed to manage the complexities of the next lighting cue. Fresnels and spots. Gobos. Gel. Barn doors. 'Close that barn door just a gnat's for me,' John Comiskey might say, while you poked at a lamp with a broom handle. Five o'clock in the morning, the new paint wet under your feet, the director throwing up outside on the cobblestones. Heaven.

There was a rat in the basement. Not often, but – like the sparks – at least once. You might see it when you crossed under the stage in order to make an entrance on the far side. You might look at it, eye to red eye, then mount the steps in your long skirts shouting, 'Burn the witch!' (*The Lark* by Jean Anouilh) or, 'Foh, foh, foh, you filthy French beast!' (*The Country Wife* by Wycherley.) This under-stage area was a dim space made urgent by the play above. A wooden ladder led to the central trapdoor that was usually shut, but sometimes open and pouring yellow light. There was a small, chaotic office to the side, with a payphone you had to take off the hook before a show. Beyond that, the basement stretched out under Front Square for room after room of old stage sets and flats, cardboard crowns and panto rubbish. I dream of it often. And I dreamt for twenty years or more about walking from the scene dock on to that stage, not sure of the play, or my lines in it.

Actually, sometimes, we really didn't know the lines. And that was like dreaming when you were wide awake.

'Prithee, sirrah!'

I wrote my first essay in the female dressing room, sitting in a black beaded jacket with plenty of whalebone and a big puffy skirt of teal and gold lamé, while listening for my cue on the tannoy. The essay was about *King Lear* – nearly all my essays were about *King Lear* – and Nicky Grene, my drama lecturer, did not seem to mind (I think he was not so much forgiving as right: there is no end to what you can learn from *King Lear*). In the spring, Lynne cast me as Everyman in whiteface, in front of a signature Parker set of simple shapes in pastel colours (she was so grown up, already). Martin did the lights. We had such a good time. We all drank too much and didn't know how to handle our drink. We fought and we romanced. We adjourned to O'Neill's, and planned a trip to Edinburgh. In the summer we staged a Joyce show for American tourists (*Joycerpts*, adapted by Declan Hughes) and, one week, we earned thirty pounds each. We lured them in with the promise of lunchtime soup, which my mother (who had heard about the rat) could not quite bring herself to eat. She mimed.

And that was just the first year. By the end of it, I was in love – not just 'in love' (though I wasn't to know that yet) – and it felt like the rest of my life. Which, in fact, it turned out to be.

How could we know? Martin Murphy had his twenty-first while we were in Edinburgh, and he got the gift of a tie with horizontal blue and white stripes. How could I look at such a thing and know, that when the next century rolled around and there was a colony on Mars, this tie would still be on the back of my wardrobe door?

Thirty years on, it still looks fresh.

Anne Enright (TCD 1981–5; Modern English and Philosophy) did an MA in creative writing at the University of East Anglia after her primary degree and, when she returned to Ireland, became a producer/director in RTÉ, most notably for four years of the late-night show **Nighthawks**. In 1993, she turned to writing full-time, since when she has written many books and won various gongs, including the Man Booker Prize for her novel **The Gathering** in 2007. She is married to Martin Murphy and they have two children.

GATEWAY TO A NEW WORLD

sean melly

IN OCTOBER 1981 at the age of seventeen I walked through the gates of Trinity and into another world. One of only two students from my school, Clonkeen College in south Dublin, to enter Trinity that year, I was the first of my family ever to go to university, never mind enter that institution's hallowed halls.

I found the place intimidating. Still predominately Protestant and relatively small, Trinity's insular world was protected from the outside city by imposing stone walls. Many of my fellow students were from the privileged class, and had attended leading private schools in Ireland and the UK. A significant contingent from the North. Brian Reid and John Bateson, who lived either side of the sectarian divide, would never have met in Belfast but became integrated quickly like the rest of us once inside Front Gate.

Trinity was not an extension of my school, my world – it was a total change. I had to make new friends and find a way of combining this new life with my pre-existing home life. I made the trip each day on the 7A bus from Sallynoggin, getting off at Greene's bookshop on Clare Street. I sat upstairs at the front of the bus behind perpetually fogged-up windows, enveloped in a cloud of cigarette smoke.

One of the first friends I made was Nyall Jacobs, the first Jew I had ever met. Our meeting was brought about by his almost fatal car crash a few months earlier. Nyall was the son of my then girlfriend's mother's employer. She asked me to deliver a get-well gift to him. To my mortification, this involved presenting him with a box of chocolates in the middle of the Lecky Library one morning. Despite that inauspicious start, Nyall went on to become my best man and friend for life.

Few students had money and I didn't have two pennies to rub together. I had been awarded a grant that paid my fees, and provided a stipend at the beginning of each term for everything else: books, food and drink – much of it was applied to the latter. I remember checking the noticeboard under Front Gate every day at the beginning of each term to see if my grant had arrived.

With only about ten hours of lectures per week we were distraught if any happened to commence at 9 am. To read for a degree in business you entered the Faculty of Economic and Social Studies (ESS) where, in the early years, we were *required* to take courses in sociology, politics and mathematics, in addition to finance, accountancy, law and economics. This broad school gave us a meaningful and liberal education beyond the narrow confines of a professional degree. The School of Business didn't have a distinct presence in my time, and business had more the feel of a discipline that emerged from the Department of Economics. This was not uncommon for the business schools that have developed in the ancient universities.

I was a denizen of the JCR, over Front Arch, home of the perpetual poker game. Lunch was a roll and a pint of red lemonade in the Buttery or the Pav, and dinner was frequently a run up to Burdocks for fish and chips, often followed by pints in the Pav, the Lincoln, Kehoe's or The Stag's Head. I cultivated a student-like appearance by carrying books, acquired second-hand from Hodges Figgis on Nassau Street, and wearing a tweed jacket from the second-hand store in Castle Market. Many events in Trinity required black tie and I sourced my first from Switzer's department store.

I wasn't from one of the rugby-playing schools, but had been playing at Seapoint, my local club. Dublin University Football Club, the oldest continuous rugby club in the world, is an institution within an institution, and, in the era before professionalism, was the launching pad for many Leinster, Ireland and Lions players. I togged out for the under-19 trials with about forty others. Many of the guys were known quantities from strong rugby schools such as Blackrock

College. It became clear that there was an abundance of wing-forwards and centres. With only two other props declaring, I decided to declare as a loose-head prop, a position of which I had some experience. I secured selection on Trinity's U19 team, which went on to contest the McCorry Cup.

The Hist and the Phil and other faculty-based societies including the Law Society were going strong but the business society, DUBES, established in 1930, was languishing and a group of us set about reinvigorating it. We organized speakers such as Albert Reynolds, then Minister for Finance; other events included a Transvestite Competition, compèred by David Norris.

By second year I was settling into my stride and time spent in the world outside Trinity diminished as I was consumed by sporting, social and some academic goings-on within the walls. The Trinity Ball was the highlight of the social calendar. Even at that age, one needed stamina to stay the course. I remember seeing Ian Dury and the Blockheads, Squeeze and The Cure. When the sun came up, we headed for an early house such as The Windjammer on Townsend Street where dockers and Trinity students in black tie drank pints at 7 am. On the way home in Nyall's Ford Fiesta, we drove straight on to Sandymount Strand, missing the turn at Merrion Gates. Bollards now block any repeat of this performance.

College was full of 'characters' – people like Dan Gaskin, otherwise known as 'Tea Cosy' (because his hat resembled a tea cosy) and Matteo, a Japanese man who roamed the libraries with plastic bags full of papers. You were never really sure whether they were students. Professor Charlie McCarthy, though no more than five-foot-tall, invariably wore a three-piece suit and bow tie. We were taught by Sean Barrett, David Norris, Dermot McAleese, Louden Ryan, Martin O'Donoghue and my tutor, P.J. Drudy, all of the Economics Department; Mary Robinson and Kader Asmal of the Law School; Basil Chubb of the Politics Department, and Ferdinand Von Prondzynski, who lectured us in industrial relations.

The provost, F.S.L. Lyons followed by William Watts in my time, was an aloof character who lived in the mansion at No. 1 Grafton Street. We rarely saw him except at official college events. The Provost's House was somewhere you never got to see, unless you dressed up in Victorian clothes for the annual Garden Party – and then you only got as far as the garden. I had heard of the

Senior Common Room (SCR), the 1592 restaurant and the extensive cavern of catacombs holding Trinity's wine supply below Front Square, but I never saw them as a student. I walked past the Chapel and Exam Hall each day but never entered the former and the latter only when I had to sit an exam.

My final year started with a bang. I had spent most of the summer working for Guinness on a management programme, and returned to Trinity having secured a promotion event for the launch of a new beer, Fürstenberg. The event was to take place in the Buttery during Freshers' Week and consisted of barmaids in lederhosen walking around with trays of the new beer. I raced down to the Buttery from rugby training and tucked into a few free pints. After a while, I saw a pretty, blonde, German-looking girl across the room and plucked up the courage to approach her. She turned out to be an American who had just arrived in Ireland and Trinity for her third year abroad to study politics. We struck up a friendship and after many cups of coffee in the Arts Block it developed into a romantic relationship. Heidi Haenschke became my wife and we now have three daughters, the eldest of whom, Clara, entered Trinity to study law and German in September 2012. I hope we have started a family tradition.

Sean Melly (TCD 1981–5; Business) took a master's degree in finance (UCD 1986) and spent ten years in banking in London and New York. He went on to become a telecoms entrepreneur, establishing businesses in the US, Ireland and Eastern Europe. He is now chairman of Powerscourt Investments, a private investment firm specializing in venture capital and private equity. He is chairman of the board and adjunct professor at Trinity Business School and a board member of the Trinity Foundation. He lives in Killiney, Co. Dublin.

EVERYBODY'S LOOKIN' FOR SOMETHIN'

luke o'neill

MY MOTHER died when I was in first year. It was the evening of 25 February 1982. Three hours earlier I had been called out of a lecture. Dr Eric Finch's face was pale as he said, 'Your aunt is on the phone in the secretary's office.' I knew she was dying – from breast cancer, which she'd had since I was twelve. My sister Helen had been called back from London the night before and my father thought it best for me to keep going to college. I went to the hospital but she was heavily sedated so I didn't get to say goodbye.

I was seventeen. A Junior Fresh natural science student who got the train in from Bray every day, ate his sandwiches and went home again, clearly still a child. My mother had been dying for months. What they gave people with breast cancer those days seems barbaric now – high-dose steroids that made her face puff up horribly, although she always had a smile for me. She was in hospital when I got the news that I'd got into Trinity the previous September. I was the first on my mother's side to go to university – it was a big deal. Not on my father's, though; my mother had 'married up'. On the O'Neill side, uncles and cousins had gone to university. Growing up, I knew about Trinity from watching *University Challenge*. I had visions of mixing with students wearing long scarves, and talking to professors who looked like Bamber Gasgcoigne and talked posh. I used to watch the show with my dad, who one night answered fourteen questions in a row, despite having left school at the age of thirteen (as he often reminded me).

He had grown up in Salford, Manchester, where his family had emigrated when he was a baby. At the age of twenty in 1941 he had been conscripted to drive a Sherman tank with the Eighth Army in the desert, fighting Rommel at El Alamein, although he didn't talk much about that. He did, however, talk to me about English literature and history and politics, on the long walks we used to take. Never about science. My mother's death threw us together, and I spent the rest of my college years living with him in Bray, just the two of us, struggling in our separate ways. Friends called us 'Steptoe and Son'. What saved me was Trinity.

I loved the place and felt like I belonged, almost from day one. I say almost, because we all remember that sickening feeling of the first few days when we knew no one and the buildings seemed so austere. I remember the smell of the burnt hops from the Guinness brewery on the cold morning air; from that first week I remember the noise and the pushing in the Chemistry Large Lecture theatre. I soon got used to it. I began to feel how Bob Dylan must have felt when he first went to Greenwich Village, or Ronnie Drew to O'Donoghue's pub: this is where I want to be.

What really saved me were the lifelong friends I made in those early months. Given the large class size, it wasn't difficult to find like-minded people. We would huddle in the Cumberland, with only enough money to buy half a pint of milk (eight and a half pence), or with a single pint in the Lincoln, which eventually became our second home. It seems unlikely now but on a Friday the Lincoln was packed to its nicotine-stained rafters, full of tobacco smoke and shouting students squeezed up against each other, barely able to lift a pint to their lips. We made phone calls from the classic black 'A button B button' phone near the side door. Jim the barman would shout: 'Telephone call for you, Luke. It's your father.' Me: 'Tell him I'm not here, Jim.' Sometimes we would go behind the bar and serve ourselves.

Disturbingly, the Lincoln closed from three to four for Holy Hour and we would then have to go to the Luce Hall library, which was brand new and smelt it. You would see where girls were sitting because they would have neat pencil cases and a Tippex bottle. Me, Brian Lockhart, Peadar O'Gaora, Joc (John O'Connor), Michael O'Flynn, Richie Porter: several of us were on County Council grants and we would constantly check the noticeboard just inside Front Gate to see if our grants were in. We'd cash them and treat ourselves to cream cakes. I would go to Peadar's house on a Friday and his mother would feel sorry for me and feed me, knowing that at home we lived off Fray Bentos tins of Steak & Kidney Pie. We were boys with Arsenal cup-winner's bags and cheap parka coats completely unable to talk to girls as we had come from all-boys schools. Our abilities with the opposite sex would change as biology took its inevitable course, both academically and developmentally.

The girls were exotic creatures from another solar system. I was obsessively drawn to them and yet completely, knuckle-bitingly inept when it came to talking to them. One girl I got to know in first year was from Belfast and … gasp! … a Protestant. Now this was exotic beyond all imaginings because our only and very limited experience was with Catholic girls who insisted on putting a phone book on your lap before sitting there. I caught sight of Nicola Smyth one morning as we sat in the Arts Block, the winter sun behind her. Eventually I plucked up the courage and sat beside her before a lecture and in a supposedly off-hand way asked what her favourite band was. She grabbed my folder and wrote, 'Making love in the afternoon with Cecilia up in my bedroom'. She handed it back and I was trapped like a rabbit in the headlights, transfixed, unable to move and in a catatonic state of excitement. I said nothing, of course. I remember Nicola coming to my mother's funeral with the others and her giving me a huge sustained hug in the graveyard. It has stayed with me to this day.

Later there was the troubled issue of condoms. In what now seems Talibanesque, these small pieces of latex were illegal in Ireland, as forbidden and dangerous as heroin. But there was a machine in the Students' Union shop in Front Square. One Friday we saw one of our lecturers – future poet laureate of Ireland Iggy McGovern – in the queue. Having bought the evil goods he also bought a Bounty Bar, which, for the rest of our time in college, became our code word for condoms. I got to know people in the Students' Union and they told me how they were under threat from the guards that unless they stopped selling condoms all their assets would be seized. This gave them the brainwave of setting up a separate bank account for the takings from the machine, which they opened in Bank of Ireland on College Green. They named the account holder 'Johnny Cash'.

For entertainment there were gigs. Louis Stewart in the GMB at lunchtime. Freddie White in the Edmund Burke on a Friday night. One night, Neil Innes came to play. He had been in the Bonzo Dog Doo Dah Band and was big friends with Monty Python, so we had to see him since we could recite the entire *Life of Brian* script, a great way to impress girls, we thought. Ivan McCormick was in our class and he was in a band called Yeah Yeah, but more importantly he had auditioned for U2 in Larry Mullen's kitchen so he was way cool in his leather jacket. He got Nicola and I didn't … predictably.

We couldn't wait to emigrate; I left after graduating, heading to London to do a Ph.D. Ireland seemed to be dying: mass emigration, no future. But before that, I had to find my way. I found it one morning, when I wasn't really looking, in the biochemistry building. I had opted for biochemistry because I thought I might get a job out of it. And then I met the staff: Keith Tipton, Jim Mason, Tim Mantle, Clive Williams, Paul Voorheis and John Scott. They seemed very clever and very peculiar but most importantly they spent time with us. They opened up the world of molecular biology and biochemistry to my hungry mind and I thought, 'Hmm … this would beat working for a living.' I remember being in a coffee shop with a friend from Bray, Ruth Brennan, who was studying maths, and telling her excitedly about a thing called ion exchange chromography, which Tim had been showing us. She said, 'Luke, can you stop, because you're boring me.'

The night before the results of the finals came out I went with Brian to Michael's house and we stayed up all night drinking his appalling home brew and watching *The Shining*, which somehow seemed appropriate. We were convinced we hadn't done well. Brian phoned the department at 1 pm, when the results were due to be released. 'Hi, Clive, Brian here with Luke and Michael, can you give us our results? Yes. Yes. Yes. Thanks, Clive.' He hung up. We stared at him. He didn't speak. The world stood still. We chased him around the kitchen. Then he told us we'd got through and done well and we whooped out of the house onto the street to the bus stop and headed in to the department to celebrate. Our lives would continue.

So what did it all mean? Trinity took an awkward boy from Bray and helped him find what he was looking for. Friends and staff were there for him through those dark days in the winter of 1982 when a boy lost his mother. They got him through. He will be eternally grateful.

Luke O'Neill (TCD 1981–5; Natural Sciences) obtained a Ph.D. in pharmacology from the University of London and carried out post-doctoral research at Cambridge before being appointed to a lectureship in 1991 in the Department of Biochemistry, TCD. He was head of the School of Biochemistry and Immunology 2004–8 and was appointed to the chair of Biochemistry in 2007. His research is in the area of inflammatory diseases and innate immunity and he has won numerous awards, including the RDS/**Irish Times** Boyle Medal for scientific excellence in 2009, and the Royal Irish Academy Gold Medal (Life Sciences) in 2012.

I ♥ PIRANHA

michael o'doherty

WE ALL DID some crazy things in Trinity. The point of going to college, after all, is to indulge in stupid, infantile behaviour that you couldn't possibly get away with in the outside world, and chalk it up to 'student high jinks'.

Climbing the flagpole outside the Pav on a balmy summer's evening, while stark naked. Hiding in a manhole just off Front Square for twenty-four hours, hoping to get into the Trinity Ball for free. Entering the august tradition of the 'Chariots of Fire' race around that same square, but running it as a team of two in a pantomime-horse costume. And setting off a large, fully functioning fire extinguisher one Friday morning in a crowded Arts Block. But more of that later.

All of the above happened during my four years in Trinity, and are but the more singular of the events that have stuck in my mind. Most student pranks, of course, involved women, drink, or a combination thereof. Mine, it still humbles me to this day to say, involved drink, of course, but also a large scissors, a bottle of Noilly Prat, and a thousand copies of *Piranha* magazine.

To trace the story of how I came to find myself one February night with this bizarre collection of apparatus in 50 Pembroke Road, with Robert Wilson, its tenant, who went on to run Nelson's homeopathic pharmacy business, and Quentin Letts, now a successful journalist and broadcaster in the UK, we go back to the first term of my second year in Trinity, October 1983.

Having spent a relatively studious first year attending a scandalously high proportion of my English and French lectures, and having found myself to be shockingly average at the two extracurricular activities I indulged in – acting and debating – I had decided to branch out into something new.

One poster, amongst the myriad of seductive inducements on display during Freshers' Week, caught my eye – '*Piranha* Magazine Seeks Fresh Fish'. I had flicked through the fabled magazine during my first year, but never thought of getting involved. Perhaps I was put off by its wordiness – *Piranha*, in those days (not to be confused with its later, down-market incarnation) was erudite, literary, contemplative, a forum for informed discussion on the burning issues of the day, with theatre reviews, cartoons and weighty interviews with leading academics.

It was also the home of the most feared pen in Trinity – that of the Sybarite, the legendary social commentator who, on the back page, entitled 'Grapevine', would dissect the minutiae of college social life, turn a jaundiced eye on its miscreants, champion the bravery of its most laudable social butterflies and, while concealing names in the most obscure of pseudonyms, list who was riding who. It always came out on a Friday – when the next Friday would be, nobody, but nobody, knew.

And while I didn't have the nerve to walk up to their Freshers' Week stall, which seemed to be populated by young men of far greater intellect and more raffish dress sense than myself, I did decide to write an article and surreptitiously submit it in time for the first issue, which was three weeks into the first term. Or thereabouts.

My first offering was a review of Commons – the evening meal held every night at 6.30 pm in the Dining Hall for students and academics alike. I wrote it fairly straight, as one would a regular restaurant review, but attempted to inject a bit of style in the last paragraph when, in suggesting that the meal left me somewhat less than sated, I wrote, 'And so this was the way the night ended, not with a bang, but with a Wimpy burger.' Nobody may admire the pun, but those with an acquaintance with T.S. Eliot's oeuvre may at least understand it.

A week or so later, I approached the desk in the Arts Block at which *Piranha* was sold on those sporadic Fridays, handed over my 10p, and sat down to flick through the magazine, still unsure as to whether my article had made the cut. And after a few sweaty flicks, there it was. Under the heading 'Commons Ye Faithful' my review appeared in full, complete with a specially commissioned graphic. Not even the fact that the last two paragraphs had mysteriously swapped order, meaning that my devastating sign-off did not appear as the last line, could dampen my joy. There was my first published article, with my name at the end. You could literally have knocked me down with a feather.

With my spirits up, I chose the topic for my next offering – a review of the movie *Heaven's Gate*. As before, I walked up to the *Piranha* offices and prepared to slip my offering under the door. It opened from inside just as I was doing this, and a staff member asked who I was. 'Oh yeah, you wrote that piece on the Commons for the last issue. Come on in …' I did. And never looked back.

Suddenly, I was welcomed into a strange and wonderful world of Pritt Stick, Cow Gum, Letraset and IBM typewriters. This was a pre-Apple world, and magazines were still being typed out on typewriters, and stuck down on pieces of paper, with headlines and photo captions inserted by hand in different type. It was an absurdly time-consuming operation, but it was 1983 and we knew no better.

After a day of selling the magazine in the Arts Block – 10p a copy, and you'd shift nine hundred of those with a good issue – the staff would retire to The Stag's Head, order pints, sausages and chips all round, and spend the entire sales proceeds in one go. Advertising revenue would cover our only other expense – the printing bill – or at least it was supposed to. I gradually assumed greater editorial responsibility after a year cutting my teeth on features, headlines, subediting, even typing. I'd suggest other features for people to write, come up with the all-important cover headlines, and deal with the mythical printers – Kennedy's. Situated on Magennis Place, just off Pearse Street, Kennedy's occupied a dilapidated building with a Portakabin, whose planning permission was of a dubious nature, perched on the flat roof out the back. Downstairs, the single printing press would churn out Trinity magazines and posters and flyers for nearby businesses, and election posters for political parties. Their biggest client, it seemed, was Sinn Féin, for whom extra-special treatment was accorded (i.e. the job was occasionally printed on time), due primarily to the fact that they were 'good payers'.

Dealing with Kennedy's was a fraught experience. Martin, the boss, had a seemingly inexhaustible supply of sob stories, disasters, once-offs and mitigating circumstances with which to appease the poor undergraduate who would turn up on the allotted day to collect his job, only to find stacks of *An Phoblacht* where his magazine should be.

On one occasion, I witnessed the magician at work when a representative of Fianna Fáil arrived to collect his promised posters. Martin pointed him to a pile of freshly printed posters, with this client's job on top, and said to him, 'That's the first thousand there, I'll get them all over to you in the morning.' With the Ógra member having departed content, Martin lifted the top poster and revealed nine hundred and ninety-nine Sinn Féin posters underneath. If he was willing to treat the then government with such disdain, imagine how beholden he felt to a fresh-faced 19-year-old arts student?

There was a tradition with *Piranha* that the editor was only allowed one full year's term, and that the outgoing editor appointed his successor. And so it was, in May of 1984, that over a pint in O'Neill's Quentin asked if I would like to take over from him the following year. I believe I took the offer with a mixture of gratitude, humility and an appreciation of the responsibility that was being placed on my shoulders. But inside I was dancing.

I returned to Trinity in October, and set about imposing my stamp on the title. An extra four pages were added, bringing it up to a dizzying twenty. The price was retained at 10p, in appreciation of the fact that Ireland was in the middle of a recession, as it had been since 1937. And the venerable tradition of coming out every third Friday, or so, would be strictly adhered to. On top of my editorial duties, I had also inherited the Sybarite's mantle – having contributed sporadically to the 'Grapevine' column in the past, I was now in sole charge of it.

It was, in hindsight, the first time I dipped my toe into the milieu with which *VIP* would, twenty years later, become synonymous. But while the latter was, and always has been, a champion of those who spend their lives on the social circuit, the Sybarite's task was to cast a more cynical eye on events. And if no such events existed, make them up.

The laws of libel, it transpired, were excluded from the four walls of Trinity. On the basis that most students would simply laugh off such grotesque mendacity as we could throw at them, and also be aware that there was little point in suing a penniless magazine, we got away scot-free. Except for this one time …

In the summer of 1984 the Dining Hall caught fire, making front-page headlines in every Irish newspaper. Strangely enough, a couple of minor incendiary incidents also occurred during the first week of the next term – one in the Physics lab, and one in Players Theatre. I decided to accuse a lady I knew of having started the last of these, on the tenuous premise that I knew she'd had a script rejected by the theatre the previous week. And while I was at it, I also made her complicit in the other two fires, just for good measure. It was all done in jest and, given the fact that no college publication had ever been sued for libel, what would she do about it, I reasoned?

I found out the day that issue of *Piranha* went on sale. As sales gathered pace I was occupying my traditional seat behind the stall when someone called my name. Turning around, I saw the lady in question, and only a couple of seconds later did I realize she had a large, red object in her hand. A fire extinguisher. Laughing demonically, she fiddled with it briefly and then set it off, directly in my face. It was gas rather than foam, a fact that saved my jacket from serious harm but resulted in the entire Arts Block being filled with a white gas, and the whole area having to be evacuated.

Not even the famously tolerant college authorities could turn a blind eye to this, and both I and the lady in question were called before the Junior Dean who, with his sternest face, informed us that this behaviour was simply 'not on', and asked us not to do it again. I left his office with a sudden awareness of the power of the printed word, a deep appreciation that it was a power to be used only for good, and that magazines were not to be casually employed for the mindless entertainment of the chattering classes. Two decades later, I launched *VIP*.

There was only one departure from the rigid Friday-only rule for *Piranha*, and that occurred every February when, following a predictably nebulous tradition, the magazine would be published on Valentine's Day. Quentin and I hatched a plan to produce a magazine that not only oozed with love, but whose very sight would make you weak at the knees: we decided to print the world's first heart-shaped magazine, as you do. There was, inevitably, one slight drawback – Kennedy's could only print on rectangular-shaped paper, and in the absence of a budget (or, come to think of it, the invention of the requisite technology) for die-cutting, we would have to do it ourselves.

The magazine was typed up and laid out as before on A4 paper, except that each page had a heart-shaped outline drawn around it in pencil, within whose confines all text and pictures would have to fit. Production for this issue would, therefore, be even more time-consuming than usual but once done it was dispatched to the printers, with the finished product collected on Valentine's eve. Nearly finished product, I should stipulate, because the real work was now only beginning.

So there we were in 50 Pembroke Road with a thousand copies of *Piranha* ready to go on sale the following morning. There remained only three problems. First, the magazines had to be cut into heart shapes by hand. Second, to guarantee the exclusive and luxuriant nature of this once-off offering, it was printed with a heavy card cover, which made cutting it with a scissors even more troublesome. Third, there were only three of us, with a thousand magazines to be cut out by 9 am, and it was already 10 pm.

In the first hour about two hundred magazines were completed and all looked rosy. We poured ourselves some congratulatory drinks – G&T for Quentin, a dry sherry for Robert, and the closest thing I could find to Martini for myself – the aforementioned Noilly Prat. But the combination of drink and 'scissors-hand' would soon take its toll, and it wasn't till dawn that the finished product was packed into boxes, and ready for delivery to our stall in the Arts Block.

Ten pence seems like a meagre return for such selfless dedication, but it was never about the money. It was about the thrill of publishing. I still have a copy of every *Piranha* on which I worked in a cupboard in my mother's house. I still occasionally, when mooching about my old bedroom, sit down and flick through them, and sigh wistfully at the joys of a more innocent time. It was never about advertising revenue, break-even sales figures or worrying about how to pay contributors. It was just about fun.

And that single night, 13 February 1984, encapsulated for me everything that college life was about, with one minor discrepancy. A late night, doing something ridiculous, fortified by alcohol.

But instead of women, there were magazines.
The story of my life.

Michael O'Doherty (left) *and Jonathan Philbin Bowman at TCD Garden Party, 1980s.*

Michael O'Doherty (TCD 1982–6; English and French), after leaving college, set up **Level 3**, the first all-Ireland third-level magazine, as well as **Career Choice**, Ireland's first guide to third-level education for school-leavers. He worked as a freelance journalist for **The Irish Press** and **The Sunday Tribune**, and was a co-director in the relaunch of **Magill** magazine in 1997. In 1999, he launched **VIP** magazine with John Ryan, and subsequently launched **TVNow** (2000), **KISS** (2002) and **Stellar** (2008). He writes a twice-weekly column with the **Evening Herald,** and is training as a barrister in King's Inns.

BIG HAIR, FREE BOOZE AND LAW

vandra dyke

I HADN'T really given any thought to my career options or what I wanted to do with my life, and for some bizarre reason found myself as a fresher in legal science. My image of life as a law student had been almost completely shaped by the American TV series *The Paper Chase*. It was, to say the very least, a crushing blow to discover that instead of being populated by good-looking, groovy guys and preppy girls my class consisted of mostly – or so it seemed – Gonzaga and crypto-Gonzaga boys and what we witheringly dismissed as 'a shower of culchies'.

The Student Handbook arrived the week before I started. I pored over it in growing excitement and anticipation of the debauchery of student life. In hindsight, chunks of it had clearly been filched from an English version *c.*1975. A huge section was devoted to sex, with the strong promise that there would be lots of it; how and where to get contraception (still contraband in early-eighties Ireland); where to go when all the sexual activity gave you crabs or, worse still, got you pregnant; and, most thrillingly, societies for gays and lesbians (transgender hadn't been invented). All accompanied by drawings of fallopian tubes and male parts. After the sex advice there was a section on drugs, which guaranteed that we would be exposed to LSD and magic mushrooms and amphetamine pushers. I have to report that the guide promised way more than it delivered; my first year passed with no offers of speed and the lesbians gave me a wide berth and, to spare my blushes, the less said about the sex the better.

With astonishing speed I seemed to get the hang of college and its real purpose, which was to spend 90 per cent of my time sitting, trying to look sultry, smoking on the chocolate boxes in the Arts Block, or having coffee and trying to look sultry in the Kilkenny Design café on Nassau Street. The eighties were a fashion-minestrone with expensive sports kit as daywear; today's student uniform had yet to be invented. My pal Lynne Byrne and I would apply our make-up on the number 8 bus on the way in. The Arts Block was the place to chat, look out for those you fancied and watch the style, which was fabulous and wildly diverse. There were old hippies, some punks, goths, Mount Anville girls (a class of their own, with Susan Maher to the fore), New Wavers and New Romantics.

The recent television serialization of *Brideshead Revisited* was hugely influential. One boy turned up in the Arts Block wearing cricket whites and carrying a teddy bear in a self-conscious homage to Sebastian Flyte. Nicola Harvey was the undisputed style queen of law, she was a whiz with a sewing machine and, in the days before cheap high-street fashion, looked the epitome of chic. Another glamour puss was Paula Reed, described recently in *Vogue* as one of the world's most stylish women.

I used to wear the most extraordinary things in broad daylight; lurid tights, pixie boots, tiny minis, pink eyeshadow and my father's hats. A UCD architecture student, Brian O'Tuama, supplied us all with enormous earrings and clunky bangles made from old baked-beans cans. A college scarf was completely *infra dig.* for anyone aspiring to trendiness, only swots and science students wore those.

The best bit about Trinity was, of course, the social life. Bang in the centre of town, we had the world at our feet. The music scene was vibrant; concerts were still held on campus in the Exam Hall or the Buttery. The Cure, Aswad and the Virgin Prunes are the ones I remember best. Debates in the Phil, Hist and Law Society were the most fun. Excoriating rhetoric and polemic from the likes of Brendan Ward and Brian Murray were always followed by a massive booze-up sponsored by Guinness.

The ball season began after Christmas with the Law Ball, held off-campus at venues such as the Powerscourt Townhouse or Slane Castle. The balls involved weeks of preparation. The first task was to find a suitable date without the indignity of having to ask him, so traps were laid and heavy hints dropped until the man was bagged. Then came 'The Dress'. Lady Di and her puffy taffeta nightmares had entered our consciousness and so Laura Ashley in Dawson Street was the go-to shop for rich girls, while the rest of us scrabbled around the second-hand shops searching for something suitably glam.

The Law School at the time had some substantial characters that we were fortunate to have teaching us. The Marys – Robinson and McAleese – taught EU and criminal law respectively. Yvonne Scannell's lectures were very enjoyable; a true eccentric and ardent feminist of the old school, she was remarkably easy to distract and we encouraged her to go off on tangents in order to waste at least fifteen minutes of lecture time.

Eldon Exshaw's real property lectures were famous because nobody bar a handful of inveterate swots ever went to them. He used to arrive wearing very old-style, three-piece suits and, in a monotone, deliver lectures on the highs and lows of the fictional Whiteacre and Blackacre estates in order to illustrate baffling laws about arcane men of straw, the Rule in Shelley's case and the Rule Against Perpetuities. Other notable characters were Nial Osborough, whose interest in legal history spiced up our evidence lectures with stories of castration in medieval Ireland, and the wonderful Regius professor, Robert Hueston, with his idiosyncratic but marvellous 'dictation' and 'commentary' method of teaching.

Patrick Ussher was a rakish don in cords and tweeds. Kader Asmal's international law was considered one of the dosser's options; he was wonderfully fluent but sometimes unprepared. Kind Gerard Hogan's administrative law classes were always oversubscribed as he was a superb teacher and a massive softy, doling out undeserved 2:1s for essays. Lovely Margot Aspel, the school secretary, would talk us down with tea and cakes during overdue-essay and exam-time panics.

The wildness and fun of the seventies had peaked and passed. Politically, early- to mid-eighties students were more complacent and conservative. Alex White, now a Labour politician, was probably the last 1970s-style ideological radical to be elected SU president. The abortion debate was raging and Bernie Dwyer of the Students' Union pursued women's rights with vigour. The campus was awash with pamphlets and posters advocating causes. Thatcherism had penetrated and there was much new-right sneering at the old guard. Maoist Tommy Graham heroically took the Marxist-Leninist banner from David Vipond, but the fight had gone out of the student body, many of which, particularly those studying ESS, were now Tory-boy *manqués*.

The epitome of this new breed was the Gonzaga crew and their ilk, with their huge confidence and ambition to match. They dressed as dandies, in jodhpurs, man-tan and berets, or as old fogeys in tweeds and waistcoats with fob watches, carrying walking sticks. Lynne and I were invited to dinner one evening by a boy in our class and arrived at a 1950s suburban house bearing a six-pack to find the male guests in black tie drinking sherry, and a table setting that would put *Downton Abbey* to shame.

College magazines were hilarious – there were a number but *Piranha* ruled. Edited by Quentin Letts and later the waspish Michael O'Doherty, you dreaded appearing, or not appearing, in their roll call. It was a no-win situation. Any kudos from getting a mention was immediately crushed by the laugh gained at your expense. Regular fixtures in *Piranha* were dashing Belgian Hugo Frey, gorgeous Greg Delany, and Amanda Cochrane and her chums Lana O'Reilly and Caroline Bourke.

I still spend a lot of time in Trinity, walking through campus on the way from the DART station, or using the Berkeley Library. I still feel a thrill and a sense of belonging. Apart from Donncha, the old library staff are gone; funny Harry with his encyclopaedic memory for names, Liz Gleeson and the others have all retired. Matteo, the deaf Japanese half-tramp, half-scholar, who was looked after so well by the Buttery staff, is now dead, but I feel sure he is carrying his plastic shopping bags and pilfering books in heaven.

The place is steeped in nostalgia and happy memories. Dancing at first light around the sphere on the Berkeley podium at Trinity Balls. Boys following girls up the stairs in the library so they could see up their skirts. The first time I ever saw my future husband sitting beside the Irish Reports in 1982, and parties in rooms filled with cigarette smoke and the smell of cheap wine and hair gel.

Left: *TCD dinner, 1984.*
Vandra Dyke (left)
and Frances McIvor.

Below: *TCD Law Ball,*
Slane Castle, Co. Meath, 1984.
David Keane second from left;
Vandra Dyke second from right;
David Sutton on right.

Vandra Dyke (TCD 1982–6; Legal Science) married Kevin Costello and lives with him and their daughter Millie in Dalkey, Co. Dublin. She retrained in land-scape architecture and has a Ph.D. from UCD School of Architecture. Vandra works as an historical landscape consultant, garden writer and academic.

THE PAST IS A FOREIGN COUNTRY: THEY DO THINGS DIFFERENTLY THERE

sallyanne godson

LOOKING BACK over thirty years, it's hard to overstate quite how different everything was in the autumn of 1982 when I started at Trinity. Charlie Haughey was the GUBU taoiseach, Margaret Thatcher's government had just won the Falklands/Malvinas War and Ronald Reagan was in the White House.

And when I walked through Front Gate at the start of Freshers' Week 1982, it really was different. There I was, an ordinary girl from safe, dull, suburban Dublin, transplanted into the architectural glory of Front Square.

While my old schoolmates were meeting each other in Belfield in places with functional names like 'the restaurant' and 'the bar', the prospect of a world where people met in the Buttery, the Pav and the Conversation Room in the GMB lay before me; they had Theatre L while I had the Ed Burke; they went to the library while I went to the Lecky or the Berkeley – even though I didn't know who either Lecky or Berkeley was.

Just how different my new world was compared to theirs came home to me at the very beginning when I went on my library tour. Among the other freshers with surnames in my part of the alphabet was a mature student from

Belfast. We got chatting. It transpired that he was a former republican prisoner in the Maze/Long Kesh who was now active in SFWP – the political wing of the Official IRA, known as the Stickies. Like everyone else, I had grown up with the Troubles as part of the daily news bulletin – the previous year had seen ten men die on hunger strike – but had always been at a safe remove, able to come to my own judgment about the rights and wrongs of assorted atrocities committed by different protagoninsts. But now I had a real, living protagonist as a contemporary, challenging my complacency from his own experience.

In the same week I also met other Northeners, from other parts of the political spectrum – committed SDLP supporters whose resistance to armed republicanism had sometimes led to their own families being targeted for not being 'green enough'. And then there were real, live Unionists – not caricature, bowler-hatted, Paisley-voting Orangemen, but normal teenagers, eager to start their adult life away from the dreary steeples of Fermanagh and Tyrone. In fact, these mild-mannered ex-grammar-school pupils were the most inter-esting of all, having chosen actively to confront their own cultural inheritance by studying in Dublin, albeit in Trinty, the last redout of Unionism in their parents' generation.

I was studying politics and so was especially taken by the realpolitik of all these Northerners, warily circling each other, keen to show that they were above the weary quarrels. But, of course, they were products of their own backgrounds, which had a direct bearing on their behaviour and opinions and nowhere was this more obvious than in the GMB debating chamber.

I had enjoyed debating in my small all-girls school and was determined to join the Hist. It took me more than one attempt to summon up the courage to approach the desk during Freshers' Week, manned as it was by seemingly incredibly confident, witty men. One of these was Ultan Stephenson who looked, dressed and sounded like Robert Brown, Just William's older brother. It was, jokingly, said of him that he grew up in an Irish-speaking household and learned English from listening to BBC Radio 4 late at night. In fact, he was a lovely gentle man, his apparent pomposity masking the shyness that we were all too afraid to own up to.

I went along to the Freshers' Debate, enthralled by the debating chamber, the ballot box, the languid, black-tied, mustachioed auditor – Eoin McCullough

– and the witty heckles from the floor. I must have been unbelievably lacking in self-awareness to have put my name down to speak in the debate – determined to fly the flag for feminism, God help me. I have no idea what the motion was but do remember being aware that I was well out of my depth. Convention mercifully dictated that maiden speakers were not to be heckled or interrupted and that the auditor invited the speaker to the committee room afterwards for a sherry. Sherry? In our house, sherry was something that went into trifle at Christmas or was served to great-aunts.

There was an air of old-fogeyness around the entire Hist committee room – although it was so shrouded in cigarette smoke that it was hard to see. The bicycles leaning against glass cases containing reports of debates from a hundred years ago just added to the other-worldliness of the place. Mary Kenny was one of the guest speakers that night and wrote about the shambolic mess she had encountered and the general scruffiness of the students compared to her experiences at the Oxford and Cambridge unions. I, however, was captivated.

Not yet suffering from self-doubt, I also joined Players and was given a small part in the Freshers' Co-op, directed by Anne Enright and Declan Hughes. Anne was small, serious, intense and petrifying – quite obviously on a whole other plane of being than someone like me. I was Vera Duckworth to her Samuel Beckett. Declan was much more down to earth, a comparatively normal boy-next-door type. I auditioned for various other productions in that first term but was never successful. I still attended every production, greedily soaking up any opportunity to experience plays like *The Caucasian Chalk Circle* and *The Duchess of Malfi*, reading *Irish Times* reviews to understand afterwards what I had seen.

The Hist, however, was where I spent most of my time. I was elected as censor at the end of first year when Declan Sheehan was elected auditor, and then went on to become treasurer and later auditor myself, so our haunt moved to the committee room, valued above all else for being somewhere safe to leave a bike or bag. I was never a good speaker but loved the politicking and intrigue that surrounded the Hist elections. While the Hist membership was well over a thousand, the actual electorate was much smaller, made up of members who had actually attended three debates and signed the attendance sheets. The election count took place late at night. Despite (or because) of the fact that I was studying politics, I was very glad to have people like John Fingleton and Simon Nugent to hand when it was my turn to conduct the count and distribute first-preference surpluses into ever-decreasing fractions of votes after lots of pints.

The debates themselves varied in quality but the best of them provided a genuine opportunity for public discourse that didn't exist in any other publicly accessible forum at the time. Michael Foot, then leader of the British Labour Party and biographer of Jonathan Swift, unsurprisingly held a packed house in the palm of his hand as he argued his case. The Northern Ireland debates offered a unique opportunity for debate: Section 31 of the Broadcasting Act prohibited RTÉ from broadcasting the voices of Sinn Féin members so the only time they got to argue their case, and be challenged in person, was at debates and public meetings. This presented a number of other problems, however, because many politicians of other parties refused to share a platform with SF representatives, so it fell to student speakers or academics to argue the case against armed republicanism.

Some of the students were not only brilliant speakers but also avoided the lazy political clichés of the day. The finest of the Northern Ireland debates were the British–Irish Intervarsities, where representatives from Glasgow, Edinburgh, Oxford, Cambridge and Durham travelled to Dublin to compete for the Thomas Davis Trophy. Our best speakers were up against their best speakers on a motion that invariably reflected the 'totality of relationships' between the islands. The protagonists argued from all parts of the spectrum: Scottish Unionists, Irish two-nationists, Belfast republicans, Home Counties' Tories and London Labourites. The Glaswegians were by far the most popular – witty speakers, politically diverse and, just as importantly, not lightweight posh boys like the others and well able to hold their own when we adjourned to our real home, The Stag's Head.

The Stag's was the one place in Dublin we were pretty certain to meet friends at any time of the day or night. We spent hours of our lives there, sometimes just chewing the fat, catching up on who had slept with whom, or navel-gazing, as well as setting the world to rights. Lunchtime pints gradually gave way to Holy Hour lock-ins (and if you did arrive while the door was locked, a sharp rap with a coin on the window saw the door open enough to slip in) and then on through the early evening (sausage and chips for dinner) to last orders. At which stage the always-helpful Tom or Peter would happily 'sell' you a bottle of gin that would be replaced the next day.

While very few of the Stag's habitués considered themselves radical, we did at least consider ourselves progressive. With hindsight it seems we were only committed to social change such as the decriminalization of homosexuality and women's reproductive rights as a way of asserting our individuality against the repressive laws of the time, rather than as a way of trying to change society as a whole. We certainly were not in favour of questioning the economic status quo lest we discover that the only reason we were so privileged was because others were not. We considered Thatcherism and Reaganomics antithetical to our own woolly beliefs yet it was the libertarian belief that the state had no role in dictating how we should live our private lives that most engaged us, perhaps because our real growing up was yet to come.

Sallyanne Godson with future husband Brian Jackson, 1980s.

Sallyanne Godson (TCD 1982–6; Political Science) followed friends to London in 1988 after two years working in Dublin for Fine Gael. She worked initially for Shell then for the BBC as a news and current affairs producer. She married Brian Jackson (TCD 1982–5) and they now have three teenage children. She returned to Ireland in 2002 and has recently re-entered the work force as a news and current affairs producer for RTÉ.

COBBLES, CORNICES AND CREAM

quentin letts

COBBLES AND CORNICES: those are the first images that come to mind. I arrived at TCD in September 1982, one of not that many British undergraduates. My mother equipped me with a pair of new shoes. She had lived in County Cavan as a girl and said, 'It's wet in Ireland – you'll need strong brogues.' Strong they were, the leather unyielding. By the time I had walked into college from Trinity Hall in Rathmines on day one, I already had whopping blisters on my feet. Through Front Gate I hobbled, to be presented by that vista of cobbles. Ouch! Ouch! Ouch!

'Cornices' takes a little more explaining. I wanted to become involved with one of the student magazines. The scruffs who ran *Piranha* seemed friendly. It was the cheeky magazine; a version (of sorts) of *Private Eye* and its editor was Alan Gilsenan. Alan was tall, blond and quite serious but his staff was less sober-minded, not above spending its generous publications grant at O'Neill's bar.

Piranha was laid out at weekends in a bare room above the Students' Union shop. Magazine design in those days was a rudimentary affair. The only efficient person was Johana Dunlop, who knew how to operate the golf-ball typewriter. She would type the 'stories' (which were being scrawled on scrap paper by the 'reporters' at another desk to cries of 'Can we call the provost an eejit?' and 'Er, how do you spell "accommodation"?'). Johana's columns of neat type were ham-fistedly glued by us on to wonkily ruled-up sheets. Headlines were done by Letraset transfers. More often than not the headlines would go awry – bits falling off certain letters, others leaning at a strange angle. If it all looked drunken that was possibly barman Eamonn's fault.

Every Letraset sheet contained some fancy patterns. These squiggles were called 'cornices' and were ideal for filling an empty page. As the printers' dead-line approached and we desperately scratched around for stories, Alan Gilsenan would examine the acres of unfilled page and drawl: 'Call for a cornice!'

I was meant to be studying medieval English and classical civilization but spent more time on magazines and Players, acting opposite people like Martin Murphy, Pauline McLynn, Lynne Parker, Declan Hughes, Darragh Kelly, Arthur Riordan and Stanley Townsend. You soon realized drama was not just about turning up and learning your lines but was about artistic vision and deep devotion. I acted opposite Darragh Kelly in a Barrie Keeffe play, *Gimme Shelter*. Darragh had trundled through the scene in rehearsals. At the first public show, however, I was emotionally scorched by his performance. Crumbs. That was the moment I ditched any foolish ambition I had to seek a career on the stage. How could one compete with such talent?

For an English boy like me, the Trinity years were not just about univer-sity. They were about Dublin and Ireland – Northern Ireland, too. The early 1980s were an unhappy time north of the border yet I never noticed any anti-Englishness being directed against me in person. On Sundays, with my Somerset friend Barney Spender, I would go to an IRA pub just north of the river and sink pints in the basement where republican songs were sung and more than a few black berets worn. Up we'd waddle to the bar and ask for a drink in our 'Brief Encounter' English accents. Barney even had a jokey habit of addressing bar staff in his most pukka accent as 'my good man'. It's a wonder the proprietor didn't boot us out.

I remember the whiff of Guinness floating down from the brewery by the Liffey. I remember visiting St Michan's church and gawping at the mummies in the crypt. Cherry buns at Bewley's, pretty girls in autumn knits on Grafton

Street, gossip in the Arts Block, motoring up to Powerscourt in my elderly Morris Minor to see the waterfall: this is what I remember about my Trinity years.

Ulster girls bewitched me. Clare Reihill, an Enniskillen Zuleika Dobson. She's a publisher in London these days. On a trip to Belfast I fell for an older woman, a painter called Naomi. What is it about women north of the border? That lift at the end of sentences? Does the Mourne Mountains mist dust their cheeks? Or is it the inventiveness of language? 'I'm so hungry, I could eat a dog with sore eyes.'

Exams never loomed too large. Lectures could be skipped with impunity, though Brendan Kennelly's poetry symposia were must-attend events. It was the extracurricular life, the Dublin swirl, the sheer, intoxicating Irishness of those four years, where the real education lay. I remember post-play parties where the drink of choice was those odd little bottles of draught stout you'd inject with air using a special Guinness syringe. I remember peaty smoke on the breeze in the evenings when walking back to my digs through pea-souper fogs. At a set of traffic lights one time I saw Taoiseach Charlie Haughey sitting in his limousine, picking his nose. He caught me watching and, even while staring back at me, ate the bogey there and then, defiant of disapproval.

After my first year in Trinity Hall I shared a house on Pembroke Road with Robert Wilson. It was an enormous place that Robert's father, Dickie, used as an office a couple of days a week. From my bedroom window I could see the distant hills, framing Dublin in her basin. Opposite our house was Le Coq Hardi, reputedly Dublin's most expensive restaurant. It was so fancy it did not have a menu outside for passers-by to peruse. Some evenings the diners would step daintily out of the restaurant, having just consumed the most heavenly fare, to be confronted by the sight and sound of a Trinity undergraduate party in full swing – the likes of Donald Clarke, Declan McCavana, Roddy Gibson and yours truly bawling for more sausage rolls while Robert uncorked another bottle of his dizzyingly disgusting homemade red wine.

Piranha had rivals. There was *Trinity News*, then a broadsheet on glossy paper. They gave me a column for a while – 'Space To Letts' – fearful drivel. 'Miscellany' was mainly poetry and arts. Ger Siggins produced a scandal sheet, the name of which eludes me ('New Miscellany'?) but it was lively, streetwise stuff and took regular tilts against the dreaded West Brits and we gallant band of genuine English. *Piranha* returned fire.

The magazine came out on a Friday and we'd flog it from a trestle table in the Arts Block. Circulation was about three hundred. Michael O'Doherty, a suave, engaging scallywag, usually managed to create some sort of scandal with his back-page gossip column. No publication day would be complete unless Michael had made some pretty Arts Block girl blush by revealing the new squeeze in her life. The naughtier the gossip, the more copies we would sell. Useful lesson, that.

Editorial responsibility was worn lightly. I would shrug my shoulders and blame Michael for the frequent libels and outrages and swung handbags. 'You Irish sort it out among yourselves,' I'd murmur, and leave them to it. When the Ethiopian famine struck and all sort of politicians and personalities started making personal capital out of the disaster, we ran a *Piranha* satire announcing an appeal for sunbeds to be sent to the poor of Ethiopia. It was in pretty dubious taste, I suppose. The head of the Students' Union hauled me in and upbraided me in the most pious terms. I briskly told him to mind his own business, saying we reserved our right to offend, thank you very much. That was the end of the matter.

O'Doherty (who has since made a mint with *VIP* magazine) succeeded me as editor of *Piranha* at the end of my third year. He was one of the most naturally vinegary wits I have known, an urbane lounge lizard with a long, dark, straight fringe that he would blow out of his eyes before taking another sip of vermouth on the rocks. Noilly Prat! How many students drink Noilly Prat? Michael did, lowering his glass to utter yet another devastating putdown of some poor mott in art history.

In my final four terms I did two more magazines. My partner was a shrewd Mancunian emigré called David O'Sullivan who handled the business side. David was brilliant at selling advertisements to banks and record companies. He got us publicity on RTÉ radio and generally schmoozed the media scene. First we produced *Mayday!* magazine for Trinity's 1985 charity week. We raised £10,000 for Concern's African famine relief. Bob Geldof gave us an interview but I was more chuffed that Frank Muir wrote us an article – his recipe for cheese on toast. We were rightly proud of *Mayday!* though David did most of the work. Then we founded a magazine called *Filibuster*, a mix of politics, arts, games and interviews. We took *Filibuster* much more seriously than we had ever taken *Piranha*. We were growing up.

I remember nights of wild windbaggery at the Hist and the Phil debating societies, when previously soft-spoken undergrads would burst into flights of Swiftian oratory, almost flicking out their tailcoats and gripping hold of their lapels. Darn you Irish. You were so effortlessly, brilliantly, wittily eloquent. I remember long nights at The International Bar, Doheny & Nesbitt and The Stag's Head. I remember the annual Pimm's party in the Provost's Garden during Trinity Week. I remember a college talent show that I compèred in the Buttery. I remember Mr Kennedy, our magazine printer, whose premises had been torched. He and his wife Gay operated from a Portakabin on the roof. You had to climb a half-destroyed staircase to reach it. Health and Safety was not a consideration in those days.

All these things I remember, through a mind whose lens is smeared with the Vaseline of time. Academic work? Sorry. I don't remember much of that. It's mainly laughter, a few love affairs, deadlines, and always, even then, a realization that these were going to be the creamiest years of my life. Cobbles, cornices and cream. Thanks, Dublin.

Quentin Letts (TCD 1982–6; Medieval English and Classical Civilization) spent a year after Trinity as a postgraduate at Cambridge University while also working as a reporter with **The Daily Telegraph**. After a stint with a corporate magazine company in Cardiff, he became a diarist with **The Telegraph** and New York correspondent of **The Times**. Since 2000, he has been parliamentary sketch writer and, more recently, theatre critic with the **Daily Mail**. Married with three children, he lives in the west of England.

Piranha, *10 December 1982.*

EARLY PRINTED BOOKS AND ALL THAT JAZZ

jane mahony

I ONLY EVER wanted to go to Trinity. My father had gone up in the late 1950s after a short, sharp and ultimately satisfactory skirmish with Archbishop John Charles McQuaid, during which the archbishop demanded an apology for my father's *lèse-majesté*, and my father replied, Certainly! Just as soon as he received one from the archbishop. Neither apology was forthcoming.

Episcopal permission was no longer required in the 1980s, and I recall filling out the CAO form with different Trinity courses numbered one to eight, with a reluctant two alternatives to keep all options open. I came to Trinity in October 1982 to read history and French with a feeling of arriving in the exact place I wanted to be. Then, as now, just being in Trinity filled me with a deep sense of happiness and satisfaction.

Freshers' Week was noisy, thrilling and colourful, like a mad medieval market with the various societies competing vigorously for members. I now regret not moving out of my comfort zone and joining more. I did join the Hist and the Phil and went to nearly every debate over the following four years; I also briefly joined the rowing club until the reality of early-morning starts on the misty Liffey outweighed the attraction of the hunky rowers, who, of course, had been the reason for joining in the first place. The Hist and Phil attracted heavyweight guests in the 1980s and there were some electric nights in the GMB.

My schooling did not prepare me for the tutorial system. Various academics had tricks to shake us out of our complacency. I remember the first history essays my tutorial group submitted to Professor James Lydon being returned with very low marks and most unkind (we thought) comments to the effect that we were university students now, these were dire efforts, and we would have to raise our game considerably. It fired us to write our second assignments very differently and those were returned with a charming smile and a murmured 'Much better!'

There was a mix of students in my tutorials from Dublin, rural and provincial Ireland, Northern Ireland and the UK, and we looked suspiciously at each other at first. The English students seemed exotic with their RP accents and tweed jackets and cords. They had floppy blond hair and were called names like Sebastian and Quentin. (Kind, clever, gentle Sebastian Morpurgo was in one of my tutorials and the very funny Quentin Letts, sometime parliamentary sketch writer for the *Daily Mail* and *Tatler*, was a presence around college.) A girl from the North caused a near diplomatic incident by worrying aloud that she and the English students would soon fall behind in French as she had an A level and we 'Southern Irish' students only had the Leaving Cert. I made particular friends with Wendy Collier from Wexford. Maura McCabe was another great friend. We stayed close throughout our four years and beyond.

First tutorials were no earlier than 10 am. A disastrous experiment with a 9 am start sometime in second year was not repeated after half the group turned up in pyjamas, clutching cups of coffee and complaining bitterly. We thought this the height of wit. At noon we would go back to our desks at the Berkeley, breaking for lunch at 1 pm in O'Neill's – an unchanging menu of soup and a toasted sandwich, then the library again at 2 pm. Tea and scones in the Kilkenny Design Centre at 4 pm; library again after that. Evenings for me might be circuit training in the gym or tennis in Botany Bay, a Buttery or Commons dinner, or the library again if an essay was due. It sounds terribly dull and timetabled, but somehow it wasn't, it was just the framework within which we explored our new world.

Wednesday nights could be jazz in the Buttery, sponsored by Guinness who sold the black stuff at half-price; not my favourite drink so I soon decamped to the Pav or the Lincoln. The Bailey was popular but O'Neill's, perfect for lunch, was to be avoided in the evening when IRA supporters came collecting money in buckets. Friday night was the big night out, and in those days before mobile phones and social networking we somehow managed to find our friends. Maura had a particular talent for looking in at a heaving pub and announcing that there was no one at all there, and moving us on to the next place. We trotted obediently after her because she had a true knack of making every occasion the best of fun and, not unimportantly, had a wide circle of rugby-playing friends. Some of those rugby players became boyfriends, but none so serious as to interfere with college life.

I could not have been described as a radical student. I did go on a student march in the first term (Freeze the Fees – Stop the Cuts!) and a garda asked me and my two equally middle-class friends what on earth we were doing. 'It's great fun,' we said and he rolled his eyes and told us to go home 'before your photos are taken'. Outside the walls of Trinity, Dublin was a shabby and depressed city with GUBU politics at their height, unemployment and a deep recession that would send many of us to London, New York and beyond, and Ulster was on fire. Who could blame us for preferring our ivory tower?

Getting through first-year exams was a relief. I spent the summer in Paris with Maura and Susan, my two very pretty girlfriends who ensured great male attention, not always welcome, wherever we went. We worked at Burger King on the Champs-Élysées right by Georges V metro station. Not the most glamorous job, but with the advantage that every Irish student passing through Paris fetched up there at some point. Returning to Trinity in October 1983, we were no longer freshers and I remember feeling more confident of belonging.

My memories are kaleidoscopic, but chronologically inexact. Some memories are particularly clear. I once wrote a tutorial paper for Tommy Murtagh on André Gide. When I got to the end of my opening sentence, Tommy (who terrified me at the best of times) expressed scepticism about my position, demanding sources. It took most of the two-hour tutorial to finish reading, citing sources and context, sentence by sentence. The usual form was to read our papers for twenty minutes or so and then for the group to discuss. This was a different experience. When I finished I looked up, shaken, to a charming smile from Tommy and unexpected praise. A longer version of that paper later earned a thrilling first.

I grew more confident after that, and increasing fluency in French made sources for French history more accessible. I enjoyed working with John Horne, who made one want to do the best possible work. I remember Professor Ian Robinson, the kind, brilliant, unworldly medievalist, passing through the Exam Hall distributing answer books together with boiled sweets. We were lucky with our tutors for the most part; strong veins of brilliance and eccentricity ran through both the History and French departments. I think we realized even then that we were getting a proper university education, rich in transformational moments that stretched our minds and altered our perceptions of ourselves and the world around us.

In the Sophister years, I often worked in the icy eyrie that is Early Printed Books in the East Pavilion of the Long Room. In my current life I am working there again. Nothing has changed about that long walk along the underground concrete tunnel from the Berkeley basement, negotiating the dripping pipes, before taking the creaking lift to emerge into one of Trinity's most special rooms. It was exciting to request a book from the Old Library stacks and find the pages had not yet been cut.

We played as well, of course. Trinity Week was the best of fun, and – false memory, no doubt – the sun seemed to shine all week every year. The Hothouse Flowers and In Tua Nua playing at lunchtime in College Park were highlights. By the Friday afternoon of the Ball, the atmosphere around college was verging on hysterical, as the Junior Dean did the rounds to rout potential gatecrashers. I recall emerging with a boyfriend from a dark dance floor to bright sunshine at 5 am on a brilliant May morning and rocking to U2 on the Berkeley podium and feeling that it was the best possible time to be alive, to be me, to be at Trinity. We went to Bewley's on Grafton Street for breakfast in dinner jackets and long dresses.

And then it was all over. Out into the world, a newly minted TCD graduate. I thought I was going to be a civil servant, but then, as now, there was a moratorium on public-sector recruitment. After a year working for Fred Hanna on Nassau Street, I went to London. The Big Bang of 1986 had deregulated the City of London, and Irish graduates were arriving in large numbers. By the time the

Department of Finance called me up in 1988, I was learning to be a publisher at Cambridge University Press, and declined their offer.

I have come back to the mother ship after nearly quarter of a century in the UK, US and Sweden and am two years into a Ph.D. on the history of publishing. I work again in Early Printed Books – which is still freezing. Donncha remembered me when I came back into the Berkeley looking for a visitor's card. The Arts Block foyer smells almost the same as it used to, although the coffee aroma is richer and the coffee itself definitely better. We wrote most of our essays by hand in the 1980s; now we have laptops, dongles and digital cameras. Despite all these advances and the extraordinary building and expansion that has taken place over the past quarter-century, Trinity is relatively unaltered. Parliament Square at dusk remains my favourite place and favourite moment in the college day, when ghosts walk and a lighted doorway in the distance is an invitation not to be missed.

Jane Mahony at her graduation, 1986.

Jane Mahony (TCD 1982–6; History and French) worked in publishing in the UK, first at Cambridge University and then as managing director of Pickering & Chatto in London. She served on the boards of the Independent Publishers Guild and the Anthony Trollope Society. Having left Ireland in the 1980s, she returned to Dublin in December 2009. She recently remarried and has two children and four stepchildren.

FRESHERS' WEEK

rosita boland

IN MY FIRST WEEK at Trinity in 1983, an enthusiastic woman with enormous glasses and a notebook politely accosted me at Front Arch. Was I a fresher, she inquired, flailing her notebook with urgency. With my blue school duffle coat, and an expression that vacillated between excitement, anxiety and joy, it was obvious I was the most emerald-green of green freshers.

I replied that I was indeed. Would I speak to her for a newspaper article about the fresher experience for *The Irish Times*? Would I allow myself to be photographed for the article? Her pen was poised. I was rendered speechless with horror. I could think of nothing worse than putting my fresher head over a parapet that I as yet knew nothing about. I explained that I would talk to her but did not want my name published, and that there was definitely to be no photo.

Christina Murphy, the well-known *Irish Times* education correspondent, for it was she, explained swiftly how newspapers needed people to go on the record, and hurried off in search of a more media-friendly fresher.

I had come to university straight from a convent boarding school where uniform was mandatory six days a week, including a special one for Sundays. Many of us even wore full uniform on Saturdays, or else wore a blue school jumper over a pair of jeans. As a result, I possessed virtually nothing that we had termed 'civvies' at school, or 'civilian' clothes. I unselfconsciously wore my school duffle coat round campus for a while; to registration, and orientation parties, and for coffee in the Buttery, until I slowly realized that I looked different from the other young women students.

Mine appeared to be the only duffle coat on campus. I started to feel as if the coat was as conspicuous as the Scarlet Letter of Nathaniel Hawthorne's novel that was on my course reading list. I had never given clothes a single thought before, but now I was in the strange position of feeling embarrassed by something as inanimate as a coat.

When my father took me out for lunch not long after I arrived in Dublin, he asked if there was anything I needed. Yes, I replied, prepared for this question. A coat. I had even done some groundwork. I marched him into Mirror Mirror on Stephen's Green, where either Oasis or Topshop is now located, and walked out of the shop with a black swing coat with two big buttons. I wore it like a carapace for the rest of that first year, and tried to pick up fashion tips by discreetly studying what my fellow students wore.

At Trinity, I became acutely aware of being from the west of Ireland; Clare, in my case. There didn't seem to be that many of us culchies in my classes: virtually everyone I met was from Dublin and was networked into a system of school friends and shared histories that had begun long before any of us walked through Front Arch. I didn't mind this at all: I was quite delighted at the thought of reinvention.

I 'read', as the formal college expression went, modern English and history. It was a combination that required the accompanying mouthful, 'two-subject moderatorship'. I soon learned I had chosen two subjects with huge reading lists, and also learned the classic lesson that just because you were good at something at school didn't mean it would sustain your interest for years when studied in forensic detail. The more I burrowed into the past of history, the less interested I became in it. I wondered uneasily if I had made a mistake, but I had my new coat now, and there didn't seem to be any going back. In my second year, I tried half-heartedly to transfer to psychology, but didn't pursue it.

My other subject was English. English departments in many universities are probably deemed to be slightly more eccentric than other departments. Ours included a man famous at the time for advertising cars on television, although he didn't drive; a man who was later to run controversially for office of president of Ireland; and a woman who never once looked at her students, preferring instead consistently to address her lectures to a point on the ceiling above our heads.

I did not drink alcohol the first three years of my four at college; my preferred drink was soda and lime on our nights out at O'Neill's on Trinity Street. Perhaps it was the fact that I had a clear head on these nights out that made me slowly realize how insidious the culture of alcohol was within the English Department. Our lecturers regularly drank with us in O'Neill's, and on several occasions we were the ones who had to help them out of the pub.

One night, I was crossing campus on my way home when I came across two fellow English classmates supporting one of our lecturers by the Long Room. He was so drunk he was unable to walk. It required three of us to frog-march him across campus and out the back gate at Lincoln Place, and along Westland Row to the flat he rented from college.

We were invited in, and he stood on a chair, swigging whiskey from a bottle and reading aloud from Martin Amis' *Dead Babies*, periodically vanishing to throw up noisily. I had little life experience, but something told me this was a bizarre form of student–lecturer relationship. Not long after that, the same lecturer, on coming home one night, fell down the steps that led to his flat and ended up in hospital with serious injuries. He did not reappear on campus the following academic year.

Then there were the English lecturers who arrived drunk to class. Today it seems unimaginable, or I hope it would be, but this was a pretty regular occurrence back in Trinity in the 1980s, and we took it entirely for granted. Drunken lecturers might sound quite bohemian, but the reality was simply embarrassing.

One lecturer in particular was notorious for turning up drunk. We never knew what we were going to get: an offbeat, mildly entertaining lecture, or an off-topic rant on virtually any subject, from politics to Irishness. I don't even know why we bothered to keep attending, except presumably we feared end-of-year exams and retaliation for non-attendance, or rather, I did. As the year progressed, we drifted further and further back in the room, leaving more and more space between the lecturer and us.

One afternoon, I was sitting beside a friend of mine, waiting for class to start. The lecturer was so late we were in the middle of debating if we would leave, when he arrived, slamming the door behind him, and spoiling for a fight. We were stupid, he informed us immediately. We were sheep. We had no original thoughts. He, however, was an original thinker and, in time, he would bring us around to his way of thinking. From the back of the class, where I ritually sat, trying to avoid attention, I could smell the alcohol off him. We were all simultaneously appalled and riveted at this implosion of authority. Some people got up and walked out. He described them as cowards to those of us still remaining.

His eye alighted on my friend and he ordered her up to the blackboard. Students were never called to the blackboard in class; they were exclusively for the use of lecturers writing notes. She went reluctantly. He commanded that she write on the board what she had learned so far in university that had made her think. It was an impossible question. She tried to write something, but at that point, between his sneers at her attempts to answer, her subsequent tears and our collective palpable discomfort, any pretence at a class fell apart. She fled the room, sobbing. I gathered up her belongings and followed.

I was happiest in my final year at Trinity. I had made good friends. My fashion choices were slightly better. I moved on from soda and lime to gin and tonic, and Guinness. I was confident enough about my work that I reversed the habits of the three previous years, and spent more time in the pub than in the library, while everyone else was doing the exact opposite.

I enjoyed the melancholic old stones of Trinity, islanded within a city. I had favourite places to sit in the Berkeley and the Early Printed Books Reading Room, which was entered via a tunnel. I regularly bypassed the queuing tourists to flash my student ID and wander through the Long Room, always ending by looking at the Book of Kells; at that time, unlike now, pages were still turned regularly.

But I could not wait to leave. After my final exam, I literally ran shouting from Front Square, under Front Arch, and into the world beyond. It was 1987, right in the middle of a horrible recession, but I had a plan: I was going as far away as possible from everything and everyone I knew. I had a one-year working visa for Australia. The USIT return fare to Sydney cost me £1250; an inordinate sum by today's long-haul standards, which I'd saved by working in London the previous summer.

These days, I very often walk through Trinity on my way back and forth to work at my job as a features writer at *The Irish Times*. Every Freshers' Week, when the stalls are out, and the slightly dazed-looking freshers wander around, I recall Christina Murphy's attempts to interview me. She died just before I joined the paper, and I am so sorry I never had the opportunity to know her. Or to tell her how I now understood what it was like to be the person with the reporter's notebook, seeking interviewees for the record, on deadline and under pressure. To this day, I regret not letting her interview me. Why? Mostly because college is a time when you should be saying 'Yes' to new experiences, instead of a cautious, qualified 'Maybe'.

Rosita Boland's student card, 1987.

Rosita Boland (TCD 1983–7; Modern English and History) has written four books; two non-fiction and two poetry. She is a staff features writer with **The Irish Times**. In 2008, she was awarded a Nieman Fellowship by Harvard University's Nieman Foundation for Journalism, and spent the academic year 2008–9 there. She has travelled extensively.

MUSICALS AND BOAT RACES

rosheen mcguckian

IT WAS WHEN the girl behind the counter at Fannin's medical suppliers handed me the scalpel, tweezers and white coat that it dawned on me that something was seriously wrong. I should have recognized the clues when I read the list of physiology, neurology and other -ology books set out as prescribed reading. I had signed up for a BSc in remedial linguistics, the degree course that produces speech therapists.

Six months prior, I had been trawling through the Trinity prospectus. There was no contest. Seduced by the aura of Pimm's and croquet with the sound of *Chariots of Fire* floating in the background, I had already decided that Trinity was going to be my Alma Mater. There was just the small matter of what degree to take. I'd had some vague notion that speech therapy would be a mixture of English, psychology and a bit of linguistics thrown in for good measure. It never struck me that I had signed up for a crash course in what was effectively to be medicine for the head and neck, with all the hours of study and clinics that it entailed, but without the kudos of becoming 'A Doctor' at the end.

I had unknowingly become an anorak. When people refer to Trinity, they think of a certain Oxbridge-influenced lifestyle. But back in 1983, two parallel universes existed within the forty-seven acres that made up the Trinity College campus. Yes, if you had the good fortune to enter by Front Gate or the Nassau Street entrance, you entered a cobblestoned world of learning, where intense discussions on love, politics and philosophy took place on the ubiquitous chocolate boxes in the Arts Block. This was the world of arts, ESS and law, where you fitted some four to six hours of lectures into your hectic schedule of rehearsals for Players, debates at the Phil and liaisons in the Buttery. However, as you headed south towards the rugby pitches at a point just beyond the Berkeley Library, you were propelled through a gateway leading to the second universe, one inhabited by medics, engineers and scientists.

The signs were imperceptible, but there nonetheless. Clothing styles shifted from Joy Division apparel with matching Flock of Seagull haircuts to Bill Cosby jumpers peeping out from under army-surplus pea coats. The height of culinary experience was a jaw-breaking ham roll washed down with a club shandy in the Pav. This wasn't how it was supposed to be.

I had it all planned out. During my university years, I was going to meet incredibly sophisticated and interesting people. Who knew, my future husband could be holding forth in the Lecky. Or perhaps he was the editor of *Piranha*, or running the Students' Union. Wherever he was hiding, I just knew that Trinity was going to open my eyes to a hedonistic lifestyle. But I had managed to select the only all-female degree course in Trinity … headed by a nun. Seventeen girls with a vocation – and me.

I was determined, with two fellow 'speechies', Karen Hautz and Fiona Bruce, to escape the confines of our base at 184 Pearse Street and experience the full, unadulterated campus life that we knew to be the real Trinity. In one sense we were an unknown entity. Remedial linguistics was a relatively new course at the time and we didn't fit the mould of the impossibly glamorous girls in ESS, nor the trail-blazing female engineers in the alternative universe over at the Parsons Building. As a result of our no-man's-land status, we gravitated towards different 'scenes'.

It took a good fifteen minutes at a light trot to get from one end of the campus to the other. With only an hour to spare at lunch (no four-hour-weekly lecture schedule for us), we made it our business to be wherever we felt the action might be. I recall how agonizing it felt at the end of lunch breaks as we watched our fellow undergraduates from Universe 1 stroll over to Kilkenny

Design for a postprandial coffee, while we galloped back past the Rubrics to Universe 2, preparing a clinical session for some poor unsuspecting patient in our heads.

We were somewhat on the sidelines for the first year or so. Of course, in retrospect, everyone spends their first year anxiously trying to identify their scene. I recall hanging with the wind-surfers (courtesy of my brother), the rugby heads, the 'Nure lads (unfortunately named after their school) and the pre-meds. I even tried out for Players. But it wasn't until second year that we found our calling.

In the Michaelmas Term of 1984, a notice went up calling fellow thespians to try their luck on the boards of the Royal Irish Academy of Music in Westland Row. This was to be the second year of the rebirth of DUMADS, the Dublin University Musical and Dramatic Society, a society that had hit hard times in previous decades, but with the energy of Mark Cunningham and others was to become a runaway success in the mid eighties. Its first foray, *Salad Days*, was postponed due to a porters' strike. Undeterred, the founders were auditioning again.

In an extraordinary turn of events, DUMADS tapped into some sort of Zeitgeist, becoming a focal point of creative energy at the other end of campus from the more erudite Players. Everyone had a go – six-foot-six varsity rowers gamely danced the Charleston five nights in a row. Voices better practised in the art of 'Swing Low Sweet Chariot' galloped through 'I Could Be Happy With You' under the expert baton of Heather Hewson. We took and slaughtered one musical pastiche after another.

And yet, serious talent emerged. Satirist Gary Cooke and actress Karen Ardiff both starred in DUMADS productions alongside the founder of the Cat Laughs Comedy Festival, Richard Cook. Behind-the-scenes attracted its own talent. David Clinch, later to become an editor of CNN news, directed, while Douglas Nichol unashamedly promoted the musicals on Gay Byrne and secured front-page photographs in *The Irish Times*. He convinced critics of *The Irish Press* and *Evening Herald* to come and review our fare. I cringe when I think of it now.

My own claim to fame was as Raquelita, the fiery love interest of Ramon, a Zorro-type villain-cum-hero, in *Viva Mexico*. My 1980s *Flashdance* perm struck an odd note for what was supposed to be a turn-of-the-century Latina look. But, not to be outshone, Michael Kenny as Ramon gyrated across the stage head to toe in leather, clutching his crotch in Michael Jackson fashion. He shot to critical acclaim.

One of the successes of DUMADS was its ability to converge the parallel universes of Trinity life. There was no distinguishing hallmark to a DUMADS 'type'. Sporting aficionados shared greasepaint with thespians, lecturers, librarians and future pillars of commerce and journalism. Through DUMADS, I established a broad church of friendships and also entered into, for a brief year or two, the world of what were fondly described as West Brits or Oxbridge Rejects (ORs).

Trinity had carved a niche in accepting certain British applicants who hadn't quite made it to Oxbridge and were shipped off to Dublin to round off their education before going home to run the family estate. These were charming people, with goofy hairstyles, velvet jackets and unpronounceable double-barrelled names. With gracious humour, they drank beer with the lads in the Lincoln and kissed one or two colleens before the inevitable call back to meet the Honourable Penelope and breed the next generation. I sound dismissive, which is not at all intended. I had no idea what to make of this social experiment when first encountering the ORs but a more generous-spirited group of people you were unlikely to meet. They wore their backgrounds lightly and accepted the constant slagging with great grace. They knew they were different and that was just the way it was. I recall in vivid detail one conversation with an OR (heir to an extensive estate in Scotland), who had just celebrated his twenty-first birthday.

> Me: 'So did your parents get you a present, then?'
> OR: 'Well, yes. Father got me a golf club.'
> Me: 'Cool. What type? A seven iron? A wood?'
> OR: 'Eh, no. I mean a club … a golf club … you know, with eighteen
> holes …'

We knew what a privilege it was to spend four years in a place of such historic significance, sheltered from the economic turmoil that was unfolding around us. We embraced the traditions built up over four hundred years – Latin grace at Commons, the announcement of scholars outside the Dining

Hall, the races around the Campanile and, of course, witnessing dawn at the Trinity Ball. We did so knowing that for most of us we were but delaying the inevitable journey overseas to find a job.

In the same way that I entered Trinity, I was preparing to depart it – clueless about what I wanted to do. In a fit of desperation, I called the careers advisory service. They were at first unable to tell me which advisor was assigned to my course, as this question had never come up before. And when I did finally sit down with a counsellor, his advice to me was to become a speech therapist. Helpful.

I did finally move on and so far I have managed to enjoy a pretty fulfilling career across many walks of life. I have never quite been an obvious fit for any role that I was lucky enough to take on. I attribute much of my career to my formative experiences in those four intensive years as a Trinity undergraduate. As I read back over this chapter I realize that almost all of my memories relate to anything but the degree that I happened to be studying for. And I'm sure that if I were to ask others, they would say the same. It was by just being there, the privilege of having to do nothing but grow up and test out so many experiences of life, that I worked out who I was and what I was capable of doing. And most of all, I made friendships that are as strong today as twenty-five years ago.

Oh and by the way, I did find my husband – not in the Lecky, but in the back of the anatomy hall. Definitely not how it was supposed to be.

Rosheen McGuckian (TCD 1983–7; Remedial Linguistics) achieved a number of postgraduate degrees in other colleges and was awarded a doctorate in business by DCU. She never practised as a speech therapist, but instead has held a variety of roles as a senior executive across the energy, financial services and waste-management sectors. Rosheen is currently CEO of National Tollroads, and a member of the advisory board to the Trinity College Dublin School of Engineering. She is married to Joey Mason.

GARDEN PARTIES, KISSOGRAMS AND NON-LINEAR VIBRATION ISOLATION

patrick prendergast

THE SCIENTIST explores what is, the engineer creates what has never been. So said Theodore von Kármán, father of modern aerospace engineering. Something of this feeling must have convinced me to study engineering rather than science. But why Trinity for a Wexford boy who had only rarely visited Dublin? That must have been divine providence.

The Trinity of the 1980s was a university in transition. The small intimate college familiar to previous generations was disappearing and being replaced by something perhaps more needed for the times – a university rising to meet the expectations of a new generation for third-level education and of a country for economic development. We were riding a new wave. Of course, we freshers didn't know any of this, but my siblings, cousins and I were the first in our extended family to attend university, and it was the same for many of my friends, especially my country friends. Maybe we were subconsciously aware of being part of an upheaval – or a quiet revolution.

Front Square hadn't changed in a century, and still hasn't. But the rest was undergoing transformation, sometimes for the better, sometimes for the worse.

At the beginning of the eighties, students still boxed or played table tennis in the Old Gymnasium and walked the Parade Ground, with its laneway out to Kennedys pub, where the raggedy backside of Westland Row still presented itself to the campus. I had my last drink as an undergraduate in the lounge of Kennedys. But a decade later this was all gone – there was no long goodbye; it seemed to go in a flash. Instead we had the O'Reilly Institute for Science and Technology, the Hamilton Institute and the Biotech Building; the Panoz and Smurfit Institutes were soon on the starting blocks. Trinity was getting ready for the economic boom of the 1990s by building new infrastructure, and it was the right thing to do.

The provost during my student days was W.A. Watts. I never met him, but, as provost, I've recently met Mrs Watts and was happy to share experiences of living in No. 1 Grafton Street. As one of Watts' successors I have to walk in his footsteps – we have in common that we both graduated from Trinity. I lived in Botany Bay, House 20, with two pharmacy students, Patrick McCormack and Brendan Fullam. Because our set was for three we had a massive sitting room, suitable for parties – if playing music to the tune of cheap spirits from mugs can be called a party. More memorably, we had a TV, and students, mainly country people like us, would drop by to watch *Glenroe* on Sunday evenings.

I arrived for my first day in Trinity on the number 45 bus from Cabinteely, where I was staying with my aunt's family. I had no clue where Trinity was, but got directions from a newspaper seller outside the Screen Cinema, who told me to follow the green railings. First encounters are supposed to be auspicious. Walking in through Front Gate under the arch of Regent House and out into Front Square is still one of my favourite vistas, anywhere in the world. Now I do that short commute every day from the Provost's House. For me this walk from the darkness of the arch out into the open space of Front Square presents a metaphor for what education should do for the mind. I want all Trinity students to feel their minds opening up to new opportunities – and more than just career opportunities: opportunities for understanding and even eventually finding what we all hope for – a little bit of wisdom about what is truly important in life.

As Junior Freshmen engineers we had much to do; the course was no cakewalk. We had four lectures most mornings, with lab and drawing-office work in the afternoons. I saw my tutor once, a very kindly man called Dr Tom Glynn with an office in the depths of the Museum Building. He told me to come back if I had problems – I didn't so we never met again. Years later as provost I received a letter from the executors of his will saying he had donated a significant part of his estate to the college 'for the benefit of graduate students'.

The great wave of expansion in Irish higher education saw Trinity Engineering School double enrolments between the late seventies and late eighties. Four new departments were founded: Civil Engineering; Mechanical and Manufacturing Engineering; Electrical and Microelectronic Engineering; and Computer Science. New academic staff arrived to teach these new students. Thinking back on it now, the college and its new staff were under some strain to deal with us all. Classes were large. Tutorial groups were also large and there perhaps weren't enough graduate students to act as TAs (teaching assistants). The buildings were not well suited to teaching engineering, being mainly converted from other uses – and often built centuries earlier. But we were enthusiastic, and so were our lecturers. A big influence on me was Dr John Fitzpatrick, later Professor of Mechanical Engineering, who taught fluid mechanics and persuaded many of us that mechanical engineering was the only option if you wanted to pursue the big challenges. Many others who taught mechanical engineering, John Monaghan, David Taylor, Garry Lyons, Darina Murray, Henry Rice and Dermot Geraghty, would also become my departmental colleagues when I returned to Trinity as a lecturer myself in the 1990s.

Our pranks were mainly with the mathematicians, for some reason. I remember we got Professor Petros Florides – now a distinguished pro-chancellor of the university – a kissogram (they were all the rage in the eighties) for St Valentine's Day. He wasn't the least bit fazed and enjoyed the performance – when the young woman appeared we could see the penny drop with Petros about why so many of us had turned up for that morning lecture.

On another occasion, Professor Trevor West celebrated a Colours victory over UCD by downing a pint of Smithwicks at the start of a lecture in the Ed Burke. Trevor taught pure mathematics, often filling the blackboard with incredibly long expansions. He recently passed away and we celebrated his life with a wonderful memorial service in the College Chapel.

One thing Trinity offered students then as now is a final-year project. Mine was on the interesting (to me) topic of 'Non-linear vibration isolation'. I had to simulate the performance of a vibration rig on a Hewlett-Packard desktop computer. I was delighted with this and would get in early to hog a little computer in the Engineering Computer Applications Laboratory. Building the rig was the best fun. Project-presentation day was nerve-racking and afterwards we all went out for dinner. This was in the great tradition of staff and students socializing together in the final years – a tradition that still continues in many departments today, but one that may prove difficult to sustain, with ever-increasing student numbers, more restrained attitudes to drinking, and staff living further out of the city.

Outside of lectures and coursework, I was a stalwart of the Karate Club – I recall our many trips to intervarsity competitions, and even winning a few times. Otherwise, I gave a lot of attention to Dublin pubs and clubs. Looking back, it's a wonder we got any work done. Certainly too much of our hard-earned cash, from summers working in London or New York, went over the counter in Kennedys or the Lincoln, or Humphreys in Ranelagh, or Slattery's in Rathmines. It was a rite of passage, then as now, for students to head abroad in the summer to earn fees and living expenses for the next year.

One major annual social event not to be missed was the Trinity Ball. In my first year I remember going, with my friend Patrick McCormack, to a girls' hostel on Henrietta Street to escort our 'dates' to the Ball. We waited downstairs in the hall with the pyjama-clad inmates looking at us over the bannisters – I'm sure we were a fine pair in our hired tuxedos. Both girls were called Eileen and both are now successful professionals – not married to either of us, I hasten to add. The Trinity Ball was always preceded by dinner even though we broke the bank eating out in restaurants totally beyond our means in Les Frères Jacques or The Old Dublin.

I never missed the Elizabethan Garden Party, either, little knowing that some twenty years later it would be *my* garden. The Garden Party was always held on a sunny day before exams and it captured something intangible about what makes Trinity unique. No matter what a person's background, eating strawberries and cream and listening to music in the sunshine is one of life's simple pleasures. I was never a straw-hat-and-blazer kind of person but I always found the Garden Party a great spectacle, and in no way redolent of a time of privilege, though apparently some people did. Unfortunately, by the time I became provost this tradition had passed into history. I hope to revive the Garden Party and with it the missed opportunity to spend time informally with students and share the beauty of the Provost's Garden with them in the last sunny days before exams.

Patrick Prendergast (TCD 1983–7; Mechanical Engineering) was a Ph.D. student in Trinity until 1990. He followed this with research work in Bologna in Italy, and Nijmegen in the Netherlands, returning to Trinity as a lecturer in 1995 and later becoming Professor of Bioengineering. He was elected the forty-fourth provost of Trinity College Dublin in April 2011.

'ONE YEAR' ABROAD

heidi haenschke

ARRIVING IN Dublin in October 1984, I wondered if I had made the right choice – it seemed such a cold, grey, damp, dirty town. I had completed two years at the University of Virginia (UVA) and wanted to spend my third year studying abroad. I searched the list of 'UVA-Approved' foreign universities (ones with recognized exchange programmes) but knew in my heart that I wanted to go to Trinity. So I bravely took an official leave of absence from UVA and enrolled as a 'One Year' student at TCD, hoping that upon my return to Charlottesville, Virginia, my time at TCD would be credited towards my studies in international relations. In the end that wasn't necessary, as Trinity stole my heart and I stayed.

My reasons for choosing Trinity were several. I had spent some time in Ireland as a child. My mother, from Stradbally, County Laois, often brought me to visit cousins (who gawked at their strange American relation and her braces) and to tour around Ireland. The Long Room and Front Square made quite an impression on me. And, thanks to *Brideshead Revisited*, I was attracted to a romantic idea of life across the Atlantic. My Trinity brochure promised parties in the Provost's Garden, tea at the Shelbourne, and – of course – the Trinity Ball. Only Trinity, and no other college, would do for my year abroad.

During the mid 1980s, Ireland was another world to a Jersey girl raised with 24-hour multi-channel TV, shopping malls that opened late seven days a week, an ethnically diverse population and the foods of many nations. Ireland was in recession and money was tight. Socially, Ireland seemed repressed and backwards. No divorce – you're kidding!? Illegal to buy condoms without a prescription – no way!? Dublin looked and felt more like 1954 than 1984.

My aunt collected me at the airport and took me for lunch at the Bad Ass Café. I think she was trying to find somewhere hip and cool. After a quick pizza (quite unlike the pizzas I was used to) I was dropped to Trinity Hall. My room was cell-like. A machine took 50p coins and produced minimal heat in return. I soon resorted to heavy duvets, woolly jumpers and fingerless gloves. At UVA, I had shared a large apartment with five other girls. It was luxurious in comparison: warm in the winter, cool in the summer and no end of hot showers. The hours spent waiting for the bus in the rain from Trinity Hall to town felt miserable compared to hopping into my little car and driving to campus at UVA.

Meals also presented a problem – I didn't eat at the Dining Hall, and often was too uninspired or lazy to cook myself a proper meal in the little shared kitchen, so lived on digestive biscuits, blocks of cheddar cheese and Nutella during term time, supplemented by Sunday dinners at my aunt's or friends' houses. Quite the contrast to UVA, with its choice of restaurants and all-you-could-eat buffets.

Despite the hardships, I loved my year at Trinity. Although many of the 'One Year' students tended to stick together, those of us that made an effort to mix had great fun and got so much more from the experience. I loved meeting people from all over Ireland and getting to grips with the subtle differences and myriad of accents and cultures: students from country farms, the Anglo-Irish, Northern Prods, working-class Dubliners, Irish Jews, middle-class Dubliners – a quiltwork of culture from such a small land. Within Dublin, subsets existed based on where people had gone to school: Alex, Loreto, 'Kings Hos', Christian Brothers, High School, Newpark, St Columba's and many more. The pecking order took some deciphering, but wasn't so different to the social order at UVA, based upon sororities and fraternities.

Academically, there were differences to manage as well. My overall courseload seemed much smaller and, with only four modules per year, my timetable was very light, leaving plenty of time for socializing. Terms were shorter by nearly two months and the breaks were longer. Massive lecture theatres at UVA were replaced by small seminars where professors knew me by name and it was impossible to hide. Continuous assessment at UVA meant that the final degree awards were based on one's grade-point average throughout four years of studying. A low grade in first year in something like 'Introduction to Psychology' counted as much as one's final-year mark in, for example, 'Advanced Economics'. Trinity was a wonderful place for students who were bright and could swot for the final two months of the year and still come out with a first-class honours degree. For the rest of us, it was necessary to put in the time at the library, and work on essays.

Campus life was also a shock to the system. At UVA, everyone either lived on campus or rented nearby. Charlottesville, Virginia, was all about UVA – the university was the centre of everything. One would have had to drive miles to see any normal life. I was surprised to find so many students living at home while studying at Trinity, and bringing in their 'sambos' for lunch. In the late afternoon and evenings, the campus became quieter and calmer as people waited for the 16B or 7A bus. I enjoyed that one could step outside the walls, wander down Grafton Street or O'Connell Street and see people from all walks of life, many of whom had never set foot inside Trinity's main gate. We went to the Kilkenny Design Centre or Bewley's for coffee and whiled away the afternoons with non-Trinity friends, which would have been unheard of at UVA. Discussions were broad-minded and not all about sorority mixers or the next term paper.

The social scene at Trinity was a little different, too, although drinking registered just as high on the agenda. UVA is traditionally a 'party' school, albeit with high academic standards, and typical nights out involved 'mixers' (intra-sorority and fraternity parties) with full free bar, live band and no time restrictions. The average night out for broke TCD students involved nursing a few pints until closing time.

Membership of fraternities and sororities at UVA is based on tradition and being 'rushed', or accepted for membership, and after a cut-throat selection process I became a member of the Delta Delta Delta sorority. This was in stark contrast to Freshers' Week at Trinity, where I was encouraged to join as many societies as possible. I loved debates at the Phil and the Hist with their unique repartee and quick-witted humour. My long-anticipated Trinity Ball turned out to be worth the wait, beginning elegantly but sliding into debauchery and breakfast at McDonald's on Grafton Street.

I decided that I would like to stay on and finish my degree at Trinity, so I consulted with the Politics Department head, Professor Basil Chubb, about this unorthodox idea. Another 'One Year' student from Canada, Brendan Kielty, also had the same thought, and we were both accepted with the proviso that we achieve at least a second-class honour in our third-year exams, a great incentive to study. Brendan and I studied hard and got the results we needed.

Transitioning to regular full-time student was seamless, and fourth year was made much easier by securing rooms on campus in New Square and later with Roisin Magee in Front Square. I no longer felt like an American imposter but a legitimate member of our little group that was studying for an ESS degree in pure politics. My favourite class memories are of Professor Kader Asmal and his often divergent, yet brilliant, lectures on international law. Professor Basil Chubb took our Irish politics lecture and managed to clear up some of the confusion I had about the complicated tangle of Irish political history while we watched the new Progressive Democrats emerge from the traditional lines. Professor Eddie Hyland would chain-smoke and wax lyrical about Marx and Hegel.

I was not a product of the Leaving Cert. so was unaccustomed to the pressure of my entire degree being dependent on final exams. Therefore, I worked hard for my results, especially as this time my place on an MBA course in London depended on them. My professors at Trinity managed to push me beyond merely reciting and regurgitating what I read. Freethinking and new ideas were rewarded and we were encouraged to debate productively and creatively. Trinity brought out the best in me and broadened my horizons in a way that would not have happened had I chosen to stay in the USA. My choice of university for my year abroad changed my life. After careers in London and New York, I came to live permanently in Dublin, a choice made primarily because of my time at Trinity.

My eldest daughter has now entered Trinity and the circle is nearly complete. Ironically, she will soon be thinking about where to go for her

Erasmus year and I wonder whether her decision will be as significant as mine was for me.

Heidi Haenschke on a TCD trip to Moscow, 1985.

Heidi Haenschke (TCD 1984–6; Politics) earned an MBA in marketing at City University London. She worked in mergers and acquisitions at Kleinwort Benson in London and later at Kleinwort's New York Corporate Finance unit, specializing in international deals. During the 1990s, she was a key player in the development of TCL Telecom with her husband, Sean Melly (TCD 1981–5), and the company was eventually acquired by WorldCom (now Verizon). After a short hiatus to raise her three daughters, Heidi qualified as a yoga teacher and owns YogaVillage in Dalkey, Co. Dublin.

MUM'S THE WORD

fiona cronin

THERE WAS NEVER really any option for me but go to Trinity. My biggest fan had always been my mum, and she had filled me with a sense of confidence and self-worth, managing to overlook my shortcomings. She had also sacrificed a lot for love – marrying my dad who was a Catholic, much against the wishes of her staunchly Protestant parents. They eloped to London to get married, and baptized us into the Catholic Church. We had a very broad and liberal upbringing: mum would still attend the local Protestant church with us in tow, perfectly happy with the conflict between an education from the nuns and Sundays with the vicar. When it came to my third-level education, however, it was clear that it had to be Trinity – I think it was her way of bridging the past, and making my late grandmother, a teacher herself, proud.

The choice of what I would do was thankfully in my control. I had originally thought that I would like to study politics, but then came across this eclectic course called ESS, which not only covered politics but a huge array of other subjects – women's studies, sociology, mathematics, law. It promised a 'broad-based education with a high degree of freedom', and seemed to provide everything I wanted.

I was completely overwhelmed by Freshers' Week in October 1984. Everyone looked so sophisticated – I remember big hair, white boots, New Romantics and punks. Trinity seemed to be a place of debate and freedom of thought and was a breath of fresh air after fourteen years of single-sex convent education.

I lacked confidence in those early weeks, probably tried too hard to make friends – laughed too loudly at their jokes and talked too much (still my downfall). Students lounged about on the chocolate boxes in the Arts Block and I thought this most elegant, so would perch nervously on the fringes when I spotted others from my course.

The dilemma was where to sit in lectures. This was completely fraught, as it said a lot about who you were. I knew I didn't want to sit at the front – it was full of mature students and earnest types who took their studying seriously. And I lacked the confidence to sit up at the very back, where the seats were occupied by the cool ones, sneaking in blearily after a late night. I settled on the back third – not too studious and not too cool.

One of the first people I met was Shana Dillon. She and I would ultimately share rooms in Botany Bay. We photocopied her notes when we missed a lecture. The other was Grainne Parker, who worked as a barmaid in The Stillorgan Orchard, and was definitely more streetwise than this convent girl. It's fair to say that the lecture schedule was not exactly taxing – one term I had six hours of lectures per week. We spent the other hours discussing the finer points of life in the Kilkenny, over one pot of tea and numerous fill-ups – how they put up with us I do not know. People roamed in and out all day and we would pop out for the odd lecture, or Shana would gamely go and take notes.

The variety offered by ESS was the making of me. I chose random topics such as agricultural economics and remember being briefly fascinated by CAP reform. Our marketing lectures bore no resemblance to the marketing I was to do in later life, but rather an in-depth journey through the perils of trademarks and intellectual property rights. We had some excellent lecturers, including John O'Hagan, Dermot McAleese, Francis Ruane and Gerard McHugh, who now heads up the Business School. They instilled in us a love of their subjects and a love of learning.

I was never a very sporty type but I decided to take up cricket because I was guaranteed a slot on the team: they were short a player. The embarrassment of throwing underarm while my friends sat on the steps of the Pav still haunts me, but it served me well on my CV and is still something I trot out now and again. A significant amount of extracurricular activities revolved around the Pav, Lincoln or Stag's Head, where we nursed bottles of Satzenbrau or West Coast Cooler. Jonnie O'Connell and Ed Hughes started up the Gun and Shooting Club, which we all joined, not because any of us had any experience but rather because by establishing a new club they were entitled to free kegs of beer from those lovely people at Guinness.

Sometimes we went to Leeson Street and one of the dodgy basement nightclubs that served only wine, port or 'champagne'. A friend of ours from overseas had access to his dad's American Express card in order to buy essential university supplies. His father eventually figured out that Strings was actually a nightclub not a bookshop. Afterwards it was the Manhattan Bar and Grill on Richmond Street for a fried breakfast and a big mug of tea.

As soon as we broke for the summer, we would head off to the US with our J1 visas, making enough money to last the rest of the year, but most of us also had at least one job to keep us going. Mine included the men's underwear department in Dunnes Stores on Grafton Street (embarrassing but well-paid); waitressing in the Westbury Hotel (less embarrassing, but very long hours); and teaching the recorder to six- and seven-year-olds in my old school (not embarrassing, but painful).

I spent a lot of time anguishing about what I was going to wear to the Trinity Ball. I remember a particularly hideous gold lamé dress that I thought was the bee's knees. We partied before the party in rooms or at friends' houses, before queuing outside the gates as lasers lit up the Front Arch. Once in, there was the scramble to get to the band or artist you wanted to see.

I spent my final year in rooms in Botany Bay, overlooking the tennis courts (which I never used, but often thought I should). The university came alive at night when Front Gate was locked. The gold dress got many an outing as we held black-tie dinner parties, the menus featuring every form of minced beef known to man (and a few more besides). I had to use the oven on the top floor and then carry the food down to our rooms on the second. Showering was equally hazardous, as you had to nip across the corridor and often found the shower occupied and the door behind you closed. You'd think you might learn to take the key after the first time, but sadly not.

I met my future husband Nigel Dawson during that year. He was a year below me, but shared rooms with a good friend of ours, David Sharpe, who was also in ESS. There was always something happening in their rooms, from curry nights to poker, but it was only during the last few months of university that I realized I was falling for him. It was during the 'Milk Round' season – I had my blue interview suit on after my second round with Mars. I spotted him in the Arts Block looking very handsome in an oversized leather jacket and that was it: smitten. We were married seven years later in the Chapel at Trinity.

Twenty-five years later, I can say that ESS was the broad experience it had promised to be, and not just in terms of education but also in friendship, self-discovery, and – ultimately – love. Sadly, my mum passed away over ten years ago, but I know she would laugh with delight if she could hear me encourage my boys to follow their parents to Trinity. It was certainly one of the best pieces of advice I ever received.

Fiona Cronin (TCD 1984–8; Economics and Social Studies) joined the Mars graduate scheme in 1988. Apart from two years spent with Pepsi in the early 1990s, she has remained with the company in various roles across its European business, as general manager of the Irish business, UK sales director, European marketing vice-president and managing director, and is now president of Mars Chocolate UK and a member of the Global Board. She is also president of the IGD and a deputy president of the Food and Drink Federation, vice-president of the Chartered Institute of Marketing, a member of the UK Government's Responsibility Deal, and a school governor. Fiona is married to Nigel Dawson and has two boys, two cats and a dog.

WAKE UP AND SMELL THE HOPS

david mcwilliams

NOT MANY Trinity careers start with a one-to-one with a nun.

The mother superior, into whose clutches my national schoolteacher mother was happy to deliver me, looked sternly over her bifocals. I knew this was it: my one and only chance. Successful prison escapees describe that one moment they have to seize – when they know that their opportunity has come. It may be a guard change, an open door or other fortuitous circumstance. That day, face to face with a nun in early September 1984, was my *Colditz, Escape from Alcatraz, Stalag 17* and *The Great Escape* all rolled into one. The next four years flashed in front of me.

It was clear. There was a choice. Down one road lay this mother superior, frigidity, *An Tuiseal Ginideach*, Lent and 1916. Down the other lay majestic Trinity College with its suggestion of gorgeous, sophisticated, willing Protestant goddesses, a cornucopia of possibilities, Alisons, Pennys and Jennifers, Dublin city, the world and the future.

We had heard stories. Older brothers had leaped from our drab, pebble-dashed suburban 1980s world into the cosmopolitan, educational nirvana that was Trinity. They came back home changed, brimming with stories of strange meetings, odd wanderings and wonderful adventures. Ulysses of the DART line – that's what we wanted to be.

The nun and my mother stood between me and Trinity.

Like every Irish mother, mum wasn't interested in what I did *in* college, it was what I did *after* college that was important. This nun was the gatekeeper to a permanent teaching job and a 'coveted' place in the national teacher-training college in Carysfort.

According to my mother, I had 'only' been accepted onto a 'make-y up-y' course in Trinity, something called ESS that had 'wishy-washy' written all over it. Sure what sort of job would you get after that? I mean it wasn't as if it was law or accountancy or medicine. It wasn't something proper. This was the 1980s after all and jobs weren't growing on trees. In my mother's nightmares, Dublin was full of ESS graduates pulling pints and waiting on tables or, God forbid, managing up-and-coming rock bands.

There and then my choice was to act to save my soul or be condemned to four years of teacher-training college followed by a plum posting to some godforsaken national school down in a part of the country I had never heard of and be banished into a twilight world of GAA and *Glenroe*.

My eighteen-year-old soul wanted to scream, 'No way, mother superior!' but thankfully, there underneath the crucifix cowed by the suffering Jesus looking down on me at Carysfort, I just lied. And with this one little lie, I was free. When the nun started grilling me in Irish, despite my decent honours Irish grades in the Leaving, I simply went mute and pretended not to understand a word she said. She persisted and the whole thing descended into farce. Shown the door, I knew I was free. Next stop Trinity College.

When you boil it all down, my career at Trinity was driven by my fear of nuns and as a result I embarked on a degree – any degree would do. I had done economics for the Leaving Cert. and thought it vaguely interesting, like biology, but it was the course I got the points for and it was the one that dropped out of the CAO grinder machine, so who was I to argue?

I walked through Front Gate in autumn 1984, locked into my Sony Walkman world, New Order's 'Blue Monday' blaring. I realized when I first walked out onto the slippery cobbles of Front Square that drizzly October afternoon that this place would be interesting, if I allowed myself to be sucked into its orbit.

I had no idea quite how interesting. I didn't know then that in my four years at Trinity I would make lifelong friends, experience great loves, have my heart broken and my mind opened while also becoming immersed in economics, which has greatly enhanced my life and without which I can't imagine what I would do for a living. As I write, in late December 2012 – twenty-eight eventful years later – it is a testimony to my time at Trinity that I stayed up half last night with some of my oldest friends and all were at Trinity with me. Flora Hunter, Marka Bowe and Amanda Cochrane now in London; Nicola Firth now in Paris; Clayton Love in Milan; Bobby Doyle and Paul White in Amsterdam; Mary McCaughey back in Dublin after years abroad; Chris McCann and Mark Hopper, too – as always doing their own thing – as well as Liam Curly, Sarah O'Doherty, Paul Scully, Vandra Dyke and Kevin Costello. Jay Bourke, my oldest friend from college, at the top of the table, laughing and holding forth. These great friends are what Trinity gave me and they are what make my memories of those four years, particularly the last two, so fond.

As part of the 1980s generation we were made for export, and flee we did at the first chance. Not unlike the present generation of Irish graduates, we have been scattered all over the world and tend to see each other at the real Irish Gathering that is Christmas. In the first few years after college we came back en masse; few of the great Arts Block loves survived the impact of the real world outside and the tedium of the first badly paid jobs in industries we had no clue about. There have been plenty of adventures since then – careers been and gone, ups and downs, a few fragile marriages smashed, others thriving and now clatters of children, but what bonds us all together – the members of my little 'tribe' – is Trinity and the formative years spent there. When I think of Trinity, I think of them and the fact that Trinity had a much greater impact on my life than school ever did.

And yet, I was one of those people who never got involved in any of what people now term 'college life'. I did not join one society, and, maybe unusually, given my subsequent career, I never once spoke publicly in Trinity, never joined a political party or even a political society. I wrote nothing for college magazines and despite being – publicly at least – invisible, I had a brilliant, life-altering time.

This reticence to engage with college in the traditional manner wasn't because of a lack of interest in, or opinion on, subjects of national and international importance. I was simply too shy and insecure. My first memory of trying to get involved in one of the big debating outfits – the Hist or the Phil, I'm not quite sure which – was one of being intimidated by the gargantuan self-confidence of the West Brits who ran these places.

Later I realized they weren't West Brits at all, but that this is what people who went to Gonzaga looked and sounded like, and back then they had a self-assured swagger and born-to-rule air that scared the bejaysus out of me. So I went along to debates and listened but never partook for fear of not being clever enough to sustain arguments against these characters who seemed to be on a one-way ticket to front-bench, Four Courts glory.

The keffiyeh-wearing activist from the well-known Rathmines *wadi* was a common sight in the Trinity of the late 1980s. Ivana Bacik was very vocal back then but it seems the rest of the politically or radically involved found worthy and rewarding careers at Ernst & Young and Bain & Company. If it was a fair enough path for the real Mitt Romney, why not the budding Mitt Romneys of TCD?

Not surprisingly, ESS – being largely a business degree – produced a certain type of conforming ambition best exemplified by the 'Milk Round', an annual beauty contest hosted in Trinity by the big banks, accountancy, auditing and consulting firms – the nexus that caused this crash, actually. In final year, they swooped into college, armed with impressive heads of HR and the cream of last year's graduate trainee intake, to snap up bargain-basement talent like football scouts in a Third World country.

By this stage I had switched from business to pure economics so was well on the way to becoming unemployable and the narrowness of my academic focus was about as far from the well-rounded, managerial jack of all trades these guys were looking for. The 'Milk Round' was in the main a monumental piss-up because the reward for having to suffer hours of corporate propaganda was a free bar.

Those who emerged from this bizarre beauty pageant with the coveted 'big job' tended to be of a type, aping the worst excesses of Thatcher's Britain without any of the Harry Enfield irony. But for all the disciples of Reagan, Thatcher and the PDs, there was another world that Trinity opened up to me: the mysterious East, the Soviet Union and Russia.

In deep winter I boarded a huge Aeroflot Illusion at Shannon beside my old mate Fiach Mac Conghail – then a member of our five-a-side soccer team, now director of the Abbey – who in February 1987 looked more like a buzz-topped Marxist member of The Housemartins than the Celtic Revival, flowing-maned bohemian of today.

Armed with The Waterboys' *This is the Sea*, cheap vodka and three extra pairs of Levi's, we touched down in freezing Moscow into pre-Glasnost, Cold War Russia. Gorbachev wasn't even a year in power and the Soviet Union was still dominated by hardliners who had no idea what was coming down the tracks. It was here I learnt about the possibilities of capitalism and arbitrage. Because Professor Ron Hill of the Russian Department had us Irish students down as some fraternal, communist, student outfit, we could get tickets for the Bolshoi Ballet at knock-down prices – part of the great socialist project of cultural expansion. In contrast, a bunch of American students we bumped into – clearly imperialist lackeys – had to pay $10. Obviously this was a great capitalist opportunity to hoard the cheap socialist tickets and flog them at a profit to the Yanks. We played this arbitrage with the enthusiasm of a young Abramovich but, unlike a proper oligarch, forgot to pay off the cops and were arrested for profiteering.

Ron Hill, knowing the ropes and possibly the value of a fist of rolled-up dollars, sprung us from the clutches of the KGB to safety. Twenty years later, I interviewed Gorbachev for TV and told him the story and he flashed back, laughing: 'They should've locked you up for a week to teach you a lesson.' Having headed to Russia as some sort of half-baked socialist, I came back with more faith in our own system. But this visit sparked a lifelong interest in a country where I have spent lots of time since.

Speaking of systems, politically Trinity then had a sort of suspended reality about it best encapsulated by the performance of and reception to Public Enemy at the 1988 Trinity Ball. Rap had yet to be appropriated by angry social revolutionaries such as Justin Timberlake and it still carried the menace of America's black ghettoes. Many of my aforementioned 'tribe' had come across it in the kitchens of New York on various summer work trips to the US, an obligatory part of the college experience. In the years before YouTube, iTunes, Spotify and shuffling, music moved slowly across the Atlantic and rap moved slower still. Public Enemy in the late 1980s must've been like the Sex Pistols in the 1970s: aggressive, somewhat alien, sulphuric and above all, black in an Ireland that was completely white.

On a warm May evening, Chuck D, Public Enemy's demonic front man, led the chorus, punching the air screaming, 'Fight the Power'. In response, the 100-per-cent white sons and daughters of the bourgeoisie, the coming power of this small country, repeated back without a hint of irony the angry chorus of Malcolm X-inspired, disenfranchised black men: 'Fight the Power'. But we were the power, so would we be fighting ourselves?

Indeed, the question of power, politics and public office is a perplexing one for the 1980s Trinity cohort. If you look back to the 1960s and 1970s, missing from the 1980s crew are political figures. Mine appeared to be the generation of Trinity students that opted out of the political life of this country. The 1970s crop produced presidents, cabinet members, political activists and party leaders. When you scan Irish public life for political titans to have emerged from Trinity in the mid to late 1980s, you find none. This is quite unusual from the university that many see as shorthand for the replication of power in the Republic. Even the Trinity of the 1990s has produced two ministers in this government. Yet those who entered Trinity in the years between 1980 and 1989 are largely invisible on the national political stage.

Possibly this is a function of the fact that a huge proportion hopped on the first Ryanair out of here, driven away by not just the gross economic misman-agement of the Garret FitzGerald government but also the crushing of political hope that the FitzGerald/Haughey years engendered. On the one hand you had Haughey – an opportunistic tyrant – and on the other you had FitzGerald – a benighted politician high on Ranelagh rhetoric, low on gritty achieve-ments. This was a man who spoke the language of prudence but behaved like Juan Perón and intervened dramatically in the economy to save Bewley's Café where he and his caste drank coffee, while proper Irish industry stagnated and an entire generation emigrated. Let's leave that to the historians, but the lack of Trinity graduates, now in their forties, possibly at the peak of their powers, is a strange absence from the political stage.

The national agenda back then was dominated by economic failure here and political failure up north. Both felt remote once inside Front Gate, despite having lots of Nordy friends. However, one memory stands out and it's the reason I still can't listen to Aretha Franklin's 'Say a Little Prayer'. In March 1988, I was in the Pav watching an Ireland versus England rugby match. At half-time, the broadcast was interrupted for a newsflash. There, as I drank pints of Guinness, I saw the faces of two British soldiers about to be lynched by the mob at an IRA funeral. I must've been listening to Aretha that morning and, for whatever reason, I still can't hear it without thinking of those murders. The fact that they were being filmed and broadcast, and the very act of being a witness, had an enormous impact on me. The North seemed to be caught in a vice-like grip of self-destruction during that period and those months in early 1988 were particularly vicious. Like most Southerners, I believed then that even the notion of peace was remote; yet five years later it was on the cards.

In final year, I shared rooms with Jay, still my oldest mate from college and the man who convinced me two years previously to go for pure economics. I had been unimpressed by academics at Trinity for my first two years. The feeling was mutual; we underwhelmed one another. At the end of second year, Jay sat me down and convinced me that there was merit in pure economics. In October of third year I threw myself into economics and, with the invaluable encouragement of our wonderful monetary professor, Dr Antoin Murphy, I began to get a feel for the subject and learned to love it and its strange hiero-glyphics. Antoin was generous with his time and kindled in me a fascination with the subject. In later years, particularly in the last decade, we have tended to be on opposite sides of the economics debate, but this reveals his success in fostering freethinking questioning and argument.

The possibilities of economics as a way of looking at the world excited me, but even then I was aware that the deeper I got into the subject academically, the less likely I was to use it in any meaningful way. The chances of getting a job as an economist were remote. As I began to crack the code of economics, I was happy and rather unfashionably keen to spend hours in the library reading the greats, Keynes, Hayek, Marx, Smith, Kindleberger, Friedman, Ricardo and Marshall. It is hard now to describe the excitement of discovering these bril-liant thinkers and their world views. The great learning opportunity that is university became apparent to me and this discovery in my third and fourth years was so much more fulfilling than the aimless dossing of the first two.

In final year, living in rooms in Botany Bay meant the city was our oyster. To say that the Dublin of 1988 was down at heel is an understatement. There was an overwhelming smell of hops from the Guinness brewery in the air. The city itself felt homeless, dilapidated and crumbling. But its pubs were outstanding. My favourite was Kehoe's. One of the 'tribe', usually Shane Henderson, was dispatched early every Friday to secure the snug and, once secured, it was defended stoutly. Old Mr Kehoe stood, ramrod-stiff behind the bar, and watched over us paternally as the place filled up with Doc Martens, Morrissey quiffs and long black overcoats smelling of damp student and coal. Dublin then was asphyxiated with dirty coal and in the cold of winter the place stank of slag.

To me the old city was the centre of the known world. We would leave rooms for the last pint every night, heading west to the Stag's or the nether regions of pre-Temple Bar, from there to the Granary or, if we were feeling particularly adventurous, out to the far west and The Lord Edward. Of course, we could go east to Lincoln's Inn, south to Kehoe's or north to Mulligan's. All points of the compass were served. Some popular spots were out of bounds. For some reason I was barred from the Bailey for years. Redheaded boys get their fair share of grief from bouncers as a general rule in Dublin, but I must have done something unspeakable in the Bailey. It didn't bother me, as in the late 1980s the punters in there always tried a bit too hard. Those who weren't in the Hothouse Flowers wanted to be – and with good reason; the Flowers, led by the messianic Liam Ó Maonlaí and sometimes featuring the mesmeric Maria Doyle on vocals, were at their zenith.

Musically, there was plenty going on in and out of Trinity. Unfortunately, this was the era of Stock Aitken Waterman, Rick Astley and Billy Ocean, so the musical world was in danger of drowning in a sea of schmaltz. But it was also the time of Talking Heads' *Stop Making Sense* at the Ambassador, Prince's *Sign 'O' the Times*, and REM's *Green*. And, of course, U2 were beginning their worldwide ascent – inconceivably, for most of us, from Dublin.

The highlight for live music was the Trinity Ball, but we saw The Clash and The Smiths at the SFX. My own personal favourite venue was the long-gone TV Club on Harcourt Street, where a few of the 'tribe' headed to see Stiff Little Fingers in their brilliant *No Sleep 'Til Belfast* live tour in 1988. However, it was those summers spent in New York that changed the way we listened to music. Coming back to a Dublin that seemed to be permanently on a depressed Joy Division soundtrack, we were armed with hip-hop records and the likes of Eric B. & Rakim. And the places to listen to and discover new music were the short-lived but brilliant and (for us, at least) very hip club Fresh in McGonagle's every Thursday night, or later Sides in Dame Street, where the first house beats of what was to become dance music were played in the guise of S-Express.

Naturally, I had my heart broken once or twice and had the intense, argumentative, first real love affair where the world stood still and then began to spin. I can recall the butterflies in my stomach as I caught a glimpse of her heading into the library and me sitting on the chocolate boxes of the Arts Block, smoking Marlboro Reds, trying to looking cool as fuck while inside I was dying. We've all been there, trying to act nonchalant and aloof, perfecting the 'Trinity Snub', that horrible casual insult where people pretended they didn't know each other. There was me giving the Trinity Snub to the most beautiful thing in the world when all I really wanted was to drag her back to my rooms like a victorious Neanderthal. Worst of all, it never crossed my mind that that is exactly what she wanted, too, until she told me months later. All that wasted time.

The clock was ticking. Happily cloistered within the high walls of College Park on early summers' evenings, sun high in the sky, drinking pints in the Pav, watching cricket, a game I never understood, it seemed that we were in a paradise. Few of us realized quite how much of a paradise it was until six months later, two hundred feet under on the Tube, going to a badly paid job with only three weeks' holidays, Trinity was over and the real world had started.

Two and a half decades later, telling a white lie to a nun in black is one of the smartest things I have done in my life – a life that has been enhanced enormously by four years at Trinity.

David McWilliams (TCD 1984–8; Economics) is one of Ireland's leading commentators and best-selling non-fiction author, publishing **The Pope's Children** in 2007. He was nominated as a Young Global Leader by the World Economic Forum at Davos in 2007. A regular contributor to radio and TV, he is also a columnist for the **Sunday Business Post** and the **Irish Independent**. He has brought economics to the national theatre with his one-man-show **Outsiders**, and also wrote and presented the documentary **Addicted to Money** for ABC Australia. He is behind the Global Irish Forum and is co-founder with his wife Sian of the Dalkey Book Festival.

David McWilliams (right) *and Jay Bourke in Moscow, 1987. A statue of Marx is in the background.*

POLITICS AND PARTIES

ivana bacik

I STARTED college in 1985 aged seventeen, full of excitement and anticipation. Having been at an all-girls secondary school, the prospect of sitting in a
class among real boys was immensely challenging. Trinity did not disappoint.
From that very first day walking under Front Arch into the frantic madness of
Freshers' Week, I was caught up in the temptations offered by student societies
trying to entice impressionable young minds. It was a whirlwind of new experiences and chance meetings with fascinating and unexpected new people.
After the happenings of that first week, we all assumed that the lectures might
be rather an anti-climax. But, happily, the Law School was a very exciting place
to be a student in the late eighties.

Among our lecturers was Mary Robinson, very well known by that time
for her battles for liberal law reform and women's rights, who taught a subject
that everyone said was up and coming: European community law! Another
highly political figure in the Law School was Kader Asmal who taught international law and labour law. His lectures brought a real sense of political
engagement. As head of the Irish Anti-Apartheid Movement, we knew he was
involved with the ANC, but as students we did not realize just how active he
had been until many years later when he became Minister for Water Affairs
in the first post-apartheid government in South Africa. He was subsequently

appointed Minister for Education, a post he held with distinction and great zeal for reform. He died in 2011, and we have instituted a scholarship in his name in the Law School.

Another highly revered lecturer was Professor William Duncan, who taught family law and has subsequently become internationally renowned in legal circles for his work on The Hague Convention on Children's Rights. We were also fortunate to be lectured by both Gerry Whyte and Gerard Hogan, who had together taken up the vitally important legal work of authoring later editions of Kelly's leading text on the constitution – Mr Justice Gerard Hogan is now a judge of the High Court, and Professor Gerry Whyte has just completed a term as dean of students at Trinity. Professor Yvonne Scannell brought a warmth and wit to her contract lectures that is still appreciated by students today. Our youthful criminal-law lecturer was Mary McAleese.

Not only were our lectures steeped in political theory and debate, but I soon found that student political life was intensely exciting. Friends who were active with me in the Socialist Society persuaded me to join the Labour Party on campus in my second year, aged eighteen. As party leader, Dick Spring was a regular guest speaker. We also engaged with members of the militant tendency, who were openly hostile to Spring's leadership. In addition, we tried to form broad-left alliances, inviting members of other socialist parties and groups to speak. I remember, as chairperson of the Labour Society in my final year, taking an irate phone call from the Labour general secretary, in which he accused me of fraternizing with the enemy – all because we had invited a Workers' Party TD to address one of our meetings. Of course, this long predated the historic merger between Democractic Left and Labour.

In my final year, I was persuaded to run for election as Students' Union president, having become increasingly involved in the union as class rep, women's-group member and activist. In advance of the hustings, the outgoing SU president gave me the only training in public speaking I have ever had: 'Grip the podium with both hands and scan the audience with your eyes.' I still often think of that advice.

I soon found out how gruelling a Students' Union election campaign can be – with formal hustings, endless rounds of lecture addresses looking for votes, and many late nights plotting strategy. Despite, or because of, all this I was soon hooked on the adrenalin, and was delighted to be elected in March 1989 after a heated campaign. The only downside was that, because I had run in my final year, I had to face immediately into final exams; most of my friends and classmates were emigrating straight afterwards. Around this time, Brian Lenihan Senior had memorably said that 'this island is too small for all of us'. I made regular visits to London to catch up with friends during my year as SU president, and moved there myself once my term of office ended.

It was a particularly intense and difficult year in the union. Teaching term had not even begun in September 1989 when a group called SPUC (Society for the Protection of the Unborn Child) took the four TCD SU officers to court and obtained an order against us, forbidding us from distributing our SU handbooks – because those handbooks contained within them the names, addresses and contact details for abortion clinics in England. Following an earlier High Court judgment, counselling services and women's health clinics had been closed down for providing non-directive counselling to women with crisis pregnancy, and students' unions were the only organizations openly providing this information. The TCD welfare officer, Grainne Murphy, and I used to take five or six phone calls or personal visits every week from distraught women who had nowhere else to turn, and who were desperate for the information. We weren't going to stop helping them just because of a court order – so we continued to distribute contact details for the English clinics when requested.

SPUC duly launched contempt of court proceedings against Grainne, our fellow sabbatical officers – Eoin Lonergan (Education) and Jim Davis (Ents) – and me. We were fortunate to be represented in court by our former law lecturer and Senior Counsel Mary Robinson, who advised us to expect to go to prison for defying the court order. We held a defiant 'last night of freedom' party in my rooms, and marched to the Four Courts followed by thousands of students protesting this gross assault on freedom of speech. Student officers from UCD and the national union, USI, were joined in the case. In an unexpected twist, the late Judge Mella Carroll was allocated to hear our case, and agreed with Mary Robinson that an issue of European law was involved. She directed that the European Court of Justice should rule on the issue and we escaped jail. SPUC, however, appealed the case to the Supreme Court and it dragged on for several more years – long after I had moved to London.

The fallout from the case dominated our time as union officers as it made many headlines – we were profiled in the national media and received a large amount of vile hate mail. My parents' phone number was listed in the directory, and my teenage brother answered the phone one day to be asked by an anonymous caller: 'Is this the abortion clinic?' He courteously and innocently replied that no, it wasn't – but could he help them? When my mother realized that calls like this were being made, the Bacik family swiftly went ex-directory. I was lucky that my parents supported our stance although they were, naturally, very worried by the legal action against us. Other union officers had a much harder time when they faced opposition from their families. I am still very proud of the stance we all took, which helped to bring about later change in the law and public attitudes. I was also very proud that Trinity students overwhelmingly vindicated our stance in a referendum on abortion information that we held during my year as president.

Other political issues were also important to us. We had regular marches and several occupations of college buildings (memorably the Accommodation Office in West Chapel in 1988) in protest at the yearly increases in fees. We ran boycotts of the Buttery in protest at catering prices; and I led a group of law students to demonstrate outside the Law Society in Blackhall Place in 1989 to protest at the restrictive entry practices of that institution. We were proud of being the only place in Ireland (apart from the Virgin Megastore) with a condom-vending machine – this was housed in 'Mandela House' (as the SU office in House 6 had been renamed by referendum the previous year) and was constantly being vandalized.

Other political issues exercised us beyond the campus. Not only were there endless debates on the 'National Question' (as Northern Ireland was usually called then) at most union meetings, but the student co-op members in the JCR above Front Arch refused to serve anything but Nicaraguan coffee. Of course, nobody would touch South African oranges – and there was heated debate about the sale of tuna in the SU shop.

But we also found plenty of time for fun. With my friend and co-conspirator, Eva Doyle, I set up a College Decadent Society towards the end of our first year – we blew all the membership funds on a great chocolate éclair-eating festival in the Buttery. A few of us in the Socialist Society took over the College

Croquet Club, attracted by the free Pimm's that the committee received every year courtesy of a sponsorship deal with Mitchell's wine merchants. We actually became very fond of the game and even helped to popularize it on campus where it is flourishing to this day. I was a regular attender at Ents gigs and at parties thrown by the Law Soc and the Gay Soc, among others, and, of course, got to as many Trinity Balls as I could – one of the best live performances I can remember was by the Dubliners, who played a storming set one year with the late great Ronnie Drew blasting out surprisingly dancey numbers.

Like most law students, I was also very involved in the Hist and Phil debating societies, although frequently finding their meetings (and some of their members) unbearably pompous. I spoke occasionally at the Hist, and was delighted to hear some great speakers in the GMB – notably the fiery orator Arthur Scargill, fresh from the battles of the miners' strike in Britain. I also protested outside the Phil one evening in December 1988 against the Holocaust denier and fascist agitator David Irving. So many of us came out to object at his presence that the meeting had to take place off-campus.

Another memorable evening the same year, this time at the Hist, was when Gerry Adams came to speak. It was the first time he had spoken publicly in Trinity, and as Section 31 of the Broadcasting Act was still in force, none of us knew what his voice actually sounded like. Security was intense and the place was crawling with Special Branch, but we managed to creep into the crammed chamber through a window to hear what turned out to be a most underwhelming speech. In all my years in college, the best speaker I heard was Tony Benn, who came over as a guest of the Labour Society in 1990. Having heard all about the SPUC case, he turned to me at the start of his inspiring talk and said, 'Don't let the bastards grind you down.' Another sound piece of advice, with general application.

It was easy to get ground down by student politics – I still believe no other type of politics is quite as intense. Union officers in Trinity are privileged with free rooms on campus but it means that you are surrounded by, and living among, your constituents all the time; there is literally no escape. I was fortunate to be sharing rooms on the top floor of House 10 in Front Square with my friend Cathy Conlon. She was the women's officer of the Students' Union but also a leading light in Players, so I regularly used to escape from the hothouse atmosphere of the SU and nip across to the dingy Players Theatre. Cathy and I also enjoyed hosting parties and at four or five o'clock in the morning we were often to be found sharing gossip and conducting a serious post-mortem on the events of the night before, as we washed up the glasses and peeled various bodies off the floor. Happy days!

Looking back now I can see that Trinity in the eighties, like Dublin more generally then, was often a shabby and down-at-heel sort of place. Nobody had any money, and we all expected to emigrate. But it was also an exciting and edgy time to be a student in the city. Before the gentrification of Temple Bar, there were funky places like the co-op in the Dublin Resource Centre and Sides nightclub on Dame Street – Dublin's first real gay club. For several years I had a part-time waitressing job at MacArthur's restaurant and steakhouse, also on Dame Street. Its exterior featured in the classic eighties film *Educating Rita* – we had a photo of Michael Caine proudly displayed inside. As this was next door to Sides, we waitresses were able to get free entry after hours. More happy days and late nights!

It's easy to be nostalgic now about a time in the history of Trinity and Dublin when we were all students together, having fun and making lifelong friends – a time, which, in retrospect, appears rather innocent. But it was also a hard time economically and socially, a time when Irish society was much more intolerant and inward-looking, with levels of political corruption and of institutional child abuse that are only now being exposed. Unemployment and emigration levels were higher than they are even now with our current economic difficulties, and people generally had much lower expectations from life. I'm glad things have changed, and very glad that we have moved on as a society in many ways – but I'm also very glad to have had the opportunity to be a Trinity student in the grim but groovy 1980s!

Ivana Bacik (TCD 1985–9; Law) was president of the Students' Union. In 1989, she and her fellow union officers were taken to court by SPUC (Society for the Protection of the Unborn Child) and threatened with prison for distributing information on abortion. The case was referred to the European Court of Justice and they escaped prison but created a legal precedent. Ivana qualified in London as a barrister before returning to Dublin to practise law, and to teach, first at the National College of Industrial Relations and then at Trinity, where she is now Reid Professor of Criminal Law and a fellow. She was elected to the Seanad to represent Dublin University in 2007 and re-elected in 2011, and is now deputy leader of Seanad Éireann. She lives in central Dublin with her partner Alan and their two daughters.

PLAYERS PLEASE, THEY TASTE BETTER

leslie williams

I ENTERED Trinity in 1986 to study philosophy and medieval and Renaissance English, but in reality I was in Trinity to become an actor.

DU Players was said to be as good a place to learn the craft of acting as any drama school – which was good news given that I had failed to get into the one I auditioned for earlier in the summer. So as soon as I had enrolled on that sunny October day in Freshers' Week, I went straight to the Players' stand with my £1 note and listened with enthusiasm as I was told of the dozens of plays that would be performed that year and (even better) how there would be a party on the last night of every run.

This great acting career I was about to pursue did not get off to the best of starts, as I failed to get a part in the Freshers' Co-op a week later. The Co-op is always the first play performed and is designed to have dozens of roles for Junior Freshmen to break them in gently and to help get their faces known.

My old school friend Tom Murphy did get a part, of course; in fact, I think Tom got almost every part he auditioned for during his time in Players. He went on to star in dozens of films and television programmes including RTÉ's *Pure Mule* and *Adam & Paul*. He also won a Tony on Broadway in Garry

Hynes' production of *The Beauty Queen of Leenane* and we remained close friends until his untimely death aged just thirty-nine.

Productions were reviewed without fail in *The Irish Times* and occasionally in the other national newspapers, and many shows attracted the general public as well as students. Dublin's theatre world was smaller in those days and student theatre could get itself noticed. An adaptation of the film *Casablanca* ran twice, first in Players and later in the Atrium to packed houses, making more money than many a play in the professional world. *Casablanca* starred Gary Cooke (of *Aprés Match* fame) as Rick and was conceived, produced and directed by Claire Kearney and the brothers Clancy (Tomás, Neil and Luke). Approximately forty plays were produced every year, so I was confident I would get a part eventually.

After a few more failed auditions, Tom advised me to begin helping out backstage to get my face known and at the very least get to attend some of the parties. Tom's advice worked, and early in Hilary Term I got my first role as Chaps in the Noël Coward one-act play, *Ways and Means*. I acted alongside some of Players' finest actors, including Tom Clinch. I remember he had an ashtray that read 'Players Please, They Taste Better'. The play went well and despite this first role and some other parts over the next year or two, I soon realized that I was not actually talented enough, or, more importantly, driven enough, to make it as an actor. But I resolved that Players was as good a place as any to hang out. I acted in around a dozen plays over the next four years and in my final year I was on the Players' committee.

My final year in Trinity allowed me to properly develop a creative outlet as an alternative to my failed acting career – I discovered that I not only loved to cook but became obsessively interested in everything food- and drink-related. Room 34.1.2 in New Square was the scene of memorable parties mostly held jointly with our neighbour, Emily. Our most memorable was a 'Concubine and Catamite Party', the name intended as an instruction to wear something outrageous. I particularly remember Sarah Clarke's red rubber dress and Gavin Quinn (now of Pan Pan Theatre) dressed fully in skiwear. Inevitably, we were busted and reported to the Junior Dean, Seán Barrett. When Dr Barrett came with the head of housekeeping the next day we had every room immaculate except for the floors, which I was in the process of washing. Sadly, this filth was a dead giveaway and all the evidence of debauchery he needed.

We were ordered to his office the following day, each made enter individually and leave by another door to ensure we did not confer or change our story. Emily went in first and insisted that no more than four people had been in her room, much to Dr Barrett's frustration (more than five people in a room constituted a party according to the college rulebook). When I came in, Dr Barrett refused to look at me but pretended to write furiously on an A4 pad.

'This was a fancy dress party, I gather?'

'Yes, a concubine and catamite party,' I replied.

This did the trick. He stopped writing, looked me straight in the eye for the first time and with alarm in his voice asked: 'Did you say CONCUBINE?' I reassured him that it had not been an orgy and he fined me £50 and ordered my stereo system removed from the campus. Through the mediation of our Students' Union president at the time, Ivana Bacik, he rescinded the stereo ban after approximately two weeks.

I have fond memories of Trinity Week and the Yard of Ale and Iron Stomach contests, which I was too chicken to enter, and the annual Twenty-Four-Hour Shakespeare, which Players performed every year. One year our chairman, Gemma Russell Brown, controversially (and to howls of protest) suggested we do a Twenty-Four-Hour Irish Drama marathon, which turned out to be one of her best ideas. I have a strong memory of performing Frank McGuinness' *Observe the Sons of Ulster Marching Towards the Somme* on the steps of the 1937 Reading Room at around one in the morning, to a snogging couple and a few heckling drunks. My one lead role in my four years was when Martin Devaney kindly cast me as Bob in his production of Peter Shaffer's *The Private Ear,* which we performed in Lombard Street Studios in what is now the Green on Red Gallery.

Academically I was a reasonably good student but I must confess that, despite the concerted efforts of Mr J.D. Pheiffer, I failed to learn more than a few words of Anglo-Saxon, sneaking through the exams that first summer by learning the translations by heart. Mr Pheiffer was my tutor and perhaps (after Dominic West) the most charming man in college. Snippets of Bill Lyons' lectures on philosophy of mind and Professor Scattergood's on Shakespeare's history plays remain with me. Eiléan Ní Chuilleanáin's lectures on many things left an impression, but in particular those lectures on Milton. I had admitted to her at the end of my Junior Sophomore year that I had managed to avoid Milton up to that point and she asked me if I honestly wanted to have a degree in English from Trinity College Dublin and yet admit that I had not studied Milton. 'Besides, he's great, you'll love him!' she said confidently. She was right – I did love him and still sometimes read him.

An arts degree is, on the face of it, a rather useless thing in terms of life skills and for many of us in the 1980s going to college was little more than a way of postponing emigration. I was lucky and managed to stay in Ireland but my time in Trinity could not have been better spent. Yes, I whiled away hours drinking pints in the Buttery and drinking terrible coffee in the Arts Block, but I do not think this was time wasted.

I heard a joke recently – How do you know somebody went to Trinity? It's easy: they tell you! And it's true. Who wouldn't want to tell people they went to Trinity?

Leslie Williams (TCD 1986–90; Philosophy and Medieval and Renaissance English) worked in public relations for a short number of years before becoming a freelance journalist specializing in food and wine. Leslie teaches courses in wine appreciation and has regular columns in the **Evening Herald** and the **Irish Examiner**. He is also a contributing editor to the **McKenna Guides to Irish Food**.

AUTUMN TESTAMENT

michael west

BLUE SKIES, leaves turning, the nights drawing in. Forget the Gregorian calendar: September is the real start to the year. This sense was particularly keen for me in my first term at Trinity, having returned from two years at a United World College in New Mexico – a peculiar educational sidestep I felt conferred a faint, exotic glamour to even the simplest tasks, such as taking the 46A or getting lost on campus.

Apart from early-onset nostalgia for Indian summers in Dublin, the immediate legacy of my time in the Rockies was a failure to possess the minimum maths qualification for entrance, a failure I grasped fully the moment I sat down and read my International Baccalaureate Subsidiary Level Paper in the Castle Ballroom in Montezuma.

'It wasn't that I hated the subject,' I explained over the phone to my former maths teacher back in Ireland, 'Or that I was bad at it. It was that I hadn't done any work.' There was a long pause before my father made a fairly tight-lipped comment and hung up.

So my first examination in Trinity was a humble O level, taken in the Exam Hall. Armed with that and the rump of my International Baccalaureate, I would be allowed in. But to do what?

I had applied to do English and Russian. This seemed a perfect match: I was genuinely keen on literature I could read, while Russian was to impress my parents with the intellectual seriousness of my incompetence.

While I waited for the results of my various experiments in avoiding the Leaving, I heard of a new course in drama that had started while I was away. With sickening certainty I knew I'd made a terrible mistake with Russian. *Russian?* What was I thinking? Miraculously, it was still possible to change my mind. Acceptance to the new department was held by interview in a decidedly old building on Westland Row. Strictly speaking, the School of Drama appeared to be a semi-derelict house, nestled under a grimy railway bridge over which trundled the new-fangled, green DART trains. I was shown into a small, dark room in which there were six plastic chairs and a very agitated Frenchman looking at a map.

'*Parlez-vous français?*' he asked.

I had no idea what an interview for a drama school would consist of, but I had heard of improvisation and role play and I was game. I didn't want to go back to *Russia*. '*Oui*,' I carefully replied and shook his hand. Thierry and I laid the map out on the table and got to work. I was quite proud of my French, but I'd a much weaker grasp of character and motivation. We kept at it, me pretending to help him find the way to somewhere, he pretending to find my questions about his origins and family anything other than extremely perplexing. His anxiety increased. I tried to put him at his ease by 'using the space' and calling him by his name at every opportunity, 'Thierry, Thierry, why are any of us here?'

Abruptly he ended the scene, took up a backpack and went out into the street, slamming the door behind him. He was clearly more experienced than I was.

I was taken upstairs for the second part of my interview. The headquarters of the School of Drama consisted of two small, carpeted rooms that would normally be described as bedsits. Or cupboards. In one of them I talked to the other two members of the department, Steve Wilmer and John McCormick, about plays I had seen and plays I had been in – probably the same number of each. The conversation was much easier in English though it had its own challenges. Steve Wilmer was tall and American. John McCormick wore black leather pants. At the last moment I remembered to say I wanted to write for theatre. Actually, 'remembered' is the wrong word. 'Discovered' would be more accurate since, although I instantly knew it to be true, it hadn't occurred to me to say it before.

I was accepted into the Drama Department and I never found out what happened to Thierry. Our first class was held in the back half of the adjoining rooms where I had last seen him. Thierry's side of the room was now the costume or set workshop depending on who was standing by the table. This was very much Clodagh McCormick's domain. She provided all the costumes for all the productions all year round and in tech weeks would occasionally emerge from the sweatshop, smiling and only moderately flustered, to ask a passer-by, 'What size is your head?' or 'Are you good at standing still?' In the classroom itself, lectures had to pause every eight minutes while a passing DART made the walls shake and the filthy windows buzz. We started with Scandinavians: our first class involved a screening of Donal McCann and Helen Mirren in Strindberg's *Miss Julie*. Now *this* was education.

I'd been too scared so far to go into Players' miniscule theatre. I felt the same way about Bewley's for over a year: they would somehow *know* you didn't belong and you would be asked to leave. But in a cunning marketing ploy, our class was offered a discount and I went to see StrangeDays – a summer fit-up company spin-off of Players – present *The Physicists*, featuring Graham Arnold, Robert Caskey and Sian Maguire, with Paul Keogan as a female psychiatric nurse. Many remarkable people passed through No. 4, some famous today, some inexplicably not. But my first impression was that the place was a tiny, shabby, splintery kip. I practically lived there until Christmas.

I was involved in five productions in my first term, possibly because it was easier to be involved – in whatever capacity – than to be in the audience. Discovering that there was a way to cross the stage via a cluttered crawl space underneath, I impaled my foot on a nail, which slightly muted the effect of my entrance and ruined my only pair of shoes. A year or so later somebody used the same pile of wood and old curtains to set the place on fire and Players had to go on tour to the GMB, the Arts Block and Lombard Street. The glamour was endless.

Over the Christmas break, we rehearsed *Icarus's Mother*, an early Shepard play, up in 4.3.2.A, the room at the top of the building above Players. Our cast comprised Karen Ardiff, Gary Cooke, Cathy Conlon and Tom Murphy. Jim Culleton was the director. Back then, a Sunday winter night in Dublin was as dark and empty as under a curfew and the light up in the top corner room was probably the only one visible from College Green. But up there we were, lying on our backs on the cold, dusty floor pretending it was a hot summer's day. I had a long speech I dreaded at the end of the play about watching a plane crash into the sea.

At some point we realized that the atmosphere had changed – not the kind of change where theatre takes you to another world, but one where the world brings you back. The light outside had shifted, the sound of sporadic traffic had gradually fallen away. It was snowing. Proper snow. Big, dry flakes tumbling silently all around.

We finished our rehearsal, stopping on the stairs on the way down to look out the window over Front Square. It was vast, deserted and white. And when we trudged outside, ours were the only footprints in the entire hushed landscape.

In our family, Trinity was a mythical place where my parents had met and my uncle lived and worked when he wasn't in Cork. My first conscious experience of it began at a party in Trevor West's rooms in 1984 before I headed off to New Mexico. I had seen *A Woman of No Importance*, which marked the revolutionary beginning of Michael Colgan's tenure at the Gate, and met its director, a gracious Patrick Mason, sitting on the arm of a sofa in Rubrics. The place was full of academics and writers and sports people, though I knew none of them. My uncle was very enthusiastic about my imminent departure. It was entirely characteristic of him that he would have been there and knew somebody on the ground.

Trevor was a legendary figure in academic, sport and college life and it was astonishing to think I not only knew him but was related to him. An anticipated pleasure of returning to Dublin and Trinity was to engage with him if not on equal terms, at least on the same ground. I saw him walk briskly across Front Square in my first week or so as a student.

'Hello, Trevor,' I called.

'Michael, you idiot,' he replied, walking firmly past.

I took it to mean I had come home.

IN OCTOBER of my second year I met Lenny Abrahamson. Trevor introduced us: 'Lenny, you're a bollocks. This is my goon of a nephew.' We instantly became friends and later shared rooms together, first in Botany Bay and then in Rubrics.

'Having rooms' was the Holy Grail for a commuting student with no means. Aesthetically Spartan, with shared toilets and running water a recent addition, 'rooms' meant you didn't have to submit to the humiliating last bus ride home and the bourgeois oppression of breakfast. I was regularly kipping on floors and sofas by this stage, so a gas fire and a cold bed in the middle of town – in the middle of college – was a thrilling luxury. In our final year, Lenny and I shared rooms in No. XXV, directly above George Dawson who could be met frequently labouring up the wooden stairs.

Among his many achievements, George started Trinity's Genetics Department and the Douglas Hyde Gallery, secured the modern sculptures on campus, and instituted the paintings-to-rent scheme for students. His rooms, which he described as a 'student bedsit', were one of the treasures of college – a single room spanning the width of the narrow building, with six windows to show off his personal collection, including works by Braque, Miró, Apfel, Jellet and Gerda Fromel, and a collection of eighteenth-century Irish glasses and modern glassware by Fromel's son, Killian Schurmann. The room had glass tables and original Danish wicker chairs and a fantastically uncomfortable chrome and black leather couch, the cushions of which would leap into the air if you attempted to sit down.

The exploding couch was also extremely difficult to get out of once you got into it and George himself, fairly wobbly on his pins at the best of times, would sometimes simply give up after a couple of attempts, sigh, and raise his hands in defeat.

His hands were enormous with long, tapered fingers, which his style of smoking put to particular effect. Owing to cancer George had had his palate removed; in its place he had a plate with teeth attached, which, I suppose, stopped food coming out of his nose. Lacking the necessary soft tissue, he was unable to get the suction required to inhale. To compensate, he would wedge a cigarette between the base of his index and middle fingers and then close off his nostrils with the tips of those fingers by pinching them and his top lip together while he sucked in the air with a gristly wheeze. On top of this, George had metal plates in his head from a fall off a horse and most of his intestine removed. He had cataracts and developed diabetes, which led to having a toe removed every other year. 'I really shouldn't be here,' he would say between puffs, 'and most of me isn't.' He would then let out one of his staccato, cackling laughs. In such moments his rooms resembled nothing so much as a Bond villain's lair.

By far the most remarkable thing about George's rooms was that he let me stay in them. Ostensibly, this was to write. Mostly, though, I hung out and received. Having one of the only TVs on campus, it was an extremely popular choice of venue for Ireland versus England in Italia 90, with supporters of both persuasions. Dominic West insisted on hanging a Union Jack out the window but it was removed to the bathroom 'for its own safety'. Kevin Sheedy's equalizer almost destroyed thousands of pounds' worth of Abstract Expressionism – not to mention the glasses.

For a year, one floor down from George lived John McGahern, where he worked on *Amongst Women*. His predecessor as writer-in-residence had been Tom McIntyre, whose collaboration with Patrick Mason and Tom Hickey and cast on Kavanagh's *The Great Hunger* remains a highlight of that time. McIntyre, for his stint in college, had required portfolios from the willing and selected a handful of those he felt met his requirements. My tortured poems didn't make the cut.

The following year it was announced that McGahern would meet *all* those who submitted writings in whatever genre, form or state in an anonymous room in the Arts Block, and return their efforts personally. He was an experienced teacher and an unprepossessing character, arriving on time and assuming a seat at the front with an alarming lack of pomp or ceremony. About forty candidates from the entire student body had braved the prospect of rejection. He began by welcoming everyone and said he was unqualified to judge anyone's work. He then handed back, envelope by envelope, the students' work. Some people left after receiving theirs. Some stayed. It was all very informal and hardly a lecture or unforgiving masterclass. Being so disarmed I was slightly bored and gently panicked. Hadn't he got my stuff? The room held only three or four of us when the pile was finished. Mine was the very last.

I went up to the table and John McGahern said, 'I liked your poems. But then I know nothing about poetry.'

The next class was held in his rooms in Rubrics. About a dozen of us showed up. The week after there was even fewer. The sessions must have involved some of us reading something at some point, but I've no recollection of it now and felt little desire at the time to submit to the process. This was not because the atmosphere was in the least threatening or intimidating. It was really that it was so much more interesting to listen to this professed non-teacher talk. He spoke about books, of course. But also about writers and their antics (usually bad). He would tell a story as if he couldn't be sure he'd got it right and then suddenly ask, 'What do you think he meant by that?' He talked about publishing. Money. Drink. Politics. People. He told marvellous stories that crept up on you, that seemed to wander off to an ending that was anticlimactic or unresolved, but would suddenly switch back on you and provoke a bark of laughter or wonderment.

From the beginning he said that writing couldn't be taught. I only partially understood at the time that instead he was teaching us how to behave: how to talk to people, how to be in a room with your work, how to be sceptical of those in power, how to be generous and respectful of others. Of course, he wouldn't have put it like that himself; there was nothing of the guru about him. It was simply apparent in his bearing and conversation.

It was the first time I was in the presence of a real writer, a proper artist at the height of his powers. He spoke of his own work honestly and without preciousness. He didn't talk much about it. Although he was very generous to me and interested in what I read and rated, he wasn't all that interested in what I wrote. I realized that this was partly because I wasn't that interested in it myself. My clotted poems fell away.

Having the odd drink with him about town, it was clear John McGahern knew barmen all over the city. And cinema ushers. And front-of-house staff at theatres. And the porters in college. And old colleagues from his teaching days. And people up from the country. He was artlessly direct with everyone, but never less than shrewd about what they were really up to. He was interested in sport and what people did with their time, in everyday tragedies and acts of kindness or bravery. I learned from him that it was possible to be a writer and not be a total wanker about it, that the task was far simpler than I gave it credit for and more difficult than I had ever imagined.

He talked openly about getting fired and banned, utterly frankly and without rancour. He was appalled by the cruelty of the Church and some of its more repellant servants but wasn't anti-clerical or disrespectful of it, either. Looking back, the 1980s was a rather frighteningly grim and depressed decade, though that's not how it felt to those of us coming of age. Church and state were positively obsessed with the human body and what it could legally do and with whom. In this, of course, Church and state shared a great deal in common with students who thought of little else themselves – and this led to a slightly false, comforting, antinomian sense of morality. (Whatever 'they' want is wrong.)

As we now know, the relentless general elections, the referenda on divorce, abortion and Europe, not to mention the hysterical venting of traditional values, only served to underline that the great unravelling of the Church's power had begun. The idea that a baggy-jumpered student activist like Ivana Bacik could by simple defiance threaten the national legislature and convulse the nation seemed both rather wonderful and preposterous at the same time. It was illegal to display a phone number. Condoms were not allowed, but you could buy them in a record store. Homosexuality was a J1 visa to damnation. It was acceptable to die in childbirth of preventable causes. It was a land of moving statues and immoveable statutes; Archbishop McQuaid's tentacles still stretched through Dublin and Trinity seemed like an oasis of enlightenment.

When I joined Players, the lunchtime slot was defined by the 2 pm Holy Hour, one of the said archbishop's attempts to encourage temperance among travelling salesmen. By the mid eighties this meant a play starting at 1 pm had to come down before the shutters of the nearest pub. If you got the timing right you'd find yourself locked in, with no hope of escape or chance of attending lectures for a glorious hour. If that was an example of the accommodation of repressive legislation with Irish alcoholism, it seemed a commodious fit. Ireland was broke and corrupt and the malign influence of the Church had to be resisted on all fronts, particularly if it involved drinking pints.

The position of right-thinking liberal was so easily adopted, at such little cost and with so little need for introspection, it lent an aura of implausibility and undergraduate silliness to the whole period. The preposterous Holocaust denier, David Irving, was invited over by contrarian fifth columnists in one of the debating societies. We, the student body – the same people who marched for freedom on the streets – howled in protest and marched around campus to deny him the right to speak. If he'd brought books to sign I've no doubt they would have been burnt in an orgy of censorship, the smoke from which would have delighted the unlamented McQuaid.

In spite of such rare examples of campus *kulturkampf*, Trinity was a fairly startlingly homogenous body. In this aspect, if nothing else, it was a microcosm of Ireland – but to me it seemed rich and 'incorrigibly plural'. If the wider context showed a country still locked in the darker aspects of the fifties, Trinity offered a more positive model of an intimate acquaintance with the immediate and deeper past.

And, of course, that's how it lives on for those of us fortunate enough to attend. I still read and reread many authors and books I first encountered there, and life would be unimaginable without them. And the people! Gorgeous, real, live humans: the best kind. I have friends I haven't seen since I left, and some I see every day. There are plenty I don't see nearly often enough and some I will never see again. But almost all my most significant relationships date from those few terms in that enclosed world, including my brother-in-law, Michael Hinds, and my wife, Annie Ryan, who came over for a year more than twenty years ago.

A lasting satisfaction, one of the most durable pleasures from those years, is seeing people who have gone on to do what they said they'd do, who have applied hard work to what was often outrageous talent or college bravado.

Some of my intimate acquaintances, like Gemma Bodinetz, Annie Ryan, Lenny Abrahamson and Dominic West are well known in their fields, but there were many others studying theatre, literature, medicine, physics, law, classics, history and whatever ESS consisted of who have gone on to confer retrospective prescience to those early claims for brilliance. Of course, most of the time things never work out quite how they're supposed to.

But for a couple of years, a handful of seasons, a clatter of terms, we had a chance to live with an imagined future. Every autumn gives it another shake. And every September still quickens the blood.

Photograph courtesy of Jonathan Shankey.

Michael West (TCD 1986–90; English and Drama) is a playwright. His latest play is **Conservatory**. He is currently teaching playwriting at the Lir Academy, Dublin, and is adjunct lecturer in drama at Trinity.

I WENT TO TRINITY, BUT ...

brian f. o'byrne

THAT'S HOW I answer any question regarding college. And I did go to Trinity. But.

I should start by saying I failed my Leaving Cert. That's important. I'm not sure you can fail it nowadays, but I failed it when you could. I will add I was also nominated for Student of the Year at my school when I failed it. Some mysteries in life are best left alone.

Failing meant that my parents somehow managed to gather money to send me to Dublin to 'repeat' in a fancy establishment on Leeson Street. I'm from Mullagh. It wasn't a shock so much as a curiosity. There were all sorts there: non-Irish, and Irish who didn't seem like Irish. To me, anyway. They all seemed to be from the south side. They all needed more 'points'. I'm not sure I met any failures like me, not that I remember. They all wanted to go to Trinity. All of them. With their polo-shirt collars turned up. And the girls wore make-up and smoked. And they all drank beers at the weekend. And they all already knew each other.

I would wait for the 46A to go home to my aunt's house, leaning against that thick Trinity wall on Nassau Street, peering between the railings. Keeping it safe from us. Gazing in at, in truth, not too much. I kept waiting for the moment when the cricketers would be playing and I could view what order and civilization looked like. And intellect. My background was Junior B football. Cavan Junior B football. But all I seemed to see were lonely silhouettes. Shuffling. In that smart, shuffling way. Not the 'I'm lonely and this country is the greyest place on the planet' shuffle. The 'inside the walls' shuffle.

The first four months in Dublin went well, my grades were good, I complied. But then I discovered cinema, and drink, and a girl who wouldn't put out. She had a boyfriend 'at home' down the country. I'm sure she put out with him. And she was going to go to Trinity. Dentistry. I could now look from the bus stop and see where she would be going. Look at the guys she would be putting out with.

I didn't fail my second Leaving Cert. I almost did, but I didn't. I tore up the results and just told my parents I did all right. I ended up in Coolock. Trinity College is not in Coolock. I was supposed to be studying communications in a secondary school with a pre-college programme. Instead, I met a great bunch of misfits. I drank, and smoked some hash. I met two particular reprobates named Brian and Declan, who liked Converse runners and Doc Martens, and our one-hour drama class. They heard about a new course in Trinity, a drama school, at the Samuel Beckett Centre. They wanted to audition.

We were in our Harris-tweed, long-coat phase. Rolling our own. We were living together. We were renting a TV and VCR, watching Woody Allen movies and a lot of dull French stuff. We would wait by a coal fire at night and charge upstairs to our freezing rooms as the last ember went out. If they were going to Trinity what the hell would I do? Join them?

And here is the stain on Trinity's history. This was not a degree course. It was not academic. It was a two-year diploma course in the mode of a British drama conservatory. Some of the kids may have failed their Leaving Cert.

We all auditioned. Having done a 'modern' piece (Pinter, I believe), I stood in a black-box theatre on Lombard Street with my right arm in the air at a 45-degree angle, desperately trying to remember the third word of my Shakespeare monologue. After many attempts, my raised arm never moving, the director of the course, Michael Joyce, sat back and asked in an astonished tone why I wasn't prepared. I did what any failed Leaving Cert. wannabe actor-student would do. I lied. Johnny Logan had won the Eurovision the weekend before (true), Ireland was celebrating (true), he was doing a tour of the country playing gigs (true), and I was back-line roadie on the tour (lie). Joyce told me to leave and come back after lunch for one last attempt.

And then I had the highlight of my time in Trinity, before I even went there. It was a beautiful day. I sat on the bough of a tree in one of the squares. I breathed it all in. I thought of the countless students over the centuries who had sat in that same spot, maybe reading the same words (okay, maybe the tree was different). I looked at the buildings; I could feel the knowledge and history they possessed. I read the words of the monologue. I understood most of them. I hoped someone would notice me, reclining, elegant. I felt like I belonged. I sat there thinking if I got in, every day would be like this. And I'd have a girl by my side who thought I was amazing. She'd put out. And I'd know my lines.

After lunch I continued in Lombard Street where I'd left off. I may have gotten to word seven. Michael Joyce told me to step outside and wait with the people who had been called back for the workshop. Dec and Brian were there. We pretended not to know each other. Joyce called everyone in and just looked at me standing on a stairway on my own. I don't know what he saw. 'Come in,' he said. He altered the course of my life. My life for the last twenty-seven years started with those two words. Turns out, theatre workshop games to see can you work with other people are remarkably like the games some people play when they are stoned. We were all accepted. I was going to Trinity. But.

We were told to despise other students, we were told we couldn't join any societies or clubs, we were told to look down on Players, we were told there were too many actors in the world and it didn't need any more, we were told that the next two years would be tougher that anything we would experience in the real world, we were told Trinity hated us. Our space was in Westland Row and Lombard Street. Not in Trinity. You had to pass through a gate to enter Trinity. I was still outside looking in.

We were an odd bunch, ranging in age from eighteen to thirty. Michael Joyce was a brilliant obsessive man, which could make him exhilarating and crushing by turn. He was complemented by a vision named Diana Theadorus, a positive, kind, American movement teacher. None of us really knew what we were doing; this was just the second year of the course's existence. This manifested itself in five of us guys purchasing the required black leotard, dance belt and shoes for our movement class. When we changed in a back room at the Lombard Street studio amongst old sets (no dressing rooms), we commented on how tight the shoulder straps were. After the initial embarrassment of the class facing each other pretending not to notice all the shapes and sizes (these were pre-gym actors), someone pointed out that we had, in fact, purchased women's leotards. We wore them for two years. We had lots of movement classes, and no showers. I can only imagine what the sensitive American nose of Diana had to go through. I don't remember washing much at home, either.

We existed on an island. An incestuous island. The doors of a class were locked thirty minutes before start time to get us used to Theatre Time. If we missed two classes in a row, the class could choose to vote us out. My memory is that I missed one, in order to work for rent money, and the vote wasn't going well for me until Dec and Brian saved the day. The boys and myself lived together, obsessed together, drank together when we could afford it, and were constantly late and a thorn in Joyce's side.

The conception of the Celtic Tiger hadn't even happened yet. Not that I noticed, anyway. Parts of Dublin still looked like they had been bombed during the Second World War. There was grime everywhere. The new coal laws were coming in. People would stand and watch a building being cleaned. They would almost look new. New! Pubs kept early hours. None of us had a future. But you could spend wonderful hours in Bewley's nursing a coffee and rolling cigarettes by the fire. And if you told a very kind lady in Bank of Ireland that your flat had been broken into (true), the door had been broken (true) and you had to pay for it (lie), the eighty pounds loaned to you could be spent over a weekend in the Norseman or the Palace with a gang.

As for studies, we spent months visiting Dublin Zoo to watch a particular animal of our choice (Sebastian the giraffe, RIP) so we could do our 'animal studies', which meant all of us in our 'cages' wearing leotards (women's) 'being' the animal for several hours while people watched. We all went a little mad. When I remember one guy, I don't remember him as a wonderful Irish speaker from the west, I remember him as a squirrel. A squirrel in a woman's leotard. Joyce was a believer in breaking people down in order to build back some kind of blank canvas. A lot of people were broken and not built back. Some beautiful young talented people never acted again. At least, I remember them as talented. Maybe they weren't. They were better than me, though. And definitely more beautiful.

We had nothing to do with Trinity. Nothing. I don't remember meeting anyone who went there, other than ourselves.

I went to the library once. I had to read some existential philosopher; we were in the middle of wonderful Beckett work. I wish I could remember who I was reading, because in an almost white-light moment, all of life made sense on the page in front of me. And then I started to have huge chest pains, which didn't stop. I smiled at the irony of finding the meaning of life, only to have it cruelly taken away, and from one so young. With such potential. I went straight to the doc. He told me to jump in a taxi to the hospital where they would be waiting for me. I went, they were. I had things stuck all over my chest and was left in the room. I contemplated my imminent death. I lay there for a long time. It was pre-cellphone so I couldn't say goodbye to my family. They obviously were finding it tough to find someone to tell me I was about to die.

After about a half-hour some little country nurse stuck her head in and said, 'God, are you still here?' She didn't mean my mortality. I was fine. Acid, or stress. I walked home thinking that the taxi could have bought me a couple of pints.

Turned out I wasn't the only student with the doc that day. Another guy, Tim (wallaby, woman's leotard), had been in with panic attacks and the doc was worried about what was happening on our course. Tim, a deep thinker with a keen intellect, had once, upon being told his eyebrows moved too much, secured said brows with Band-Aids for a week to keep them in check. This seemed like a correct approach that hardly warranted comment.

I did bump into the Dentist Girl (who didn't put out) once, coming out of a dentist pub with all her dentist friends and she dragged me on a bus to Slane where I was the oddity. I seem to remember she was getting engaged or something. Not only did I not feel like we were at the same college, I felt like I may have existed in a different universe.

We finished the two years. We were told to look ourselves in the mirror and with all honesty ask ourselves if we could contribute anything to the acting world. It was an easy answer. No.

I left the country immediately.

I think I was awarded a diploma. I don't know. I never received one. I have not kept in contact with anyone. The occasional meeting suggests no one else did, either. It's sad, really. College shouldn't be like that. I meet people who talk about being friends from college, who have reunions. That must be fun. My classmates were brave kids who gave their all, for an idea that hadn't yet been tested. It didn't work. And yet I learned most from those years. The intensity and passion. But it didn't feel like college. It didn't feel like Trinity. I don't know what it was and neither did Trinity; they didn't want us. It became a degree course (you'd have needed your Leaving, I'd say) and was ultimately canned.

I've returned often since I left. I get a thrill every time I see Front Gate and people waiting as I did countless times. What a fabulous place to wait for people, don't you think? Walking though the arch I read all the handwritten notices. Turning into the shop I find myself looking at the sweatshirts and T-shirts with 'Trinity' emblazoned upon them. I did buy a scarf once. At least, I think it was a Trinity scarf. I don't know Trinity's colours. I do always buy a Curly Wurly and a Ribena, though. I walk outside and watch the students traverse the cobble-stones. Probably on their way to a library, or a club, maybe even their rooms. Filling themselves with knowledge and friendship. The lucky bastards.

I wish I'd gone to Trinity.

Brian F. O'Byrne (TCD 1988–90) attended the Samuel Beckett Centre. He has lived in the US for a long time. He started acting there and has been awarded, well, awards for it. It's a fascinating way to make a living. But he might try something else sometime. Maybe.

ANCIENT MELANCHOLY

patrick healy

One of the earliest attested uses of the word for melancholy is to be found in the Corpus Hippocraticum, *which can be dated to the last third of the fifth century. The treatise in which it appears is entitled* Peri aeron, hudaton, topon, *'on air, water and places'. The context in which the word appears is a discussion about the effect of climate on health, and in particular what today we would call depression.*

THAT PRONOUNCEMENT was circulating in my ear as I strolled down from St Stephen's Green to College Green, and finally to the manuscript reading room, west end of the Old Library, in Trinity College, where I sat most days in the late 1970s and much of the first half of the subsequent decade, and from that curious vantage point I came to know the college and some of its life and people. It should seem physically impossible that this was a room through which college passed by, and all of Irish history. To write such a history, Joyce once suggested, would be the task of the supermen of the future. I hasten to add I am not such a one. The *Übermensch* of Irish history? Is it possible Joyce had Roy Foster in mind?

It had been a very long time since I asked my mother, as we made our way to Lord Edward Fitzgerald Street for my eye examination, why the lawn in front of TCD was so small. I rang my fingers along the railings, and wondered, 'Do people live in there?' When we returned from our mission the sun was already setting on the sooty facade. I wanted to see a cat slip through the spears of the railings and hear a chatter of heads on spikes tell the story of the place, and where it came from. I liked the blue clock. My mother suggested I read a book and stop 'romancing', and then threw me – a single fact, as a sop, to stop me talking, and with some emphasis – the unanswerable observation: 'Bram Stoker studied in there.'

The bus came by, its windows steamed up and carrying a hoard of damp passengers. On the back window someone had scrawled, 'The republi'. My mother winced as I completed the word. It was as if the whole city was being swallowed and absorbed by this fast-fading *graffito* in the breath and damp of the late evening, the last glimmer of twilight.

It is remarkable how places start and unfold through people, and vice-versa. Mr William O'Sullivan was the keeper of manuscripts, his movement rapid and intense, dressed in tweed with hints of speckle and heather, probably from Kevin & Howlin of Nassau Street. Unflappable courtesy, and a most delicate affability. It was charming and strange when we spoke at the Kilkenny Design Centre, about talking heads. On that topic he was a mine, literally, of information. He knew the antiquarian research backwards: Sir William Betham's arguments on the link between Ireland and the Etruscans, Betham's unkind, perhaps hasty, dismissal of O'Brien's theory of the round towers, and his linking of Newgrange with the tumuli and menhirs; and had I read Colonel Charles Vallancey? Much of the material was legendary, but there could be a grain of truth; after all, Troy existed. Yes indeed, the reports on the Celts and talking heads was of considerable interest. Women fought ferociously.

'It really is about words.' When I said this he looked amused. You could take just forty Etruscan words and end up in the Boyne Valley. I suggested that this fascination was important for Joyce, in *Stephen Hero*, with the mishmash the students exchanged in a kind of polyglot pidgin, or cant, that was also a feature of many of the manuscripts he had studied. He nodded, clearly wondering why I had mentioned Joyce and surprised as if an unmannerly intruder had caught the ferocious women of his phantasmic tribes bathing.

I thought it best not to add the details from Posidonius via Diodorus

Siculus, on the innate love of gold shown by Gaulish men and women: 'the women of Gaul are very beautiful, but the men prefer to have sex with other men'. Apparently, the custom was for the men to sleep on animal skins, and other bedmates to roll around on the ground, and the oddest thing, thus Posidonius: the young men didn't care about their appearance and, I better quote: 'will gladly give their bodies to anyone who wants them, and have no sense that this is shameful, but rather, are highly offended if anyone refuses them'. Not that this mattered; as Joyce had argued, the current tapestry was made of a lot of different threads. There was not much left then of the pure gold weft of Celtic belongings. Ireland, shaped as a saucer, was a melting pot, and there was no virgin thread. Further, only one man in Ireland had declared at this date for such ancestral predilections.

I put in my spoke, as they say: 'Stephen Hero, when they are looking at the old yellow copy of the *Daily Graphic*, and Cranly, that is John Francis Byrne, I think, replying to Temple tells him *"Feuc an eis super stradam … in Liverpoolio."* Joyce had been learning Irish from the bearded priest O'Growney's grammar. He has a very intricate and delicate joke about that. I wouldn't want to bore anyone with it, but I think it worth mentioning.'

'Please, please', he clearly braced himself without betraying any irritation.

'Joyce availed of the Gaelic League lessons as he was learning Irish. The class were using O'Growney's *Simple Lessons in Irish*, and Joyce tells the story how serious everyone had been until they came to the word *gradh*: "Stephen found it very (hard) troublesome to pronounce the gutturals but he did the best he could." The class, he said, was very serious and patriotic. Of the ten students five laughed and five remained grave; those who laughed, Joyce mused, "finding something very funny in the Irish word for 'love' or in the notion itself" .'

'We know', the sudden royal plural caught Mr William O'Sullivan's attention, 'that Joyce mentions the "loveless Irish" as an epithet in his essay "Ireland: Island of Saints and Sages". However, to get back to O'Growney, I looked up the publication and found indeed that this meant the class were then at part two of the lessons, lesson LVI, section 330. Anyway, section 330 sets out more observations on the consonants and especially the broad consonants, in this case *dh* and *gh*. At the end and middle of the words they are silent, an example of which is the writing of *Gaedhlic*, given in figured English pronunciation in brackets as (Gael-ig). A previous short vowel or digraph could be lengthened, such as *magh*, and pronounced *mau*, and so on; but, in the beginning of a word these broad consonants have a sound not heard in the English and might be best represented by the Greek gamma. O'Growney suggests one takes the English word *auger*, a carpenter's tool. I don't remember the details, but that in pronouncing this word the tongue is pressed against the back part of the mouth in bringing out the sound of *g*, and he advises to try and pronounce it without allowing the tongue to touch the back part of the mouth and the result will be *avver*, thus giving the sound we want; but the gamma of Greek is not so hard as the g and thus we know it is only a partial consonant sound. I think that's right … Joyce must have been very amused at the blushing of Michael Cusack, a fellow student learning Irish, on hearing the word *gradh*, or at the appearance of Arthur Griffith and his circle that met in Cooney's tobacco shop, which reminds me: O'Growney mentions that some words adapted from foreign languages have retained the foreign accentuation, and indeed he gives the example of *tobac* (thub-ok). I have the impression that Joyce sides with the O'Growney view that the model is what is happening with Welsh, and that his involvement in the *Kulturkampf* is Parnellism by other means, but troubled by his awareness of another stream of nationalist rhetoric, from MacHale to Pearse. Oh, and in the paradigm sentences the name Nora appears frequently!'

I blew rings from a rolled Egyptian cigarette, a packet purchased in Kapp & Peterson, and smoked lazily, savouring the delicate bright paper and the tapered slimly edged tip tasting of marzipan. In the eighties it was no longer easy to buy single cigarettes, such as Sweet Afton. Kapp & Peterson smelt of Mick Mc Quaid tobacco, 'irrespective', as we used to say.

'Hadn't Joyce played chess somewhere along this street with Parnell's brother?' I suddenly asked. I had been too detailed; it was easy to see through the dissembled 'hesitancy' of such tedious remarks. I beat a retreat, left an opening. The language revival had failed because of scholarship, and tying it to the speech of the people; an urban population couldn't … moreover, the pedantry was killing. Such a polemical and imprudent rush of talk must require upbraiding.

'Yes,' he quickly remarked. 'The problem had been how to have a standard. There was that German transcription of the speech of Aran, Franz Finck's *Die araner mundart*, a phonetics windfall for all of us, before recorded speech, and it confirmed, you know, that Parnell was pronounced with emphatic stress on the first syllable.' He made the transcription and quoted the phrase, supplying the Irish, the phonetic version and the German. A little bristle of light rippled along the folds of the tweed.

It was time to go back, and we left the lamp-filled clutter of the ground floor of the Kilkenny Design Centre, not caring to look at the Jim Fitzpatrick Celtic mural over on the left. I thought of Mr Belton, lolling down the brick steps coming from his night club, the Pink Elephant. He always wore braces. I had just been turned into a renegade nationalist, and we took to the mean huckstering streets and passed Fred Hanna, the bookseller, whose spectacles glinted with deep respect at an ambling philological troupe returning to the hub of the world. Philology was the future.

The keeper of the Douglas Hyde Gallery went by, a dark beard, hooded eyes and a busy mien. Students could have art on loan in their rooms from the gallery: Vasarely optical cubes, posters of Kandinsky, Klimt's neurotic nudes, Nolde's ferocious flowers; originals, pochoirs, prints, copies and reproductions of twentieth-century art replacing pristine paperback printings of *Ulysses*, Che Guevara, a solitary image on a wall, or table mats of Malton or Piranesi. Nigel Rolfe had rolled naked in flour once, downstairs in the gallery, a kind of performance berserker, and Laurie Anderson had introduced the repetitive minimalia of Steve Reich there. The beat of being enlightened, and thus, it seems, modern, took curious turns in the race to exchange religion for art. Punk rock in Temple Bar; U2 were on the way to the National Stadium; sometimes from a window you might hear Echo and the Bunnymen. But sounds were on the move. Kraftwerk was definitely only for the truly initiated.

Back at the reading room, a patient unfolding of a little text, from the *Liber Hymnorum*; word by word, I was being instructed in the arts and mysteries. This polite scholar picked his way through each word, and then produced a translation. It was the request for protection by St Patrick, an elaborate joke at my expense. Such amiable superiority was adorable!

In another conversation on Joyce, I mentioned his Trinity reference in the essay on James Clarence Mangan, who had gained work as an assistant librarian at Trinity, become an opium addict and was the 'most distinguished poet of the modern Celtic world'. The absurd demand for chastity would impede Irish recognition of such heroic figures as Parnell and Mangan, Joyce had argued, and an obsession with respectability. No, I had not been able to work out if Joyce had spent time in the library, although he mentions it, and describes it to his Italian audience in Trieste in 1907 as being three times bigger than the Victor Emanuel Library in Rome. He mentions the Book of the Dun Cow, and the Book of Kells, among others.

Professors Webb and McDowell were busy finishing an updated history of the college. The botanist with his interest in *Saxifraga*, and the historian who flickered like Chaplin through mounds of archives, talking to himself and moving as he wrote little notes, scarf and coat and hat permanently attached to an ageless murmuring being who was omnipresent and utterly industrious. McDowell, nicknamed 'urbi et orbi' by the students, later told me, in confidence, that as a young man in the very late twenties he had carried a copy of *Ulysses* around in a brown paper bag, as the work was thought to be somewhat 'smutty'. At the same time, Trevor West passed by – wisps of sandy hair and a tight tweed jacket – and seemed to overhear the word 'smutty'. He smiled, as Joyce might have said, 'wanly'. A word was a spit on a whetstone, and then the great scholar was put to flight with Christopher Daybell's asking: 'Do you read poetry at all?' I was treated to an impassioned reading of 'My Last Gitane' and invited to coffee in Bewley's, where I reminded Christopher we had met before and talked about Rimbaud. In all the chaos he deposited a copy of every pamphlet in the library. I contributed 50p and owned my own Gestetner example of an original Daybell.

Trinity hosted the Joyce centenary conference in 1982. Thanks to its president Conor 'Apollo' McElroy, the Phil organized a one-day reading of *Finnegans Wake*. Borges attended in the afternoon, and Christopher Daybell was ecstatic for days.

A spectacular passer-by, busy and intense, was the bearer of ionized water, David Malcolm Lass. The water was used to prevent the books drying and the skin of the calf bindings cracking along the heavy shelves. No one could have realized that David Lass was the true revolutionary force that only a long future would reveal. He had policed smoking on the lower deck of buses for a decade; with his briefcase and brolly, dark-blue navy coat and Trinity scarf, he would object to anyone who lit a cigarette in non-smoking areas, which was at times to put himself at great risk. His own curriculum vitae, which ran to five hundred pages, included all his letters on behalf of the no-smoking campaign to *The Irish Times*, and included achievements such as winning an egg and spoon race when a boy of five. He had also worked on an article on Nicholas of Lyra, Santa Claus, and was the secretary of – yes – the Bram Stoker Society; various other interests included science fiction and vegetarianism. He would attend plays with copies of the text, and cough and splutter if actors made mistakes. Yes, here was the eccentricity that Joyce loved, and it wasn't James Clarence Mangan, but a mirror avatar, and a sub-librarian, the greatest lobbyist of twentieth-century Irish history.

The keeper of manuscripts was amused to hear I had discovered Samuel Madden's volume of the *Memoirs of the Twentieth Century* at the other end of the library, the Printed Books Reading Room, and that it had been brought from the shelves by Miss Pollard, who was always called 'Paul' and not Mary. Miss Pollard had the colouring of a seventeenth-century Dutch vellum binding with an embossed and gilt centre piece. I had filled in a green slip to call up the work, which had been written by a fellow of the university sometime in the 1720s, published and mostly pulped in 1733 or thereabouts. Then Charles Benson actually brought it to the table, and reminded me notes could only be taken in pencil. I had a little shoe box of reference cards, and looked up at his 'loveless' gaze. It was a blind wall, a surface never to be penetrated. There was no need to say 'Thank you'. Keys jangled from the hip of a heavyset woman who passed through the room and handed someone their requested copy of John Dee. It was the receptacle for the advanced study of magic and satanic grimoires. The Burgh Barracks.

The book was a fabulous concoction. Very involved with the furnishing of the library, with books, that is, Madden had written a futuristic work containing the mother of all conspiracy theories. The 1980s had already been foretold, and yes indeed, it was a world dominated by Jesuit intrigue and popish superstition. The Jesuits had subtly orchestrated the conversion of Russia to Rome, and a printing house in Oxford five times the size of the Sheldonian would only print the classics, as there was too much information around. There is a character, the Professor of Weather, whose publication was leading to a final triumph over nature.

Madden saw a future that held much in suspense. There is nothing more amusing in his work than the list of the relics on sale that he found in a catalogue, when Rome, in 1997, would clear out the shop and the Jesuits have taken over banking. The list is nearly fifteen printed pages: the tail of Baalam's ass, the Judas lantern, the cradle and manger of baby Jesus, the table of the Last Supper, the cross of the good thief, somewhat worn, the rather rotted towel that washed the feet of the disciples, Mary's hair, the brains of Peter in a jar, a tooth of Mary, the rope of Judas, Pilate's handwriting, the tear that Christ shed over Lazarus enclosed in a crystal by an angel who made a present of it to the Magdalene, whose body (*vessali prope Aliss – odorum* [*sic*]) was also on the block. The trumpery and foppery goes on and on.

However, nothing about mass emigration from Ireland, the increase in student numbers, Mary Robinson's brilliant advocacy, David Norris' declamatory exultation, slapping his thighs with his left hand and then screaming with a nasal twang, 'shite and onions'; not a word about the struggle against colonial oppression, political prisoners, learning Irish in west Belfast; not a word about Joe Duffy and Aine Lawlor shaking the board to its cocktails, nor anything of a plan to blow up the library; nothing about the Bernie Inn, just that milk and cheese of Mary sent from Mexico to Rome, which never curdled; no premonition of Bishop Casey, or the moving statues; not an inkling of the IT revolution or that the fifty broad acres of Trinity was a battery farm for exporting new batches of graded emigrants, the children of lower postal codes of Dublin, to eternal well-being, when they could have stayed at home and looked down on the flawed pedigree of fellow lapsed co-religionists, especially from Clontarf and Raheny. No, not a whiff of it: that the last bus left at 11 pm; that rooms in college were a warren of hospitality for those who were straggling from the Buttery; that Barry Desmond abolished the medical card for students; that Provost Watts, with his great egg-head a scion (pronounced 'sion', not 'Zion'), was the greatest provost since Hely-Hutchinson introduced French and dancing classes for the sizars, scholars and students of the holy and undivided college, juxta Dublin, and not a smidgin, or the faintest notion of a president of a republic attending the Garden Party in top hat and tails; the difficulty of getting marijuana in Kehoe's; the closing of the Toby Jug; David Norris' pin-striped suit; Kennelly reading his work in O'Neill's, or that Brian Lenihan had rooms in the GMB. Oh! What else can one end with but a question mark and a colon?: *COLONS ÜBER ALLES!*

Patrick Healy, St Patrick's College, Maynooth (Pontifical University), University College Dublin (NUI) Philosophy; Semitic languages; Researcher Dep. Hist. of Medicine, RCSI, Frankfurt am Main (1973–84). Elected honorary life member of TCD's Philosophical Society (1982–3). Recent publications include **The Papyrus Dream**, poems (2011); Carl Einstein, **Bebuquin**, translation (2011); for further details see patrick-healy.com.

OUT OF THE BLUE

gerald dawe

THE TRAIN I took from Galway Monday mornings would get me in on time. I'd go to the rooms, dump my bags, and head over to the Arts Block and give my first class of the week. It was 1988 and I was newly arrived as a lecturer in English at Trinity, moonlighting in a colleague's rooms for the year. That train had its very own community of TDs and civil servants and we all knew one another and had the patience of Job when the engines periodically failed – outside Woodlawn, for instance, or when there were problems with 'signals on the line', usually of a Friday evening as we were heading home.

Sitting in a stalled train for hours pre-mobile communication was 'no fun'. But we got to know one another, CIÉ food and drink, and the newspaper back to front. I also started to use the train as an office or extension of my workroom and ended up writing some poems out of those years of 'commute'.

> The second *o* in Portarlington has gone
> and under the shed's Bangor Blues
> a yellow breakdown truck.
> Into the sky's concealed entrance
> head a line of sheep, but what,
> pray, are we waiting for?
> —'Out of the Question'

The taxi ride to college was also often in a state of delay because of perennial work on the roads along the canals. The city then was still in disrepair and decay nestled alongside bolder architectural initiatives but what I recall most about the contrast between the Galway I'd left behind and the inner city I inhabited, was the air. Dublin in the eighties was very much a smoggy city with Trinity an essential lung.

Occasionally, I'd need to come up on Sunday and arriving in Dublin in the late evening the frosty sparkle of winter could hardly conceal the spores of smoke and coal-dust – 'cheap Polish coal' was the by-word back then – that settled on the plates and cups and saucers in my rooms. The scent of bitumen seems to remain in the after-burner of those years although how that could actually be the case, given that the world and its mother all smoked incessantly *everywhere* – it's hard to fathom a quarter of a century later.

That first Trinity year was a new beginning. The preceding year things were looking grim. The economy was precarious, tax onerous and weighty on even the most modest of salaries, friends were leaving the country, the future seemed to be elsewhere and the poet's life I had been hoping to maintain on the back of teaching was snapping shut. We had gone to Australia for a look but returned for family reasons when, with great good fortune, out of the blue, an opportunity arose in Trinity and I took it.

Previous contact had been sparse. In October 1979, I'd been part of a Poetry Ireland reading with the grandly Miltonic John Heath-Stubbs and other Irish poets. So relatively rare were such events then that it was reviewed in *The Irish Times* by fiction writer Lucille Redmond. A few years after, I 'delivered' a lecture on the 'thirties generation' of Irish poets, still languishing in relative academic neglect. The glass of sherry beforehand – a custom long since abandoned – limbered up the voice, whatever about the mind.

And there I was, some years later again, somewhat dazed and detached on Commons. The two elderly scholars, one to my left averting his gaze ceiling-wards, the other in front of me addressing his plate, were debating the correct times of British Rail connections at Crewe before the war, or was it Carlyle?

I was only saved by the wondrous presence of Petros Florides who asked me about George Seferis, the Greek poet. For a mathematician to know so much I guessed I was in the right place after all. Thereafter, from the soliloquies of George Dawson on his latest artistic 'find' to the ruminations of physicists, philosophers, geneticists and visiting dignitaries, the world of the Commons brought me inside Trinity at a point when college was itself changing. The body language of the place was altering for good. It was as if the beckoning of its four hundredth anniversary in a few years' time – and what a ball that turned out to be – was making its own kind of music as an older style of belonging *to* Trinity and of Trinity's belonging in the wider world, was also being refined; a quiet revolution, perhaps, but a revolution, nonetheless.

From House 33 none of this was apparent. That winter the cold and rain matched the dank morning in which I used to rise and catch a first glimpse of fellow dwellers moving about in this inner world as the buses started up and the tooting cars and the lorries – lots of lorries – clanked about outside. When winter set in and the frost became a palpable mist, the magic of Front Square at evening time was beguiling.

On Sunday evening there was a sense of solitariness about as dusk fell. I and a colleague the same age, also living in rooms and teaching in the English Department as it was then known, would nip through the squally rain to the Oscar Wilde, a pub at the corner of College and D'Olier Street.

Dublin too was on the cusp of change and though those streets surrounding Trinity had their famed local histories – of Bowe's, the Palace, the Lincoln, O'Neill's – there was a sense that *that* past was losing its grip and the great literary tales of the 'shocking charactors' who'd spent much of their lives on the bar stool or ensconced in a snug, that it was all slowly but irreversibly disappearing.

Barmen, who'd worked in the same place for ages, left, died away, pubs changed hands, were renovated, started to serve 'hot food' and the bell-ringing of last orders or the solicitous retort to finish up turned to counter-slapping and the opening of doors unto the chill breezes of the street.

It always seemed to be dark by mid-afternoon and men still wore hats and smoked pipes and couples had 'dates' outside pubs or cinemas as if time had indeed stood still for the last half-century. But nothing could compare with the onset of spring and the first flush of the cherry blossoms – so entrancing I started making or imagining poems.

Removed from the west and the family life that I had known there from the mid 1970s, and in my temporary home, this new beginning – which I didn't know at the time – would become permanent, or as permanent as anything ever is. A home from home with the grass verges, the cobblestones, the humane dimensions of the buildings, and the light of the fields and gardens and trees that we all walk around, half-seeing, half-knowing each other, in a bit of a rush.

Then it was all new and the sense of what had gone before unassumedly present – like the two old chaps rehearsing their lives *entre deux guerres* or the friendships that grew out of the teaching day and the sociable late afternoons willingly spent in each other's company. And there were the records I could hear at night in my rooms with the accompanying noises that ended up in the poem I finally wrote about that first year at Trinity. The excitement of expectation between then and now never left me.

Good Night

Since we haven't met yet
and more than likely won't –
things being what they are –
I felt a little note, off-the-cuff,
might do the trick.

Between us there is next to nothing,
but I have heard you cough
early morning and have begun
to expect to hear your window
rattle on its sash at any time,
and guess that when you turn
you face me in bed in this
Hall of Residence.

I have heard too, at midnight,
you laugh and shuffle about
with some bloke whose voice
mumbles against the stereo.
(Your taste in music is not mine.)

And now, having spent the night
reading the work of friends,
I wanted to jot this down
because in some way you have
entered myself as much as the room –

a silent partner sleeping out
the police car's shocking klaxon,
and the equatorial heating pumps
in the background a steady beat,
and somebody's alarm goes off
prematurely, although we all
still sleep, or are meant to.

The magnolia and cherry trees
flower in the gardens below.
In the labs, experiments are timed
to perfection, but the invisible dust
descends on books, paintings,
maps, busts, the executive aquarium,
even the washed dishes on the rack,
and on our faces upturned in the dark.

Gerald Dawe (MA) is Professor of English and fellow of Trinity College Dublin. His most recent publications include **Selected Poems** (2012) and, with Darryl Jones and Nora Pelizzari, **Beautiful Strangers: Ireland and the World of the Fifties** (2012).